"...A major strength of this introductory text is its demonstration that three theologians can incorporate their individual strengths (Hill in religious education, Knitter in interreligious dialogue, and Madges in systematics) into a presentation which flows smoothly, laying a foundation for what is to come and recapitulating ideas which have gone before....The book is very well-written, easily accessible to a non-specialist audience, without over-simplification. The unobtrusive summaries at the end of each chapter will be helpful to both students and instructor. The discussion questions can also be used as tools of classification as well as to stimulate further reflection."

Mary Ann Hinsdale
College of the Holy Cross

"...I admire how much information and challenges the authors have packed into this volume. If students studied this book diligently, they would come away quite sophisticated about the areas it covers and the challenges that faith, religion and theology present....The book is filled with issues and examples that students should fine relevant. It offers some of the terms that students need to negotiate in religion or theology, without being jargon-ridden or overly technical. And it serves up many of the names and notions that one would hope students exposed to religion or theology would take away as part of their adult repertoire...."

Denise Lardner Carmody
University of Tulsa

"This work unites excellent scholarship with eminent readability—a real introduction to theology today."

David Tracy
University of Chicago

Brennan R. Hill
Paul Knitter & William Madges

Second Printing 1990

Twenty-Third Publications
185 Willow Street
P.O. Box 180
Mystic, CT 06355
(203) 536-2611

ISBN 0-89622-415-5
Library of Congress Catalog Card No. 89-51578

Acknowledgments

We would like to express our thanks to a number of people who have contributed in a special way to this project.

First, we wish to acknowledge our students of the past several years in Th 111, Introduction to Theology, who provided much of the inspiration and incentive for creating a contemporary introduction to faith, religion, and theology. In particular, we express our gratitude to the theology majors and a few other interested students at Xavier University, who listened to our proposal for the book, made concrete suggestions, and criticized certain portions of our project. Among this number explicit mention must be made of Melanie Koop, Mary Kay Rehard, David Nissen, and Douglas Hudson. Second, we wish to acknowledge our colleagues in the Department of Theology at Xavier University who, in diverse ways, stimulated our thinking and promoted our project.

In addition, we would like to recognize publicly the contributions of a few other individuals: Stephen B. Scharper of Twenty-Third Publications for his gentle, yet insightful criticisms and for constant encouragement. Mrs. Linda Loomis, secretary of our Theology Department, for typing a large section of the manuscript and for her unfailing cheerfulness. Our wives, Marie Hill (who, in addition to her comments and support, also compiled the index), Cathy Cornell, and Marsha Erickson, for their comments on the manuscript and their ongoing personal support.

To Our Children

Ami, B.J., John, Moira, and Kate

Contents

PART THREE—THEOLOGY

Introduction

The need for this book arose out of our ongoing search for useful materials for our introductory religion course at Xavier University in Cincinnati. For the last ten years we have had success with our introductory course, but there has been a constant problem with finding a suitable text. We experimented with a number of books over the years, and even put together our own collection of articles, but we could never quite find a text that would deal with the range of topics we treated or that could be easily understood by our students.

We hope that this text will adequately meet the needs of those pursuing an introductory course in religious studies. In order to ensure this, we have included a number of attractive features: 1) We have made what we consider to be a proper distinction between *faith*: the gifted relationship with Mystery, *religion*: the context wherein most live out such a covenant, and *theology*: the process of reflection on the experience of such an ultimate commitment. 2) We have made a serious effort to address the book to the average reader, unfamiliar with the vocabulary and methods of religious studies. Although we have used the best scholarly resources available, we have made great efforts to avoid the use of overly technical language and jargon. Moreover, we have used the comments and questions of our own students as valuable resources. The learners using these materials will hear the voices of their peers, honestly struggling with questions and doubts concerning a wide range of religious issues. 3) We have worked within what we consider to be an inclusive religious perspective. Although this book is primarily an introduction to the Christian tradition, the authors have openly engaged in conversation with other religious traditions. 4) Attempting to blend the theoretical with the practical, we have synthesized what we consider to be the best theoretical work on faith, religion, and theology. At the same time, we have addressed the issues that most concern religious thinkers today, especially those that arise out of oppression and social injustice. The following is a brief overview of the areas dealt with in this book.

Faith as Gifted Covenant

Brennan R. Hill views religious faith as an invitation to trust in ultimate reality. The act of faith is a free choice by the whole person and includes the mind, feelings, imagination, will; indeed, all human capacities. Authentic faith culminates in action, especially in action toward peace and justice. The life of faith is integral to the rest of human living and is intimately related to the stages of human development. Each of the stages is discussed in terms of its bearing on the growth in faith. Special attention is given to the young adult stage of development, since so many students are in that period of human growth and faith formation. This section ends with a chapter on the young adult struggle to integrate faith with a concern for social justice.

Religion as Context

Paul Knitter begins his introduction to religion by facing the many modern criticisms of religion. While admitting the validity of some of the charges against organized religion, he counters with a number of positive values attached to religious movements. Then the very nature of religion is discussed in terms of a commitment to "Something More." This is followed by an explanation of how such a commitment is worked out differently in the various world religions. The question "Why so many religions?" is explored realistically, seeing such diversity as not only acceptable, but as an opportunity for valuable dialogue as well as for vital cooperation in facing contemporary crises. After an overview of positions on the uniqueness of Jesus, this section closes with a lively dialogue between Jesus and Buddha, which should serve to stimulate extended class discussions.

Theology as Reflection

William Madges begins his section with a discussion of the various approaches to Christian theology, including the fundamental, historical, systematic and practical ways of dealing with religious tradition. He then addresses the crucial relationship between Scripture and tradition, dealing with both the Protestant and Catholic points of view. The next section concerns the crucial debate between those who approach Scripture as fundamentalists and those who study the Bible contextually and critically. We have found that this is one of the most eye-opening and thought-provoking issues in the entire introductory course.

Madges then moves on to a timely exploration of the relationship between experience and tradition, pointing out the religious dimension of common experience. This is followed by a discussion of how contemporary experience has challenged traditional Christian beliefs, most notably the experiences of human suffering and the discrimination against women. This section concludes with an explanation of liberation theology and a practical application of contemporary theological insights to the crucial nuclear and ecological crises.

Educators are beginning to reconsider the role of religion in the contemporary curriculum, on both the secondary and college levels. Public schools are rethinking their exclusion of religion from education, and higher education is once again coming to an awareness that religious thinking is integral to an authentic liberal arts education. The many social and political crises that surround us have brought many educators to realize that religious values, beliefs, and "praxis" are crucial not only for world improvement but indeed for world survival.

It is our hope that this text will offer educators the materials they need to introduce many learners, whether college students or other interested adults, to the challenges and opportunities that the religious dimension of life offers.

Part One

FAITH

CHAPTER ONE

What Is Faith?

Most young adults have faith in something, complete confidence and trust in a thing or in a person they can turn to. For some, their trust is in themselves, in their ability to achieve, to get ahead, to be a success. Sarah, a sophomore majoring in mathematics, puts it this way: "It may sound cocky or proud, but I like myself. My parents and teachers have always shown that they like me, and I have been popular with my classmates. I am proud of my intelligence and personality, and I am confident that I will achieve the goal that I have set for myself in life, to be an accountant for a large firm."

Others place their faith or confidence in their family. Bill, a factory worker and an expert skier, says: "I am close to my family and I believe in them because they have never let me down. Any time that I've been in trouble or suffered injuries in skiing, my family always came to my rescue and helped me through the tough times. My parents have sacrificed a lot for me, and I have always been able to turn to them for anything I needed." Kati describes the trust she has in her mother, a single parent: "My mother has brought joy into my life ever since I was born. She has been there for me no matter what the situation was, and there have been some horrible ones. My love for her is so deep that death could not separate us. I don't know what life would be like if I did not have my mother there for me."

Still others place their faith in their friends, people who accept them, listen to them, keep their confidences, and who show up when help is needed. Tim, a junior business major, has several friends like this, and he maintains that without them life would be grim. He comments: "I grew up basically alone and without friends, probably because we moved a lot and I never had much of a chance to get to know people very well. Then I went to college and there I found two friends who are loyal, interesting, and like to do the things I enjoy. They aren't perfect, in fact, they have the same troubles with studies that I do. But both of them don't mind listening to me, and I really feel that they care about what happens to me. And they are really fun to be with."

In order to go in life with any sense of purpose and meaning, we need to have some degree of faith in ourselves, in others, in the system, even in the future. Someone has said that faith is like some kind of "ontic sap" that enables us to keep it together, enabling us to somehow believe in ourselves and in the world that surrounds us. Without such faith, we have little confidence in our own abilities, and we become alienated from our surroundings, constantly threatened by other people and by the realities around us. Faith is the X factor that enables us to trust in reality and in the possibility that life does have a meaning and a purpose.

Faith—Uniquely Human

We can observe that even animals have a certain trust. New pets usually take a while before they begin to trust their environment and the people taking care of them. Those who work with such amazing animals as dolphins and even killer whales observe that a mutual trust gradually begins to build up between these animals and those who care for them. Even wild animals can come to trust in a trainer; they can acquire a confidence that they will be fed, cared for, and never abused. Neglect in any of these areas quickly breaks down this trust, and the animal begins once again to be hostile.

Human trust is similar to the trust we observe in animals, but it is uniquely different in that human trust is reflective, freely given, and the basis for growth and development not known by other creatures. Well-known Lutheran theologian Paul Tillich (1886-1965) describes faith as "the courage to be." Trust in ourselves and others enables us to move ahead with confidence and become more than we are. Faith gives us vision, goals, and the motivation to reach beyond where we have been and where we are. Faith is an energy that can drive us to incredible accomplishments.

Consider the story of Stephen Hawking of England. He was a brilliant student in college with a promising career as a professor ahead of him. While he was doing his doctoral studies, he was suddenly stricken with a rare disease. The disease gradually crippled his entire body, so that he can barely move, and has to be permanently in a wheelchair. Even his voice is affected, and Stephen could only communicate with a faint hum. On the face of it, it seemed like this was the end of his career, and perhaps of his life. But Stephen would have none of that kind of thinking. He believed in himself and his abilities. He would not give up on his dream to teach. Stephen finished his Ph.D., fell in love, married, and fathered three children. Moreover, he proceeded to win the coveted Lucassian Chair at Cambridge University that Issac Newton once held. Today, Dr. Stephen Hawking is one of the world's leading experts on the physics of the universe, and a witness to the incredible power of human faith.

Religious Faith

Religious faith is a unique kind of faith. Religious persons place their trust in a reality that is beyond observation and proof, the mysterious reality often referred to as God. Religious faith accepts the existence of such a reality, convinced that God is not an illusion, a projection of some need for security or for answers to the puzzling questions of life. Religious faith is, as Paul Tillich describes it, ultimate concern. Such faith believes that there is an ultimate source for all existence and an ultimate goal in life. It "rests assured" that God exists, that God can be trusted, that God gives ultimate meaning and purpose to life.

The faith of Jews, Muslims, Hindus, and Christians trusts that all life somehow comes from a God who is creative, powerfully involved in the world, and the mysterious architect of the future of this universe. Ancient Jews called this personal presence of mystery Yahweh. Followers of Islam called this mystery Allah. Hindus refer to this Ultimate Reality as Brahman, and they worship this one great God in many forms and under many names. Christians refer to this ultimate mystery as God, and believe that this God has been uniquely revealed to humankind in the person of Jesus Christ, the Son of God. Similar to the Hindus, Christians worship God in various "persons": Father, Son, and Holy Spirit.

Faith as Gift

There seems to be a consensus among Christian theologians that faith is a gift, a grace freely given by God. Raimundo Panikkar makes a useful distinction in his discussion of faith. He points out the difference between "faith" and the "act of faith." Strictly speaking, faith is an invitation, an inner urging, a feeling of being grasped by some reality beyond us. Faith is a call to relationship, a beckoning to friendship, a loving and inviting call to be one with God as Creator and Savior. Young people that we have interviewed report having experienced such a call or urging in many different ways. Jose, a Puerto Rican who was raised Catholic, turned off religion early on because of the threatening ways in which God and the church were presented. He was inclined to reject the notion of God in his life until he was befriended by a priest who enjoyed good laughs with young people at parties and at the beach. This experience began to move Jose to rethink his religious position and attracted him to a different kind of God, one who was loving and kind. Mary, a sophomore drama major, was stunned one morning when she found the baby sister she loved dearly dead in her crib. At first, Mary was angry that God would be so cruel as to cut this innocent baby's life short. At the funeral, Mary was moved to a new insight. She writes: "I was really feeling let down by God, and I prayed hard for strength. Then I began to realize that my baby sister, who had been very ill, was now relieved of her suffering and was now peacefully with God." This inner call to faith can come in many different ways and forms. For some, it comes watching a beautiful sunset on a camping trip; for others enjoying a family gathering after a long separation. For many, these urgings toward faith come in the midst of a tragic loss of a parent or close friend.

Faith as Universal

One of the most often debated religious questions might be summarized this way: "Does everyone get invited to accept faith, or is the offer only made to a chosen few?" Those who approach religion in an "exclusive" fashion hold that God picks out certain people to be saved and bypasses others. For instance, John Calvin (1509-1564), the Protestant reformer, believed in "predestination," the position that only a certain select few are chosen to be in relationship with God. Similarly, the Mormon religion teaches that there are a limited number of places in heaven, and those will be filled by a select few. Other versions of such religious exclusivity are heard in statements such as: "You have to be baptized to be saved," or "Outside the church there is no salvation," or "Unless you belong to this true faith community, you are not among the saved." From this perspective, God makes the invitation to a faith covenant only to "the chosen," and that is how one can explain why some people have faith and others do not.

Those who oppose the exclusive view of religion suggest that God's offer of faith is made to every person. They argue that since we are all created by God, we are all somehow drawn to be related to God in friendship. Such an invitation is extended somehow in all religions, all churches, and indeed outside of organized religion altogether. Salvation, then, is not so much a matter of belonging to the "true religion" or being part of some designated "chosen people." Instead, salvation involves the sincere following of one's inner urgings and the living of a good life. Faith implies commitment and fidelity to one's religious beliefs, but it also properly includes a way of life that evolves out of these beliefs. From this point of view, it is ultimately one's behavior that indicates whether or not a person has chosen to share friendship with God.

Faith as Holistic Response

But the question still arises: "Why do some believe and others refuse to?" The answer seems to lie in the dispositions each brings to human experience. To hear the call, to experience the "grasping of God," one must have a certain openness, a posture of listening, a sensitivity to these movements deep within the self to accept the reality of God. Of course, this is true of any relationship or friendship. Unless one is open to the invitation of friendship, sensitive to the signs that someone wants to be close, many opportunities to be joined with others go unheeded. If one chooses to be closed, to not listen or respond to signs of friendship, relationships simply do not happen. The same applies to a faith-relationship with God. We are free persons, and we need not respond to the gift of faith offered to us. This is the position of Bob, a senior marketing major from Los Angeles. He writes: "I don't need God in my life. Most religious people I know are either superstitious or hypocritical. They go to church all the time to sing and talk about love, and then they swear at each other trying to get out of the parking lot. Religion is a crutch for weak people. I put my faith in myself and in my abilities to achieve my goals. I try to live a good life and, frankly, I think I am more honest and caring than a lot of people who claim to have a faith in God."

The choice to respond in faith is always a free choice of every human person. None of us can rightfully be forced to accept the existence of, or be pushed into a trusting relationship with, this personal presence we call God. The decision is always ours, and, to be made properly, such a decision should be made knowingly and freely. Just as others cannot force any of us to love them, neither can we be forced to believe and trust in the existence of the divine. Faith is a freely spoken "yes" to God's invitation to friendship: It is a profound surrender to a covenant of mutual fidelity. Even though the offer is made to everyone, many have turned down the invitation.

As humans, we respond to things in many ways—with our bodies, minds, imaginations, emotions, and wills. The faith response, it would seem, should involve all of our human dimensions; to accent one over the others can well lead to a distorted response. Those who stress the physical can identify working themselves into a lather of perspiration with a religious experience. The "holy roller" or the "whirling dervish" then becomes the model of the faithful person. In contrast, those who accentuate orthodoxy or fundamentalism seem to identify faith and salvation with correct thinking. Such people are often quite intolerant of those who would differ with them in belief, even to the point of condemning others as heretics or religious outcasts.

Likewise, limiting the faith response to the imagination can produce distortions. This would be the case of those who take myth, symbolism, and religious metaphor so literally that they identify all such religious elements with Mystery itself. It is easy here to believe in an illusory world where God is an "old man in the sky," a world populated by angels and devils, where history actually consists of worldwide floods and the divine slaughter of first-borns. By the same token, such stress can be placed on emotions that religious faith can be identified with "feeling saved" or with a kind of feverish frenzy experienced in a revival meeting. Finally, it is possible to so stress action as the religious response that one can be satisfied with legalistically "practicing" religion, that is, carrying out all the prescriptions of a religion meticulously.

Indeed, there is a place for all of these human elements in the faith response, but to stress one at the expense of the others can indeed result in religious distortion or even fanaticism. The challenge is to maintain balance in the faith response so that such a commitment comes from the whole person. In the following, let us consider each of these human dimensions of the faith response in some detail.

The Physical: Friend or Foe?

Historically, there have been two major tendencies in approaching the physical or the material in religious thinking. On the one hand, the body, the senses, sexuality, and material things have been viewed as inimical to the life of faith. One sees this tendency in early Buddhism's view that the body and material things are the source of all suffering, in the flight from the world and its pleasures by the early Christian desert fathers, in the negative thinking toward the body and the world on the part of the early Gnostics, Augustine, and some of the Protestant reformers. This is the position of the Puritans who came to this country, and of those today who believe that drinking, dancing, and participation in what they call "secular humanism" is a participation in evil.

Conversely, physical attractiveness and material success have been viewed as a sign of God's blessings, to the exclusion of those who are physically or materially less fortunate. Ancient cultures often elevated physical and material things to the level of idols worthy of divine homage. In some instances, sexual orgies were viewed as worship and participation in divinity. The Renaissance often viewed human beauty and artistic achievement as the ultimate in spiritual achievement. Liberal Protestantism of the nineteenth century identified social progress with spiritual progress and set out to establish the kingdom of God on earth. One gets the impression from some of the television evangelists today that material success, social acceptability, and an attractive physical appearance are indeed concrete signs of being "God's chosen people." One television evangelist recently put it this way: "God wants you to have lots of money, so stand up, raise your hands to heaven, and say after me: 'God, give me lots of money.' " There are actually some fundamentalist institutions of higher learning in this country where admission is allowed only if one has a certain physical appearance, or if one is a member of the "proper race." Externals are of ultimate importance in this approach to faith.

Perhaps the traditional split between body and soul, secular and the sacred, matter and spirit can be overcome by what theologians call "incarnational thinking." This Christian approach to reality maintains that through Jesus Christ, God has entered humanity and the world. The reign of God, or God's presence within all of reality, is revealed in Jesus Christ. From this perspective, there are not two realities, the material and the spiritual. Rather, there is but one reality, with both spiritual and material dimensions.

Christian faith offers the believer this view of reality. The body is seen as integral to the person and to the faith response. While granting that the physical senses can be a source of temptation, the emphasis here is on seeing the senses as a means of perceiving the presence of God in all of reality.

As Anthony de Mello (1931-1988), a well-known expert on spirituality, has put it, Christianity helps us "come to our senses," so that through them we can perceive and experience the presence of God within ourselves, others, and in our world. Those who enjoy nature can appreciate what de Mello is saying. Ellen is such a lover of the outdoors, and cites a camping trip as an illustration of an incarnational experience. She writes: "Last spring break I went backpacking with some friends in the Red Rock country of Arizona. One evening we were all tired and stopped to watch the sun set in total silence. I don't know why none of us spoke; I guess we must have been overcome by the beauty. I remember coming away from that experience feeling refreshed, alive, and with a better attitude toward myself and my friends. I had experienced something or someone that afternoon—I guess I might have felt God's presence in that sunset."

Rather than fearing the body, sexuality, sensible pleasure, and the wide range of physical activities, this approach to Christian faith views them as means to experience the divine, as ways to express one's commitment to faith. Here faith becomes integral to participation in athletics, to achievement in dance, music, and the arts. Bernard Meland, a renowned American cultural theologian, thus links faith with our ability to appreciate aesthetic experiences, our human ability to somehow sense something beyond ourselves in physical and artistic activity. There is within our physical dimension the power to transcend ourselves, and the person committed to faith uses that power to somehow be in touch with God.

All of this is not to idealize the physical, not to deny that many experience disabilities and handicaps that make life, including faith life, extremely difficult. There is a dark side to the physical, the side that includes suffering, breakdown, and even death. But, even here faith offers a promise of hope. Consider the inspiring story of Joni Eareckson. In high school, Joni was an outstanding student-athlete, a popular leader in her school, a girl whom everyone thought had a promising future. That all changed one summer morning when Joni dived into Chesapeake Bay, struck her head on a rock, and became paralyzed from the neck down. Joni was crushed, physically and psychologically. Her friends could not bear to look at her yellow color, and her boyfriend broke off their relationship. Joni contemplated suicide. Then a young friend came to her, prayed with her and searched the Scriptures with her for some answers to the many agonizing questions she had about the meaning of her life. Joni writes that gradually she came to realize that Christ loved her even with her twisted and distorted body, even with all her despair and doubts. In the midst of all her physical suffering and pain, Joni discovered the presence of an empowering and healing God.

Joni eventually became an accomplished painter, holding the brush in her teeth. She has written several bestselling books, made a movie of her life for television, and has dedicated herself to helping other young people overcome their handicaps. Joni's story is an illustration of incarnational faith, a faith that can experience God in the physical, even when tragedy strikes. Moreover, her faith commitment to God is now that of her whole person, including her broken and paralyzed body.

The Rational Dimension of Faith

Thomas More (1478-1535) once said that one of the things that marks us humans off as unique is that we like to work things "in the tangle of our minds." We seldom accept things we don't understand, and we constantly struggle to figure out the meaning of things. The same applies to faith. Our minds are integral to the faith response. While some are satisfied with an unquestioning and "blind faith," most want to make a reasonable response to Mystery.

Our culture tends to take a "show me" approach to reality. In a very real sense, we are all children of the Enlightenment. We tend to take a scientific and analytic approach to reality and we do not accept things unless there is factual evidence, clear proof. We examine, measure, calculate, and then come to conclusions. Especially today, young people have been trained to be critical, evaluative, and questioning. They will not simply accept things "on faith" the way many former generations did. Young adults today feel free to voice their own opinions on things; they carefully protect their right to put together their own personal views on all matters.

The critical approach to reality works well in matters material, but it faces difficulty when applied to matters of religion. The content of faith, God, and matters of revelation, is not measurable or provable. Spiritual reality cannot be seen, heard, touched, or subjected to scientific investigation. While it may be reasonable to accept the existence of a supreme being, and plausible to believe the truths of revelation, a certain "leap" beyond observable phenomena is needed to make an act of faith.

Theologians have often struggled with this question of how we finite and limited persons can make an act of faith in the infinite, the unfathomable. In the fourth century, the great Christian genius, Augustine (354-430), suggested that faith is made possible by a God-given "light" that enables the mind to perceive the supernatural. In modern times, Paul Tillich proposed that there is a "depth of reason" within the human structure that allows us to perceive divine mystery. Karl Rahner, the outstanding modern Catholic thinker, held that humans have been created by

God in such a way that they have a "transcendental capacity," a unique "openness" whereby they can be receptive to the revelation of God.

Each of these thinkers in his own fashion is suggesting that human persons are actually equipped with the capacity to somehow go beyond the observable, the measurable, and relate to a Reality that is both beyond and within. With this capacity, we are able to perceive all reality with a new vision and grasp a deeper dimension in all phases of life. When a baby is born, we can experience the wonder of creation. When someone loves us, we can actually be put in touch with the love of God.

Faith and Doubt

It is often said that we now live in a post-Enlightenment era, a time wherein our original confidence in science's ability to answer all of our questions has given way to a certain disillusionment. While science has indeed given modern culture a tremendous amount of progress, it has, at the same time, made it possible to destroy all life on earth. While science has unlocked many of the mysteries of life and death, it has now come to the brink of being able to genetically and chemically manipulate life and "play God." It has so mastered techniques of preserving life that it can rob humans of their right to a natural death. The advances of science have not so much solved the mysteries of life and death as much as they have opened up an infinite number of new mysteries, seemingly beyond science's capacities. In this technological and scientific time there are increasingly more questions than there are answers.

A similar disillusionment has appeared in the area of faith. In former times, answers seemed easier to come by. One had only to listen to religious authority to discover absolute truths. Now church authority has often lost credibility. Church officials frequently speak in such absolutes that there seems little room for dialogue or compromise. Moreover, in most churches there exists such a plurality of views on nearly every issue that any sort of doctrinal consensus is extremely difficult to achieve.

Young adults are normally moving through a phase of questioning the beliefs that they received from their families and their church. As children, we usually accept the religious truths we are taught without question or critique. As we become more autonomous and independent, we may begin to realize that our religious beliefs are not really "owned" by us. It becomes necessary to examine our belief system and decide whether or not we as individuals want to place our faith in the truths we have taken for granted throughout our childhood. Theologian Monika Hellwig points out that as we mature, we want to better understand our beliefs, and that increased understanding can only come about by questioning, puzzling, and challenging. New discoveries in the area of belief involve risk, hesitation, perhaps even infidelities. Yet, any honest search, any effort to discover, will by necessity involve mistakes and setbacks.

The questioning of belief can be done in two ways; one destructive, the other beneficial to faith. Questions can be asked cynically and rebelliously, in such a manner that there is not actually an openness to the discovery of new understanding. This approach to questioning says: "I don't know and I don't care." Here, the former beliefs are simply pitched overboard with little effort to re-evaluate and come to a better understanding of them. This is hardly a sincere search for religious belief; rather, it is more a search and destroy mission that tends to annihilate the belief system.

The more positive approach to questioning sincerely searches for deeper understanding, is open to new data and fresh interpretations, and is prepared to seriously consider other points of view. The religious quest here is characterized by honesty, openness, and the willingness to change if the arguments are convincing. The questioning here proceeds from our natural desire to inquire, to go beyond where we are, to grow in our perception of things. This is a constructive questioning that can move the believer into new horizons of understanding and commitment.

Such questioning might well also lead to religious doubt. Some traditionalists have taken a dim view of doubt, even considering it to be a "sinful lack of faith." Paul Tillich, on the other hand, suggests that doubt is integral to the life of faith, even an indication that the faith is indeed vital and growing. Our uncertainties regarding belief indicate that creedal formulas do not have an ultimacy in themselves. They are limited statements about the Mystery of God, they are not the mystery themselves, nor are they exhaustive of the Mystery.

As Tillich says, doctrinal formulations point to the Ultimate, but they are not the ultimate. The believer, therefore, must constantly go beyond statements of belief. Herein lies the uncertainty or doubt. For the searching person, the questioning person, doubts are inevitable. Doubts are not unbelief, which is directed toward God and represents a lack of faith. Rather, doubts are the result of the critical questions we ask about our religious traditions. Religious doubts can in fact lead us to new interpretations and a deeper commitment of faith.

Faith and Belief

It is important to make a distinction between belief, which is our rational acceptance of certain formulations about ultimate truth, and faith, which is our personal commitment to and trust in God. While beliefs and faith are closely related, it is useful to see them as distinct for several reasons. First of all, some young adults at times feel that they are losing their faith, when in fact they are simply examining and questioning beliefs they received as children. For example, Richard Chaput was struck with polio when he was nine and left paralyzed from the neck down. Richard had faith in God and trusted that God would show him a way to live a happy and successful life. However, the beliefs people were giving him were filling him with bitterness and despair. People would tell him: "Oh, you poor child. It is a terrible thing to see you this way, but it's God's will." Others were speaking of beliefs about God that would indicate that God sends us suffering to test us or even to punish us.

He refused to believe that God sat in heaven pushing buttons marked "accident," "polio," or "cancer." For him, God was a loving and caring Father who would help him through anything. He decided that his condition was part of an imperfect world. As a Christian, he believed that if God could bring salvation out of the unjust and horrible death of his own Son, Jesus, God could also bring meaning out of this crippled condition for himself and for many others. Richard set out to get his high school and college diplomas through the use of tutors and correspondence courses. Then he set out on a national lecture tour, and lying on his back, he taught hundreds of thousands of people that God can bring goodness, love and meaning out of suffering. Richard had to change his beliefs in order to maintain a healthy and strong faith in God.

Beliefs of individuals and communities change, and though such changes do affect our faith, our beliefs still remain distinct from our faith commitment. Indeed, some young people find that their faith in God grows stronger when they alter their beliefs. Pamela, a freshman drama major, found that she had been going to church all her life because this was what her parents wanted. She also attended church because she was afraid that if she didn't go, God would severely punish her. Pamela came to realize that none of this was healthy for her relationship with God, so for a while she stopped going to church altogether. She wanted to change her beliefs about churchgoing and make sure that if she went it was because she freely chose to go out of the love of God who cared for her, and not from fear of a God who was waiting for her to step out of line so he could punish her.

Naturally, a change of beliefs can also be detrimental to one's faith commitment to God. Some young people stop searching for new understanding, give up on prayer because they don't feel they get what they want, and perhaps begin to believe that ultimate happiness consists in accumulating things, gaining success, or seeking self-indulgence. This, of course, will affect the faith relationship that they have with God, and the commitment can well fade away to nothing. We choose the direction of our beliefs, and the choices that we make affect the faith relationship that we have with God. A conscientious and searching examination of one's beliefs can ultimately be beneficial to one's faith. On the other hand, a careless and cynical approach to one's beliefs can be most detrimental to a faithful relationship with God.

Faith and Imagination

Paul Ricoeur, a well-known philosopher, points out that people are more inclined to be moved to do something when their imaginations have been touched than through direct appeals to their minds or wills. We speak of something "capturing our imagination," meaning that we have become excited about something and turn to it with great interest. It is in this amazing power of imagination that we conjure up our dreams of the future, fantasize about the possibilities for us, and formulate images and models that move us to action. Athletes have recently discovered the tremendous value of having the race, the game, the event etched in their imaginations before they begin. For instance, if a skier can imagine coming down the slalom perfectly before even beginning, this can be a tremendous asset when actually skiing the event itself.

The world of imagination exists within the often neglected right side of the brain. This is the area where story, image, fantasy, archetype, symbol, and ritual operate. For the ancients, who laid the groundwork for the great revelations and religions, the imagination was a significant way of knowing and experiencing. It was through the imagination that they could reach out to ultimate mystery and come to understand and experience that which is beyond conceptualization. So much of our religious literature, whether it be the Gita of the Hindus, the Koran of the Muslims, the Dhammapada of the Buddhists, the Hebrew Scriptures, or the New Testament, is imaginative literature. It is religious myth, a library of imaginative literature attempting to share with us the religious experiences and beliefs of the ages. Through stories, metaphors, images, and poetic creations these authors of sacred writings try to touch our imaginations with the possibilities of reaching out to God and to ultimate reality in faith.

The Western mind, which has been shaped by the Enlightenment, tends to be empirical. We want the facts, the evidence, the proof—before we are convinced. The "real world" for us is the world that can be measured, observed, touched, heard, and directly experienced. The world of imagination and fantasy is perhaps acceptable for entertainment or diversion, but it is not where we will often put our faith and trust. Yet, in fact, much of the energy of our lives is directed toward dreams and fantasies of future careers, achievements, and dreams that do not actually exist. So much of our striving is toward goals that are really imaginative. Isn't "the American dream" a fantasy for which many of us strive, an idealistic success story that may or may not ever materialize?

Young adults often become disillusioned with religion when they discover that much of its content relates to imagination rather than fact. As children, they are exposed to the images and myths of religion and in childlike naiveté take all of them literally. Children normally equate imaginative images with reality and easily conclude that fantasy really exists. There really is an Adam and Eve, an ark of Noah, a manger in Bethlehem, and an old man in the sky whom we call God. For the child, these religious realities exist just as really as do toys, parents, and the rest of the visible world around them.

As we grow older and mature, we begin to realize that much of what we considered in religion to be literally true is indeed myth and symbol. The first reaction is perhaps one of cynicism and disillusionment. We have been had! We have been led to believe something as true that is really fantasy. We have been given fiction as though it were fact. This was one student's reaction when she discovered that creation occurred through the "Big Bang" and through evolution, rather than through direct creation by God. She was brought up to believe that everything was indeed created by God as portrayed in the myths of Genesis. She accepted this all her life, and then suddenly in college she became aware that the universe and the earth are products of an extremely complicated process that has been moving forward for billions of years. She concluded that religious stories are nothing more than fairytales for children, and became quite disillusioned with her religious tradition. Another student of ours had always accepted the image of God as an all-knowing and all-powerful Father that took care of him and protected him from all harm. Then this young man found his own father dead one morning. Where was this God in whom he had believed? If God was such a protector, why did he let this terrible thing happen to his family? Serious doubts about the existence of God still linger with this student.

There is a way out of such religious disillusionment. First of all, there is the necessary recognition that in the area of faith we are not dealing with empirical reality. We are dealing with mystery, with a spiritual reality that can neither be measured nor proven with evidence. In faith, we are dealing with actualities similar to love, beauty, and life, realities that indeed exist, but can never be defined or tested scientifically. Second, one must come to appreciate how common it has been for religious people to use poetic image, myth, and symbol as an effective means to describe their understanding and experience of the divine. There is indeed "real" experience of the spiritual realm in this imaginative literature, but the metaphors and symbols never exhaust the mystery, nor should they be equated with the mystery. The image of "Father" we use for God is just that, an imaginative image, used to describe the strength, protection, and fidelity experienced in God. Its purpose is not to reduce God to an ancient patriarch who controls all of life. Feminine images are also used in the Hebrew Scriptures and New Testament to describe the compassion and tenderness one can experience in God.

Neither should religious myth be mistaken for historical or scientific fact. The Creation stories (and there are two of them) in Genesis carry the ancient religious beliefs that a single and good God is somehow responsible for the universe and all life. The myths conjure up a sense of grandeur and awe in the imagination and "enchant" us with a belief in an all-powerful Creator. No attempt is made to scientifically portray just how the world came into being. Likewise, the myth of the great flood imaginatively conveys the belief that somehow the good overcome and the evil bring destruction upon themselves. If we go away from the story believing that God drowns bad people and keeps all good people from harm, we have missed the point of this classical piece of religious literature.

The response of our powers of imagination is part and parcel of our faith response. God's revelation comes to us in symbol, image, and myth. God can be experienced in symbolic ritual. It is in our dreams and fantasies of a future for ourselves that we can touch the kingdom in our midst. If we can move beyond literalism, we can be open to the faith experiences that are accessible in religious literature, symbol, and ritual. Scripture, sacrament, and religious celebration can touch us with the holy only if we struggle to understand the meaning of these imaginative creations and allow ourselves to be open to their power.

The Aesthetic Dimension of Faith

Many young people who find it difficult to discover the experience of God in traditional church rituals are, however, able to encounter God in the beauty of nature, in art, music, literature, dance and athletics. Bernard Meland calls this approach to faith "appreciative awareness." Here, faith is approached more on a feeling level, more from what is now often referred to as "right-brain" experiences. As humans, we have this unique capacity of experiencing enjoyment and excitement watching a magnificent sunset, or on a solitary walk along the ocean. We can be deeply moved by a work of art, a wonderfully formed statue, a classical or popular piece of music, or by reading a powerful novel, poem, or play. We can become excited by watching or participating in a dance. And many of us can be thrilled by observing or taking part in a sporting event. Watching a basketball star doing one of his amazing slam dunks or seeing an Olympic skier soar off the 90-meter ski jump can thrill us.

Such experiences lift us beyond thought and ordinary experience. They involve our senses and our minds, but at the same time they cause us to move to an area of experience that transcends both. For the person of faith, such experiences can somehow touch the presence of Mystery in life, the powerful and creative presence of the divine. For the person who through faith is in a relationship with God, such experiences are indeed religious and sacramental. Appreciation for the beauty in life can move us to an appreciation of the Author of such beauty.

Experience and Faith

Karl Rahner has given us a useful image to help us understand the experience of faith. He speaks of the "horizon" of our experiences. The horizon is what appears to be the boundary between the earth and the sky. While the horizon seems to be reachable, in that we can point and move toward it, it somehow constantly eludes us. The horizon always is there and yet is beyond us, and as we move toward the horizon it constantly opens before us into infinity. Rahner uses this image to describe our experience of Mystery or God. In a sense, Mystery is always with us and available to our experience, yet it is also beyond us, ever opening to new vistas.

Our human experiences are "horizon experiences." In many of our everyday experiences we can get glimmers of Mystery, yet ultimate reality constantly moves beyond our reach. Consider friendship, for instance. Many young people today report that they are aware of experiencing God in the people with whom they feel close. While these same young people might not be able to have an experience of ultimacy in church rituals, they do find that when they are with their friends they experience something that is beyond description or analysis. The very experience of loving and being loved is unique and seems to be able to grow on and on without limit.

In friendship, there is the experience of trust and union that can convince us there is something here that goes even beyond the relationship. Somehow, the caring love of God, the power of God, and the forgiveness of God are able to be felt among friends. In friendship, we can feel a peace, a joy, a security, that is a very real experience of God for the person of faith. In friendship, we discover a mutual trust that is the very foundation of faith. When we trust someone, we know that we can put our very lives in that person's hands and safely surrender ourselves in love. Such an experience can offer us an appreciation for the trust that is involved in religious faith.

For instance, in the case of the Christian, faith is a matter of trustfully accepting a friendship with Jesus Christ. Here there is a confidence, a sureness that Jesus Christ is the Savior, and that his message about eternal life is worthy of trust. All of what we have said indicates that human friendship can well be a good place to start in one's attempt to relate to God. The mystery of the other, which opens more and more as we get closer to friends, can somehow put us in touch with the ultimate Mystery underlying all of reality.

The Experience of Limits

As we have seen, the horizon includes both infinite possibilities and visible limits. Such is the nature of human experience. There seem to be infinite possibilities for human growth and progress. Each of us can be always open to more extensive knowledge, a deeper experience of love, and greater personal growth. At the same time, there are obvious limitations to all of this. First of all, there are the individual limitations of intelligence, talent, health, and opportunity. A young person raised in poor conditions in the inner city experiences many more limitations than does someone who grows up in financial security. In addition, the actions of others, as well as so many random happenings, can set limits to personal freedom and progress. An athlete can be in perfect condition and have trained rigorously for an event, only to experience failure because of some fluke. Violence, accidents, failure, and collapse are all givens in human experience. And though we avoid the thought of it, the ultimate limit of death stands as another given for each and every person.

Limits imply something beyond, something out of reach. Limits imply horizons that are there and yet elude us. We want to move beyond ignorance to fuller understanding. We want to go beyond hostility and violence to reconciliation and peace. There is a drive within us to overcome handicaps, sickness, and lack of opportunity. There is a desire to go beyond failure toward success. And, even in death, there is the inner hunger to live on. Does not all this imply that there is a something or someone within all of reality that is ultimate and infinite, something or someone that transcends the limits we experience? Faith trusts that there is a creative and personal presence in reality that creates, sustains, heals, and offers eternal life. Faith has a sureness and confidence that somehow there is meaning and purpose to the limits we experience. Faith is in touch with a Mystery which can bring love and fulfillment out of the dark side of human experience. As an illustration, consider Thelma Boston who opened her house to children no one wants, the "throwaways" of society. One day she took in little Billy, who was severely retarded and constantly screamed and banged his head on the floor. Thelma gave Billy lots of love and care. She taught him sign language and showed him how to eat properly. Gradually, Billy was transformed into a happy child who scampered around the house laughing and having fun like other children. Through her deep faith, Thelma was somehow able to help this little boy transcend his severe limitations and experience the loving and healing power of a caring God.

Active Faith

Authentic faith moves beyond understanding, feeling, and experience to a way of life. The early Christians referred to their movement as "the Way." Faith is a commitment, a fundamental option to be active in loving others and pursuing justice. Genuine faith is not only concerned with privately being a "good person," it is also concerned with making the world a better place in which to live through public action.

Recent studies have shown that the contemporary generation of young adults tends to be much more concerned with personal careers than with bringing about social and political change in the contemporary world. Given the financial pressures on young adults and the fierce competition that surrounds them, this is understandable. Though many young adults are idealistic and would like to help others, they fear that if they take time to do so, they will lose ground in the race to be successful. Moreover, many college students point out that there is tremendous pressure from their parents to select a "practical" major and to be financially successful. Students who would like to major in the humanities, the arts, or in social service find their parents as well as their peers saying: "What are you going to *do* with that?"

A college education for many adults has become a time to prepare pragmatically for a successful job, rather than an opportunity for personal growth and for becoming sensitized to the needs of others in their society.

Many young adults also report a certain feeling of powerlessness in the face of the overwhelming problems that surround them. The nuclear threat, world hunger, homelessness, ecological dangers, and many other serious dilemmas seem to be so vast and unsolvable that many young people today simply abandon the possibility of their making a difference. Some simply ignore the problems; others simply choose to conclude that those who are deprived have only themselves to blame. Many settle for working to establish their own little niche of security in a threatening world, and hope that somehow they will not be touched themselves by want or oppression. Injustice and deprivation are just "someone else's problem."

On the other hand, many young people attempt to act out of their idealism, believing that they can make a difference. Consider the recent incidents of campus demonstrations against racial prejudice. Young blacks are pointing out that in spite of advances in civil rights for minorities in the United States, racial prejudice and even violent racial oppression still exist on campuses. There have been incidents where interracial couples have been verbally and physically abused; occasions where minorities have been openly attacked or socially ostracized for no other reason than the color of their skin. Many white students are appalled by this kind of hateful treatment and are publicly demonstrating against such racism on their campuses.

Critique of Western Faith

The approach to faith in the Western world has come under severe criticism from liberation theologians in the Third World. For instance, the Chilean theologian Segundo Galilea has pointed out that First World Christians too often are satisfied with a faith that consists largely of an intellectual assent to certain beliefs and religious practices, and to a spirituality that is quite private. This approach to faith tends to blind them to the plight of the poor and oppressed. It also excuses them from any practical involvement in confronting injustice and violence in their own country and throughout the world. Some have observed that Marx's criticism of religion as the "opiate of the people" has now been given a new twist. Now, instead of making the poor impervious to their affliction, religion renders the wealthy apathetic to the plight of the marginalized of the world. This Western approach to Christianity not only blinds believers to injustice, it can even stand as a justification for colonial domination and the economic manipulation of poorer countries.

There is a strong tendency in much of North America to see religion as a private matter. The old Platonic dualism between body and soul, secular and sacred, matter and spirit, tends to prevail in our approach to religion. Religion pertains to the private life of the spirit, to individual worship on Sunday, and to personal belief and prayer. The stress on separation of church and state has accentuated this dualism to the point where many Christians hold the view that church leaders have no business meddling in politics, economics, or other public matters. Any talk of faithful people getting involved in prophetic criticism of the culture or in liberation movements throughout the world makes many American Christians quite uncomfortable. In our surveys of young people, we have found that many students identify liberation theology with violent revolution and want nothing to do with it.

Peruvian theologian Gustavo Gutiérrez is quite critical of such a private approach to religion. He maintains that often Christians are committed to a form of idealism that affirms the gospel in the mind and on the lips, but gives little commitment to concrete deeds of service. Gutiérrez holds that genuine Christian faith should generate a strong resolution to assist others, especially the poor and the helpless. Such resolution grows out of listening: listening to the gospels in a new way that is sensitive to the gospel themes of freedom, detachment, sacrifice, and prophetic stands against injustice; listening to the homeless and the have-nots down the street and throughout the world as they cry out for freedom.

Active faith, therefore, moves beyond mere orthodox belief, which so often sees salvation as a reward for correct thinking. Active faith implies more than merely being a "good person," who doesn't commit crimes and who lives out the faith sincerely but privately. Genuine faith is concerned with what theologians refer to as "praxis," or reflective action. Here the Christian is not only a believer, but also one who is both aware of and active in the struggles for human dignity. From this perspective, the faithful Christian is not a mere spectator of life, watching from the safe distance of private prayer and churchgoing. Rather, faith moves one to be an agent of change. There is a need to change the sinful structures that make individuals into non-persons. One thinks of the prison systems that dehumanize and generate hatred, rather than rehabilitate. One thinks of the social service systems that render people helpless and dependent. Another obvious example is the corporate mentality that uses individuals until they are middle-aged and then discards them for younger and less expensive employees. There is the industrial attitude that would pollute our land, air, and water with toxic wastes, all in the name of efficient productivity.

The crucial question that needs to be addressed here is: "Does the faithful Christian need to be informed about and engaged in efforts to challenge violence, injustice, and oppression?" Is it enough to simply be a "nice person" committed to one's own education and career development? Or does the act of faith imply more in terms of sensitivity toward and involvement in the service of others? This is not an easy question to answer, especially for a young person already overextended in working to pay tuition fees and burdened with studies. Yet, the question needs to be honestly faced and reflected upon in any discussion of Christian faith. We will deal with this connection between faith and justice in some detail in Chapter Four.

Faith and the Community

It is possible to respond to the gift of faith on one's own, but as Anglican theologian John Macquarrie observes, such a faith is somewhat defective. Traditions develop within communities as groups of people commit themselves to a certain revelation. The Jewish faith grew out of a chosen people accepting the covenant of Yahweh with Abraham and Moses. The Islamic tradition developed as followers of Mohammed accepted his prophetic revelation from Allah. And the Christian tradition came about as disciples of Jesus Christ accepted him as their savior and gathered in a fellowship known as the church.

Humans are social by nature, and the religions that they follow bind them together as communities of believers who accept the same beliefs, follow the same moral codes, and worship together in common rituals. To say, therefore, that one accepts a certain tradition and yet does not wish to be in communion with fellow believers is somewhat of an anomaly. This is especially true in the case of one who professes to be a follower of Jesus Christ, and yet does not recognize the intimate brotherhood and sisterhood that is central to the Christian religion. Christianity is by definition communal, both in its beliefs and in its traditions of worship.

In this chapter we have attempted to describe the nature of faith. Human faith is a trusting attitude toward others and toward reality. Similarly, religious faith is a trusting response to ultimate reality, to Mystery, to God. Christian faith begins with the freely offered gift, a call to accept Jesus Christ as one's Savior, to follow his gospel of love and sacrifice, and to live eternal life hereafter. The act of Christian faith is the free choice to accept this gracious invitation and live in friendship with God and others through the Son of God, Jesus Christ.

The Christian faith response is a holistic commitment, involving the total person. This response is physical, rational, imaginative, aesthetic, and volitional. Christian faith offers the believer a new vision of human life, and enables the faithful person to experience God within all of human experience. Christian faith goes beyond belief and becomes a way of life, a way of action, especially on behalf of those who are oppressed. Finally, Christian faith is communal in that it is a commitment to a community of believers, a community dedicated to worship and self-sacrifice.

Questions for Reflection and Discussion

1. Explain your understanding of Panikkar's distinction between "faith" and "the act of faith."

2. In the church or religious group with which you are most familiar, is more stress placed on thinking, emotions, or actions? Give examples to explain your answer.

3. Discuss your point of view on Tillich's position that doubt is an integral part of faith.

4. How do you answer the Marxist critique of religious faith as the "opiate of the people"?

5. Do you think it is acceptable to view faith as a strictly private matter? Explain your answer.

Suggested Readings

Cabestrero, Teofilo, ed. *Faith: Conversations with Contemporary Theologians*. Maryknoll, N.Y.: Orbis Books, 1980

Kasper, Walter. *Introduction to Christian Faith*. Mahwah, N.J.: Paulist Press, 1980.

Monden, Louis. *Faith: Can Man Still Believe?* New York: Sheed and Ward, 1969.

Nelson, C. Ellis. *Where Faith Begins*. Richmond: John Knox, 1967.

O'Donnell, John. "The Mystery of Faith in the Theology of Karl Rahner," *Heythrop Journal* 25 (1984), 301-318.

Panikkar, Raimundo. *Myth, Faith and Hermeneutics*. Mahwah, N.J.: Paulist Press, 1979.

Tillich, Paul. *The Courage to Be*. New Haven: Yale University Press, 1952.

CHAPTER TWO

Human Development and the Growth of Faith

The life of faith is integral to the rest of our lives, and is deeply affected by how we develop as persons. Individuals who have never been able to achieve a trust in reality and in other people often find it difficult to trust in God. Likewise, those who have never learned to relate socially usually find it hard to belong to a religious community. Human development, then, is integrally related to the life of faith. Thus, the more we understand about our growth as persons, the better are we able to understand the dynamics of our faith.

In this chapter, we shall examine three main stages of human development: childhood, adolescence, and adulthood. (Treatment of the young adult stage will be taken up in the next chapter, where it will be given extended attention.) I have chosen the developmental approach to both human and faith development because it is my conviction that this approach has had the most profound influence on the contemporary understanding of personal growth. Of course, we realize the limitations of the developmental model. As so many critics have pointed out, developmental studies are often limited to Western males who are well educated and financially secure. These studies usually do not consider all persons, both male and female, or those who live in the Third or Fourth Worlds or the Orient. Thus, the results are considerably narrow. Moreover, if applied too rigidly, the "stage" approach to human growth and faith development can result in a definite elitism where a person in one stage of development is viewed as superior to another who has not reached that level. In spite of these limitations, developmental studies have contributed immensely to our contemporary understanding of the maturation process. It is for this reason that we have chosen to make use of them in the following discussion of the relationship between human development and the growth of faith.

Childhood

We begin as infants, completely dependent on others for all of our needs. We have to be fed, changed, cared for at almost every moment. Infancy is a totally self-centered time of life. As far as the infant is concerned, it is the center of the world. The infant seems to control the world about it, identifies its wishes with reality, and assumes that its every wish will be gratified.

Trust Erik Erikson, one of the most influential thinkers in the area of human development, points out that it is in infancy that one acquires to one degree or another the first ingredient for a healthy personality—a basic trust. We are not born with trust; rather, it must be gained from the way others respond to our physical, social, and psychological needs. If people respond to us with care and nurturing we begin to trust those around us and our environment. If, on the other hand, we are neglected and mistreated, we develop a mistrust that will significantly affect our later lives.

One touching example of this comes from a hospital in Boston. One day, a tiny, ten-month-old baby that had been neglected, beaten, and abandoned was brought into the emergency room. This little "Mr. Nobody" was curled up in the fetal position, looked very sad, and made no response to efforts of care and kindness. After trying all kinds of ways of getting a response and failing, the doctors and nurses decided to place the baby in a crib at the entrance of the nurses' station. It was agreed that everyone who passed Kevin (his new name) would show him some sign of love and affection and say "Hi, Kevin." For a while the infant showed no reaction, but gradually his little body began to uncoil. One day an amazing thing happened. As one of the nurses stooped down to kiss Kevin, he gave a little smile and reached out his arms. At long last, Kevin had gained some trust that others loved him. He was now able to receive as well as give affection, one of the most rudimentary stages of human development.

Autonomy and Individuality The time of total infantile dependency is brief, and before long we begin the next crucial task of human development, establishing independence, or personal autonomy. We begin to see ourselves as separate individuals who can move under our own steam, first by crawling, then by walking, and we begin to insist on doing things on our own. We begin to toddle off and explore as much of the world as we can, and we also start to get more assertive and willful. Very early on we learn the word "no."

Our individual personality begins to unfold early in childhood. We learn our name, we know our family, we are quite vocal about what we like and do not like. By the time we are three, we are aware of our sexual identities, knowing whether we are a little girl or boy. Carol Gilligan, a psychologist at Harvard University, points out that this individuation takes shape differently in boys and girls. Since women generally hold the major role in nurturing, the girl's individuation takes shape through identification with the mother. Perhaps this is why females are more capable of intimacy, empathy, and emotional attachment. Little boys, on the other hand, forge their identities as males by separating from the mother. Thus, males often have a stronger sense of independence, are often more comfortable with competition, and are more prone to want to achieve than to relate.

Going to School "Then the whining schoolboy, with his satchel and shining morning face, creeping like snail unwilling to school." This is Shakespeare's description of a most significant event in our personal development: going to school. Until this event, much of our time has been taken up with play, where we exercised our lively imaginations in creating all kinds of worlds of fantasy. The preschool years were times of wonder, stories, games, and endless hours of playing with toys.

Now, school comes upon us and demands that we also develop a sense of work, of industry. We have to develop skills for study for the first time in our lives, and we are constantly evaluated (marked) on how successful we are at mastering the content that is given us in more and more abundance. School is a time of testing us, measuring us, putting us in categories of "A," "B," "C," pass or fail, move ahead, or be held back. School also broadens our social world. Now authorities other than our parents come into our lives: teachers and a much larger circle of peers.

The Development of the Child's Faith

Our faith life takes place in the context of our personal development, and is affected by how successfully we pass through the various stages of personal growth. John Westerhoff, an expert on religious education, notes that the first stage of faith development is what he calls "experienced faith," that is, faith as we experience it from others. Since children tend to mirror the actions of those around them, they reflect the faith life that they experience in the significant people in their lives, especially parents. The faith of children is not so much their own personal faith as it is the faith that is modeled for them by others. If a child sees a parent devoted to God, that faith deeply affects the piety of the child. On the other hand, if a parent is filled with fear of God and divine punishment, this attitude can move the child to become very intimidated by God. This "experienced faith," according to Westerhoff, is largely communicated through feelings and experience, rather than through ideas. At the child's level, the faith is "caught" rather than "taught."

The degree of trust in others definitely affects the child's religious development. If the child has been well nurtured and has confidence in his or her reality and in the surrounding people, it becomes more possible for this child to place trust in God and in God's creation. Conversely, the child who has been mistreated often finds it more difficult to believe that God is a protector. As one student, who was physically abused and then abandoned by his father, put it: "It is hard for me to call God my Father, when the word 'father' conjures up such bad associations for me."

By the same token, if personal autonomy has not been successfully achieved by the child, the notion of an all-powerful, all-knowing God can be quite threatening to such a fragile ego. Several reactions to such a God are then possible. The person might so rely on God and religion that personal autonomy is further inhibited. Or, the person might feel forced to reject God simply to be able to achieve some degree of independence. How many young people have felt forced to turn from God so that they will no longer be plagued by guilt or be haunted by the notion that everything they do is being watched by a punishing God? How many young people have abandoned religion for no other reason than to gain their personal freedom?

James Fowler, a major contributor to today's discussion on the development of faith, points out that children begin with an "intuitive-projective" faith. This means that a child comes to faith more out of intuition and imagination than out of reasoning and understanding. At this stage of faith, the child is powerfully affected by examples, feelings, images, and actions. The child does not yet have sufficient powers of logic and critical reason to make up his or her mind about faith. Long-lasting images and impressions about religion are instead picked up from the beliefs and practices that children see going on around them. Thus, the child is as easily susceptible to distorted and frightening images of God and religion as it is to positive and comforting images. A child raised in a religion of fear will no doubt carry these impressions throughout life, whereas the child who is brought up in a healthy atmosphere where God is trusted and loved will carry the same religious feelings into adulthood. These impressions can be changed later on, but only with great effort and determination.

Fowler points out that when children enter school they often move on to another stage of faith called the "mythic-literal." At this point, the child can move beyond intuition and imagination and exercise concrete thinking about the stories and religious beliefs of a religious community. Now able to deal with time and space, the child can understand the myths of the tradition, identify with religious figures of the past, relate to the symbols and rules of the community, and rationally accept the beliefs of a community. At this stage, however, the young person is still quite literal in accepting religious myth. Adam and Eve are, for the child, real historical characters who lived in a garden many years ago. Noah is a real person who actually built an enormous ark to save his family from a worldwide flood. And God is often seen as an old man in the sky who created everything and now watches, ready to reward good people and punish those who are evil.

This same literal approach is taken toward religious symbols, which the child often approaches superstitiously, attributing magical powers to them. The child does not yet have the capacity to step back from the stories and the symbols in order to reflect on the meaning within them. This is the reason why some children approach communion with apprehension, thinking that somehow they will be forced to drink blood from the cup or eat a piece of flesh. They have taken the words of the Lord, "This is my body, this is my blood" far too literally.

Communal Faith If the child's experience of faith has been positive and good social skills have been developed, a new stage of faith (which Westerhoff calls "affiliative faith") is entered. This stage meets the child's need to belong, to be accepted and loved by a community. The child is usually drawn first into the parents' community, especially if the emotions of the child are touched by the warmth of the community members, the sense of awe in the liturgy, and by a feeling of accomplishment in participating in the work of the congregation. In affiliating with the community, the child loyally accepts the authority of the community's leaders, and adopts the beliefs, values, and lifestyle of the group. It is obvious here that a religious congregation that lives out its beliefs and shows interest and care for the child will deeply affect that young person's commitment to it.

One can easily see how vulnerable a child is with regard to a religious community. If the threats of punishment or rejection are too harsh, the child can lose spontaneity in faith. Religious actions like going to church can then be done out of fear or merely out of conformity. The child will go along for a time, but as he or she grows older, there may be a great deal of resentment and even rebellion. Consider the number of college students who refuse to darken the door of a church because they were for so long forced to attend church without any consideration given to their feelings or their personal freedom. Or how many young adults leave religious communities because the leadership has been overbearing or uncaring for them when they were young and vulnerable. Religion is a social phenomenon and, if religious experience has not been a good social experience, many young people are inclined to turn away from it.

The young woman who did not as a child experience sufficient value placed on bonding, friendship, affectivity, compassion, and service to others in her religious community might look elsewhere in another religious community or perhaps abandon religion altogether. The young man, who as a child experienced his congregation as either bent on taking away his independence or given to a sentimental emotionalism, might be inclined to "go it alone" in his faith life, or even set aside religious faith altogether as "unmanly" or irrelevant to his goals of future achievement. However, young women and men who found as children that their religious communities contributed positively to their personal and sexual development are usually inclined to continue in their loyalty and dedication to the life and work of these communities.

Moral Development There can be no doubt that churches and congregations affect the development of one's moral values. This is another instance where our growth as persons relates to our growth in faith. In teaching moral values, churches and congregations have to be aware of the stages of human development and sensitive to the damage that can be done if morals are forced upon individuals in such a way that healthy human growth is curtailed.

Lawrence Kohlberg, an expert in moral development, has given us an elaborate description of the various stages of moral development. The child usually passes through several of these stages. First, there is the "pre-conventional" stage of the infant, where pleasure and satisfaction determine what is good and what is bad. "If it feels good, do it," is the moral position of the small child. Thus, children will often be seen taking candy from the supermarket rack for no other reason than that it will taste good. Quite early on, the child begins to get reaction from others regarding its behavior and moves to the "reward-punishment" stage of moral development. At this point, something is good because it brings a reward; another is bad because it brings with it some punishment. The toddler will refrain from hitting a brother or sister, not because of some value like human dignity, but because the little one knows such behavior will bring on a spanking.

Gradually, as the child matures, it moves to a more reflective morality based on its own personal needs. At that point, children are inclined to go along with rules, provided there is something in it for them. For instance, the child might be inclined to clean up a room, knowing that this will mean being able to have a friend over. A final stage of moral development applicable to a child is that called "conventional morality." Here, the child accepts the values and rules of the community because the child wants to please the group and be accepted by its members. For instance, the child follows the rules of a game, not so much out of a sense of fairness, but because to ignore the rules would mean being rejected by the group. Conflicts begin to appear when young people are getting different values from their peers than those held by the parents. Since the youngster wants to belong to both groups, moral tension becomes a part of many decisions.

One can easily see the damage that can be done if religious communities are not sensitive to the moral stages of its individuals. If threats of punishment are too harsh (the hell and brimstone approach to religion), or if the threat of rejection or expulsion is too overbearing, the child can be subjected to frightening images of God and church that will distort the life of faith. If faith implies a loving and trusting relationship with God, how can this be maintained in an atmosphere of fear and excessive guilt? Consequently, to use either the reward and punishment or the conventional model improperly with regard to religious values can seriously impede faith development as well as damage personal freedom and responsible decision making. Mature faith and mature moral development, not controlling individuals or dominating them with childish restrictions and threats of punishment, are the goals of faith communities. Responsible church leadership is done through inspiration and persuasion, not through intimidation or force.

Adolescence

Adolescence is generally a tumultuous period in anyone's life. For some, it is an exhilarating time of challenge and growth. For others, it is a time of excruciating pain and depression. For most, it is a mixture of both. The teen years are a period of "rebirth," a movement from childhood into the adult world, from security and simplicity to independence and complexity. It is a time when tremendous changes take place in one's body and in many areas of one's life.

Adolescence is a time when we need lots of mirrors to observe all the changes that are going on in our appearance; a time when we need friends who can empathetically listen to all the inner turmoil and searching. The teen years are a time of storm and stress, an exciting time of transition that can move one on to a challenging future, or, tragically, end in collapse and failure. It is a period of tremendous highs and lows, filled at times with positive energy and optimism, and at other times characterized by depression and cynicism. While the issues of identity, questioning, and socialization are with us all through life, these issues take on a unique intensity during adolescence.

Identity One of the most difficult struggles during the teen years is with personal identity. "Who am I?" suddenly becomes a question, perhaps for the first time in one's life. In childhood, our identity seems to be rather simple and tied up with externals: where we live, where we go to school, what teams we play on, and what our parents and teachers tell us about ourselves. In many ways, our identity has been a given from outside ourselves, and most of our personal decisions have been made for us by others. As we enter the teen years, this childhood identity suddenly begins to change and we are faced with the challenge of building our own inner identity. We have to make more and more of our own decisions, and somehow put ourselves together in such a way that we don't lose the approval of the others, and yet are an authentic and independent self.

Questioning The many questions about personal identity and our place in the world, along with newly acquired capabilities of abstraction and intellectual critique, help make adolescence a time of questioning and searching. As children we accepted what we heard about ourselves, reality, and religion on the authority of those outside ourselves. Adults had to be right, because we thought they knew everything and had all the answers. In the naiveté of childhood, everything seemed to be rather simple and clear. Now that we start to become "our own person," we begin to wonder: Do we really accept all that we have heard? Are these things we have heard from parents and teachers really true? Now that our own personal authority is growing within us, everything will have to be brought before our own "court," re-examined, challenged, and perhaps even rejected.

Since teens are trying to detach themselves from dependence on parents and other adults, the latter often lose authority and appear to be "stupid" and "out of touch" to teens. Consequently, the resulting teen theories on reality often appear egocentric, and condemnatory of what they see going on around them. Some teens experience a total estrangement between themselves and the world. Richard Parsons, an expert in adolescent psychology, points out that such alienated youths often feel that they are consistently letting down themselves and others. This can ultimately lead to a feeling that they are valueless and unworthy of love.

Socialization Most teens need to have their friends around them. Adolescence is a period of life when we aren't too sure who we are, a time when we are vulnerable to criticism and attack, and so always in need of a little help from our friends. This seems to be particularly true of teenage girls, whose identities, as we have observed, are so often linked to relationships and require emotional intimacy. Adolescent girls are constantly looking for the "best friend" in whom they can confide and trust. And, since often there is not enough maturity to keep such trust, there are many infuriating experiences of betrayal, with a constant shifting of relationships. The "best friend" of today may be the hated enemy of tomorrow.

Adolescent boys also need friends, but perhaps for different reasons than girls. Boys often tend to be more aggressive, more competitive, and less given to sharing on an emotional level. Boys need friends to affirm their prowess, to recognize their achievements, to "stand with" in times of difficulty and danger. And, among boys, there usually does not seem to be that urgency to gather, share, and trust with feelings that we find among girls.

During the pre-teen and teen years the first moves are made toward friendship and intimacy with the opposite sex. As we formulate the new self-identity, we want to share that self, at least tentatively, with another on a sexual level. We often need to have someone tell us if our "new model" of young woman or man is acceptable and lovable. We may want to see if we are capable of responsible caring and fidelity in a relationship with a person of the opposite sex. At times, we might feel the urge to dominate and possess the opposite sex; at other times, there is the need to hand ourselves over in submission. Regardless, we find within us new stirring for relationships on levels of depth that we never experienced as children. Moreover, there is a new appetite stirring within us that was never there before, the appetite for sexual gratification. And, as we start to head down that road, it often seems that all that we see are stop signs!

The Development of the Adolescent's Faith

In discussing the stage of faith he calls the "individuating-reflective" stage, Fowler points out that many teens enter this stage when they decide to take responsibility for their own identities and religious commitments. He points out that during this time adolescents usually encounter a number of tensions: between wanting their own faith and not wanting to leave their religious community; between their own personal positions and doctrine that is presented objectively; between their need for absolutes and the relativity that surrounds them. At school, work, and in the media they encounter many who speak with a new authority to them about matters which, as children, they thought were settled. They encounter teachers and peers whom they respect who have no regard for organized religion, or who doubt or even reject the whole notion of the existence of God. Conversely, those who have been brought up with little or no religious background suddenly meet those who are strongly committed to religious beliefs.

Because of the inability to accept such relativity, many teens are forced into an extreme position either for or against religion, a position that might well last for the rest of their lives. In Fowler's terms, they establish a highly individuated approach to faith. The religious stance in this stage might remain unexamined until some other critical time of life occurs, such as mid-life, or old age.

Fowler points out, however, that many young people never get to the stage of individual faith. Many remain in the conventional stage where they continue to accept or reject religious beliefs simply on the authority of others. Those who live in strong families and communities of faith might let their beliefs go unchallenged. It is more important for them to belong than it is to begin disputing the traditions of the community. We see this particularly in fundamentalist communities, where the young are extremely enthusiastic about the beliefs of their communities and accept the tradition without question. More commonly, however, young people find themselves among peers where it is not "cool" to speak of religion or to give any indication that one belongs to a religious tradition. Here, the pressure of the group can well lead to a rejection of religion in order to gain acceptance, or at least to remain a "closet religious" and live out one's religious faith privately.

A Searching Faith Naturally, with all the changes going on externally and internally for the teen, faith life is usually affected. Westerhoff points out that many youngsters at this time enter what he calls a "searching faith." The independence and autonomy gained by the individual often require that the beliefs that have been handed on by parents and the religious community be examined critically. The teenager often reflects: "I have believed all of this because my parents and others have told me so. Do I really believe all this on my own?" Few teens have chosen their own religious tradition. That decision has usually been made for them from the time they were infants. In fact, they have accepted someone else's faith, and it is time now to look at this religious faith and determine whether they want that as part of their new identity. Thus, there are doubts, challenges, questions, and even rejection of former beliefs.

Teens will often feel a need to distance themselves from religious beliefs and practices just to gain perspective and be free to make their own decisions on what they believe and don't believe. Up until now, perhaps, religious faith has been more on a feeling level or has been maintained in order to belong and to be accepted. The child usually does not have either the mental capacity or the independence to challenge the religious beliefs of surrounding adults. But the adolescent is beginning to acquire sufficient critical capacities and autonomy to question and challenge. Truths need to be tested, examined. Practices like going to church or participating in family prayer often need to be resisted, just to see if one is freely choosing these on one's own, and not merely out of a childlike obedience.

Maryellen, a teen from Chicago, recounts the story of how she and her sister used to tell their parents they were going off to church every Sunday, when they were actually playing miniature golf. She remembers: "We weren't trying to be defiant or anything, but we had been told that if we missed church we would go to hell and be evil people. We just wanted to see if that were true. Actually, we missed church for many months, and we didn't feel any different than before. We felt that we were still good persons. During college we both got back to going to church, but now it is our decision and for our own reasons."

During this period of searching faith, many teens question some of their deepest beliefs and commitments. Do I really believe that there is a God? Is God really responsible for creation? Did Jesus really exist, and if so, did he really perform all those miracles in the stories? Is there a hell? If God is as loving as they say, why would God send someone to be burned for all eternity? Is there really an afterlife, or has all that been concocted by people who were afraid to die? Does one really have to be a member of a church to be "saved?" Are the Scriptures true or are they just stories made up a long time ago by primitive people who were superstitious? Is it really wrong to have sex with someone that I love? Why is it evil to steal when the rich corporations don't really miss what I take? Is it really sinful to cheat in school when so many around me are doing it? What is wrong with getting bombed out of my mind when it feels so good and is the only way to party with my friends? Aren't a lot of our church laws put together by stupid old men who are living in the past?

These and many other religious questions are seriously raised by teens and they have to be listened to and taken seriously. Often, when they raise such questions, young people merely face speeches and even outrage. Consequently, they either settle these questions on their own or with their peers, often in an inadequate fashion, or they simply put the questions aside as irrelevant to everyday life and move on without a religious commitment.

It is common for teenagers to drop out or "take a leave of absence" from organized religion. Social researcher Dean Hoge shows that the leading reason for young people dropping out of church is tension with their families. When many young people reach the age of searching, they are not given the space to ask their questions and carry on their search. Families are often shocked at what they perceive as religious rebellion, and will hear no more of such talk against the church. Parents often feel that it is their responsibility to "pass on their faith" to their children. When they hear religious questioning, they interpret it as failure on their part and take it as a personal attack, rather than listening. The young, who are frequently hypercritical, charge that the church members are hypocrites, that church is boring, and that all the ministers talk of is money. Religious alienation quite often sets in, and the young person drops out at the first available opportunity.

Adolescents and Religious Communities As we have seen, many teens are in a state of confusion regarding their religious faith. They are beginning to shape their own religious identity, and are searching for answers to their new religious questions. As a result, many young people are inclined to be attracted only to churches where they can find friends, both young and old, who will accept them and listen with interest to their questions. More often than not, churches are concerned with adult and family questions, and have little time for the young. Some churches tend to sermonize at youth, determined to show the young "the evil of their ways."

Teens often have a deep sense of loyalty. However, they will not give this loyalty to a community unless the group shows real concern for adolescent struggles and offers young people sufficient room to grow and develop their own personal faith.

Few young people will be inclined to be loyal to a religious community that lets them down in one of the most difficult periods of life.

We have seen earlier how important it is for teens to have a sense of belonging and to have access to friendship with both sexes. Churches that recognize these needs usually do well in holding on to younger members. Churches with youth groups, teen liturgies, and counseling services for teens are often successful in nurturing the faith of the young. On the other hand, those churches and religious groups that are child- or adult-centered rapidly lose touch with the teenagers. Dean Hoge's study of religious dropouts shows that one of the main reasons the young leave the churches is boredom. Teens are interested in school performance, their looks, making friends, sex, their future, and many other practical matters of youth. The issues they hear addressed in church gatherings many times simply have no bearing on these concerns.

Friendship with God The relational, however, does not only pertain to the teen's faith life with the community. It is also an issue with regard to the teen's personal relationship with God. Teens find personal relationships of ultimate importance, and many place a value on having a healthy relationship with God. They are, however, attracted to a positive and loving image of God, a God who is concerned about all the changes that are going on inside of them; a God who listens and supports them in need. Harsh and judgmental images of God tend to drive youth away from religion, especially the alienated who are convinced that no one accepts or loves them.

Overemphasizing the male, patriarchal image of God can also turn young people away. Young men who are reacting to a strong, dominating father, as well as young women who are becoming more and more aware of the value of the feminine side of God, are searching for new images of God to which they can better relate. Thus, during the teen years the notion of God as friend, companion, or mentor is much more appealing.

Moral Development In terms of Kohlberg's stages of moral development, teens may operate out of several levels of moral decision making, and vary as to how they accept the ethical teaching of their churches and congregations. It is possible that a teen still follows church laws strictly out of obedience, or from fear of punishment from parents, the church group, or even from God. Possibly, the youngster accepts the community's moral values simply to please and win approval.

Some move on to what Kohlberg terms the "law and order" stage, where they accept the moral values of the religious tradition because they believe that maintaining such rules is necessary to promoting order in the community. From this point of view, it is necessary to fulfill one's obligations to maintain the established system. Others move on from this "don't rock the boat" approach to morality to a genuine concern for human rights and justice, even if that means challenging the traditional value systems of their religious communities. Such a posture, however, would be unusual for an adolescent.

Whatever stage of moral development teens find themselves in, many of them discover that there are often sharp contrasts, perhaps even contradictions, between the moral values of their culture and that of their churches and congregations. Many of the traditional churches have simply lost credibility with the young when it comes to such areas as sexual morality, social ethics, and many other areas of personal morality.

Adulthood

It is only recently that psychologists have given serious attention to adult development. In the past, the adult stage of life was seen as a final stage achieved in the early twenties. The adult was viewed as a finished product, rather than a person who is as much in process as any child or teen. Now we understand that the same developmental principles are operative throughout all of life, and that there is a series of developmental stages or seasons unique to adult life. Contrary to Freud's view, the adult life is not merely a scene for the reenactment of the child's conflicts. As Erikson has pointed out, life is a journey from birth to death, and human development follows universal principles, as well as uniquely individual patterns that are influenced by our personal make-up, our sexuality and a variety of environmental factors. In this section, we will discuss the various stages of adult development and comment on the faith development that is often associated with these stages.

The Settling-Down Period By the time they have reached their late twenties or early thirties, most adults have "settled down." They have made their key adult choices: the single or married state, occupation, lifestyle, what contribution they hope to make to society. If they have chosen marriage, they have decided by this time whether or not to begin a family of their own. If they have chosen to have children, they have begun the process of nurturing and educating these young ones. At this point in life, adults are usually at the height of their physical and mental powers and will remain at that peak until middle age begins to set in.

During these years of "getting established," there is a great deal of youthful energy, and ambition drives the adult to succeed in fulfilling the dreams and goals that have been set ahead. In Erikson's terms, the mature adult has now completed tasks necessary to be intimate with others, and settles down in close relationships with family and friends. The adult ideally has become separated from parents and is now self-sufficient and independent. A new inner life structure has been formed in which adults live their own lives and plan their own futures.

We have become more aware in our time how this settling-down time often differs for young women. Commonly, their identity is developed in terms of their husbands and children. Instead of having their own dreams and ambitions, women often act as supporters of their husbands, and do not get sufficient opportunity to use their own personal gifts or to achieve the life goals suited to their talents and skills. While marriage and family offer these women more than ample opportunities to nurture and care for others, they may not have the chance to develop decisiveness, assertiveness, and qualities of leadership. Men, on the other hand, are usually caught in the competitive race to move ahead or go up the corporate ladder. They get many opportunities to achieve, aggressively compete, and be successful in the public forum. Yet, men may not have the chance to develop the more compassionate and tender dimensions of their personalities. Of course, much of this is changing as more women enter careers, and as the traditional roles in marriage become altered.

Middle Age In our culture, the age of forty signals the beginning of what we refer to as "middle age." The physical signals of change become apparent as adults begin to have gray hair, baldness, wrinkles, and often, weight problems. Inner changes are also experienced, as adults begin to realize the limits of their accomplishments, to look at past failures, and to recognize the fact that all their dreams and ambitions did not work out quite as expected. Death becomes a very real possibility at this time as one or both of our parents die, and we see the beginning of the deterioration of our bodies.

Middle age can be a topsy-turvy experience for adults, often including more turmoil than adolescence. Job changes, divorces, depression, mental and physical breakdowns frequently occur during this period, giving clear evidence of the storm that is going on during this season. For men who have not achieved their ambitions in life, there is often the feeling of failure. Even those who have achieved their goals may begin to experience boredom with the routine, and they desire to start over. Sometimes this urge results in bizarre behavior, such as affairs with much younger women and adolescent adventures with "the guys."

For women, the so-called mid-life crisis usually takes a different turn. Commonly, a married women comes to realize that her identity has always been in terms of roles and has been so linked to others that she has not had the opportunity to be herself or fulfill her personal ambitions. If she decides to "go for it" and build her own career, she can put tremendous pressures on her marriage and family life. More often than not, women who decide on careers find that not only do they have to compete in the marketplace, they also have to do the bulk of the housekeeping and parenting. For many women, this role of "super mom" brings on a great deal of stress, with accompanying anger and resentment. Women who have decided to remain single often experience an intense loneliness and the need to get more in touch with the nurturing dimensions of their personalities.

Erikson points out that the polarity that must be dealt with during the middle years is between generativity and stagnation. Generativity refers to the task of caring for the younger generation, whether as a parent, mentor, coach, teacher, or a supervisor on the job. This is generally a key role for the middle-aged person, who stands in a position of stability, and is responsible not only for the generation coming up, but also for the elderly who begin to depend more on them. Erikson points out that if, for one reason or another (selfishness, attachment to material things, personal ambition, or a poor self-image), middle-aged adults aren't able to respond to the challenge of being generative to others, they can easily stagnate and lose their sense of purpose in life. Failure in this challenge can have dire effects when the person approaches the next season of life, old age.

Old Age There is a great reluctance in the United States to use the term "old," or even "elderly." The thought of being old in our culture is frightening for many, largely because the Western culture does not hold old age in reverence, as Eastern cultures often do. We speak of "senior citizens" or the "golden years" in an attempt to avoid the notion of being old. But the fact is that during the sixties each person begins a unique period of life. Like all seasons, it has its own challenges, assets, and liabilities. Old age can be a time of great freedom since older adults usually no longer have the earlier career or domestic responsibilities. Many elderly achieve in these years a marvelous degree of wisdom and creativity. On the other hand, old age has its difficulties. Illness, the death of friends, the loss of a spouse, neglect by children, and the approach of death are severe challenges during this time.

Erikson holds that the main tension for old age is between integrity and despair. The elderly person must reflect on his or her life and how it has been spent. Now there is mostly past and little future; many yesterdays and fewer tomorrows. Instead of dreams of the times to come, the elderly have memories of the way things were. The elderly person must find integrity in accepting the triumphs and the failures of life and look back with a sense that life has been meaningful and purposeful. Otherwise, the elderly person succumbs to despair, to the feeling that life has been a waste, a failure, a "tale told by an idiot," as Shakespeare expressed it. Death is then fearsome and bitter.

The Development of the Adult's Faith

Since religious faith is an integral part of human life, its development is deeply affected by the various seasons we pass through. The Christian tradition is based on a notion of personal conversion, a continuing process of radical change toward being more unselfish and loving throughout all the stages of one's life. Therefore, there is an integral connection between gospel living and the various life stages. The person of faith views each season of life as a time to relate uniquely to God, a sacred time in which to discern prayerfully how he or she is called to grow, and what God calls that person to accomplish.

Autonomous Faith The person of faith views the important decisions for making one's own life in terms of "vocation," or "calling." Thus, personal ambition and the desire to construct one's individual life are colored by discernment of what God might want us to do with our lives. This discernment provides the person with a caution that life choices not be made purely out of selfish motives, or out of a desire to be only materially successful. Christian discipleship implies that we will be better human beings if we are "other-centered," people of service to others. This, of course, often flies in the face of the current secular approach to choosing one's life goals.

Separation from parents and the home, which began in adolescence, now becomes more final, and this often brings with it a great deal of religious upheaval. Most adults make up their own minds about religious belief and affiliation, and that decision can set adults into conflict with their parents. Adults today, in choosing a marriage partner, will frequently move out of the church traditions in which they were raised. Parents who feel that it is their responsibility to pass their faith on to their children can easily interpret such a decision as failure on their part, the same way they have reacted during their child's teen years.

Westerhoff describes the adult faith that can be achieved as we separate from parents as "owned faith." Whether or not we choose the faith tradition of our parents, the "owned faith" is ours, chosen as a result of our own personal search and evaluation of religious beliefs and our careful choice of church affiliation. Adults need images of God that are more compatible with personal autonomy and independence. They need to affiliate with church communities that will allow for the formation of a responsible conscience and for the individual expression of religious values. This faith brings together belief and deed, as the mature adult makes the commitment to actually live out his or her beliefs.

To reach this stage of faith development, of course, requires the space in which to search, and the personal interest to do the necessary and often painful discernment about what we really believe, and how authentically we actually live out these beliefs. Too often, even mature adults remain in a searching stage of faith because they have neither the internal freedom nor the interest to move beyond a state which might be described as a quiet agnosticism. Here, one slips into an attitude toward religion which says: "I just don't know, and honestly I just don't care to know."

The American Dream The persistence of the "American dream" as the ultimate goal of many adults has affected the faith development of many. Key life choices, such as who to marry, what job to select, and which lifestyle to pursue, are often dominated by this dream's promise of material success and comfort. For many, particularly with the financial pressures that exist today, pursuing this dream can be so all-absorbing that there is not time or energy to pursue the life of the spirit. Material things replace spiritual realities as the ultimates of life. As Paul Tillich has pointed out, this results in a sort of contemporary idolatry, a distortion of faith that can approach the demonic.

At this point, a word should be said about the dilemma of the many who never get close to the so-called American dream. The homeless, the destitute, the people who want for decent shelter and food often feel that somehow they are without dreams and ambitions. So many individuals have neither the education, the parental modeling, nor the employment necessary to be a part of the American success story. Doubtless, this affects their faith life as well as their church affiliation.

Such people often feel embarrassed to even show up at any gathering of organized religion because they feel they lack the proper clothing and personal appearance. For them, religion seems to be for the "haves" and not for the "have-nots." Church affiliation appears to be a way the prosperous and comfortable can isolate themselves from the needs of others, a kind of private faith which blinds many from the oppression and injustice that is around them. Thus, the poor can find themselves alienated from religious communities, and are forced to develop a private faith life for themselves that will at least help them survive the hard times they experience. At this point, it would seem that religion becomes more a divisive factor in life than a way of bringing people together in friendship and love, as it should be.

Parents' Tough Questions Having children of one's own is often an important faith transition for adults. Our children ask the difficult questions about who made us, who God is, what happens after death, and what it means to be a good person. Many adults have not asked these ultimate questions for a long time, if at all, and are forced to address them for themselves if they are to give sincere and responsible answers. As parents, we carry the serious responsibilities of explaining spiritual reality to our young ones and of modeling for them what it means to be a faithful person. Those who take this responsibility seriously often have to go back to the drawing board regarding their own beliefs and faith life, and make some hard religious decisions.

One observes many adults at this time of life once again getting more seriously involved in faith matters and in church attendance. This was the case of Bill, a young executive in Pittsburgh. Once he got into college, Bill had little time for religion. He took a long leave of absence from his faith life and became totally preoccupied with his career, his marriage, and establishing a home. All of a sudden, it came time for his seven-year-old daughter to make her first communion. Bill remarks that both her questions and the simple faith she had in Jesus caused him to look at his own faith and take stock in how he was living the Christian life. For Bill, his daughter's communion was a turning point in his life, an event that brought him back to his own following of Jesus and his own appreciation of going to church and joining in communion with his local congregation.

In Fowler's terms, Bill has reached the "individuative-reflective" stage of faith. He has critically examined his own beliefs and takes responsibility for his own religious commitment. Bill now accepts his faith, no longer on the authority of his parents or because this is the conventional faith of his associates, but because this is the tradition that he, as a free and independent individual, holds to be true. In Kohlberg's terms, Bill is also prepared to move beyond a conventional morality of merely pleasing others or keeping rules out of obligation to external authority. He is heading toward a post-conventional morality, where he operates out of his own internalized moral principles and is concerned more about gaining individual rights for others than he is in simply maintaining public law and order.

Faith in the Middle Years Of course, it is improper to generalize about the faith development of individuals, but there are certain patterns that are observed during different seasons of life. Those in their middle years are once again brought to ultimate questions by the fact that they are facing their own finiteness and the limitations of life in general. In middle age, people often ask: "Is this all there is?" If they have been successful and now have acquired a good deal of material things, all this can now seem to be rather meaningless. Some react cynically to this "failure of success," an experience of disillusionment with all the achievements that were supposed to bring happiness. Some find little solace in their religious faith at this time, especially if there has been little development in their faith along the way.

Others find this to be a time of deepening faith, when they rely on true ultimates and meanings that reach beyond the limitations that are now being experienced. Still others kick aside the traces of their religious values and experiment with much that has been previously forbidden, only to face guilt and self-recrimination later.

As Erikson has observed, the middle years allow many opportunities for generativity, for nurturing and assisting the younger generation. Since religious values place a great priority on service to others, this is a time when the mature adult can make great strides in growth psychologically as well as spiritually. It is a time for reaching out to others; a time that calls forth great energies to be of service. Those who, for one reason or another, pass up these opportunities can dry up spiritually, becoming isolated and extremely self-centered. Such a posture doubtless makes it difficult for a person to relate authentically to religious belief, or to share a sense of community in any religious sense.

Fowler speaks of a later stage of faith development, which he calls the "conjunctive" stage, wherein one acknowledges the grays of life, its tensions and paradoxes. This is the stage where one can accept the mysteries of life, admit the limitations of religious symbol and myth, and live with partial truth. The mature adult can also accept the religious positions of others as having validity. This is particularly useful for the parent, who at this point in life might have teens or young adults taking religious positions which challenge the parents' tradition.

Faith and the Elderly This is a crucial period of life that challenges on all levels—including that of religious belief—anyone going through it. In this period, one experiences great losses, perhaps the loss of health, loved ones, or even financial security.

Here one faces death as something that can come at any time—a part of life. For the faithful, this is a time for religious integration, a time to take stock in their lives, to accept both failures and successes, the good and the bad, and, with trust, to put one's life in the hands of God. The challenge to the belief in life beyond becomes intense. It is only when one really faces death that one can understand the stress that there is in facing what appears to be annihilation, but which to the person of faith is a transition to new life. The elderly person who experiences great love and support from others, perhaps the tender love of grandchildren, and who has sustained a purposeful life, can weather the storms of old age and make great strides in spiritual development. The ultimate questions are pressing during this period, and yet there is leisure time for reflection and prayer. There is also more time for reaching out to others in service, and for developing dimensions of personal life that were neglected during busier times.

Fowler describes a stage of "universalizing" faith, which he says is rare. Who is to say? It is quite possible that many elderly people do reach such a stage of universalizing faith where they are indeed detached from material things, are emptied of self-concern, and are experiencing a unique freedom from fears of what might happen to them should they continue serving others. Kohlberg also describes a moral stage of universal ethical principles, where one moves out of one's own conscience, has a deep respect for all people, and is committed to struggling for peace and justice in the world. Since this in fact describes the Christian gospel life, it is conceivable that many faithful elderly people achieve such a stage of moral development.

So far we have discussed the developmental tasks that face all of us as we move through childhood, the teen years, and then on into the various stages of adulthood. We have seen that the growth of one's faith is integrally related to these stages of human development. In the next chapter, we will focus on the young adult stage of development, and examine the unique challenges to personal and religious growth that often present themselves during the college years. This does not imply that all college students are young adults, for we realize that many older students are appearing on the campuses throughout the United States. It is hoped that these older students will find relevant material for themselves in this present chapter, where the later stages of adulthood were discussed.

Questions for Reflection and Discussion

1. What were some of the key events or turning points in your movement from childhood to adolescence?
2. Would you describe your religious faith as predominantly "searching" or "owned"? Could you think of another term that would perhaps better describe your present stage of faith?
3. Give examples of people close to you who are either middle-aged or elderly. Describe how they exhibit some of the characteristics of these stages that are discussed in this chapter.
4. Discuss middle-aged adults you know who demonstrate healthy generativeness in the way they relate to and assist younger people.
5. Are there any elderly people that you know who are now influencing your religious views? If so, give specific examples of how these individuals affect your religious attitudes positively or negatively.

Suggested Readings

Chamberlain, Gary. *Fostering Faith: A Minister's Guide to Faith.* Mahwah, N.J.: Paulist Press, 1988.

Dykstra, C. and Parks S., eds. *Faith Development and Fowler,* Birmingham, Ala.: Religious Education Press, 1986.

Fowler, James. *Stages of Faith: The Psychology of Human Development and the Quest for Meaning.* San Francisco: Harper & Row, 1981.

____. *Becoming Adult: Becoming Christian.* New York: Harper & Row, 1984.

Gilligan, Carol. *In a Different Voice.* Cambridge, Mass.: Harvard University Press, 1982.

Spencer, Anita. *Seasons: Women's Search for Self through Life's Stages.* Mahwah, N.J.: Paulist Press, 1982.

Stokes, Kenneth. *Faith Is a Verb: Dynamics of Adult Faith Development.* Mystic, Conn.: Twenty-Third Publications, 1989.

Westley, Richard. *Redemptive Intimacy: A New Perspective for the Journey of Adult Faith.* Mystic, Conn.: Twenty-Third Publications, 1981.

Whitehead, Evelyn and James. *Christian Life Patterns.* Garden City, N.Y.: Doubleday, 1979.

CHAPTER THREE

The Young Adult and Faith Development

Sharon Parks, a leading expert on the young adult stage of development, maintains that this stage is the birthplace of the adult vision. Young adults are people "on the way" to a new life; people engaged in putting together a uniquely personal and individual journey. As such, young adults are in a transitional time. They are neither adolescents, nor are they mature adults. They are, if you will, "novice adults," who are engaged in the difficult task of building inner structures that will be adequate for them to take adult places in the everyday world.

On one side, young adults experience dissolution, the coming apart of the past child and teen identity. Former assumptions about life, past images of self, old rules and values seem to lose the absoluteness they once had and must be seriously examined. On the other side, this is a time for recomposing, for "getting it together," for constructing a new adult self that can handle the future with confidence. Young adulthood is a time for recognizing one's own values, beliefs, talents and handicaps; it is a time to decide how one can make a difference.

Change usually produces tensions, and no young adult is a stranger to tensions both inner and outer. There is the pull from parents who want to keep protecting and parenting, while there is the tug within the self to listen to its own voices. There is the call from religion to be orthodox, while there is the urge to "chuck" religion as irrelevant. New thinking urges us to treat people as dignified and equal, while old ideas recall us to prejudice, sexism, and discrimination. The voice of moderation teaches us the value of peaceful settlement and reconciliation; while the Rambos around us advise violence and a "nuke 'em" mentality. On one hand, our conscience tells us of parental values of sexuality and other moral issues; on the other hand, experience may tell us something rather different.

Establishing Identity

Each sex has its own singular challenges in reaching maturity. The young woman might feel called to a successful career, and yet at the same time want to get married and raise a family. She wants to establish her own identity, have her own dreams, and yet she searches for a man, suspecting that she will often play only a supporting role in *his* dream. However, it is no simpler for the young man to establish an adult identity. Tradition has told him to be strong, tough, independent, and reluctant to show emotion. He is told that he is to be the protector of the weaker sex, the breadwinner, a leader in a male-dominated, patriarchal society. But other voices make him suspect that all of this is of a passing age, and that the future will expect him to be a person of feeling and compassion, dedicated to equality and justice.

There are a number of obstacles that can stand in the way of our establishing a mature adult identity. First of all, fears can prevent us from going through the necessary changes and taking the needed risks to grow. Maybe we have made mistakes or possibly failed at something, and we are afraid that this will happen once again. Some young people get so paralyzed by these fears that they simply escape into drugs, drinking, apathy, cynicism, or some other way out of facing change in their lives. Another obstacle to growth is the pressure we receive from others who want us to be something that they have in mind. Parents can pressure us to be what they want us to be; peers can manipulate us to play roles that are out of character for us; even friends can force us to be what they want us to be by threatening to withhold friendship if we do not cooperate.

Finally, those who have authority over us can force us to play artificial roles that do not really fit our personalities at all. Teachers can use their power of passing or failing us to make us seem as if we are interested and cooperative students, when we might not have the slightest interest in the course at hand. Bosses can intimidate us into all kinds of roles where we seem to be industrious and dedicated, when we couldn't care less about the job we are doing. Churches and religious congregations can attempt to force us to believe and attend services, threatening us with rejection or punishment. All such role-playing, even though it seems necessary at times, actually inhibits our personal growth and prevents us from formulating and acting out our true identity.

Establishing one's identity is always a process, but the young adult period is a crucial transitional time for growth in this area. The young adult takes up the pen to write the future of her or his own story, to establish the foundations of a personal maturity, knowing full well that many inner changes will have to be dealt with, and that numerous obstacles will be in the way toward mature development.

Gaining Independence

One of the most important and yet painful tasks of young adulthood is gaining independence. As children, and even as adolescents, we depend on our parents for security, for psychological and financial support, and for many of our values and religious beliefs. Going off to college is an important step in changing all of that. We begin to separate from our home, our family, our neighborhood, our parish or congregation. Even though we usually still depend somewhat on our families for financial support, we are getting more and more independent in our decision making, our living circumstances, and our thinking. We are moving to a new position of living on our own, and the challenge is to separate from the past without rejecting our parents and all that has been important to us. We don't want to end up alienated and isolated, but neither do we want to remain in a childlike dependence on our parents and the past. There is a new freedom, but it often has its risks of painful mistakes and hurts for ourselves and for those who care for us.

Part of gaining independence is making a break from the voices and the authority that exist at home. Young adults usually want to be different from their parents and their brothers and sisters. They want to be "their own person" and make their own decisions about what they will be and what they will do with their lives. As Abraham Maslow has pointed out, to be "self-actualized" we have to listen to our own inner voices and make our own decisions about what our future will be.

Separating from parents is not always an easy task. At times, young people want to cling to the safety and security that existed at home. Parents have been the providers, the protectors, the supporters. It is not easy to give up the comforts and luxuries we have enjoyed. To go off on one's own often means to give up the things one has been used to having. It means sacrifice, struggle, hard work; this may not have a great appeal to the young person who has gotten used to being carried along for many years. It is easier to "keep one foot on base" and not risk independence. Moreover, the college student's independence is usually only partial. With today's costs for higher education, few students can go it entirely on their own. When the going gets tough, it is still necessary to turn to parents for help. And we know that when the term ends, we usually still have a place to go where they will take us in and care for us. Most young adults are on the way to independence and are not in a position to be entirely on their own.

On the other side, many parents are reluctant to allow their young to have independence. The parental instinct to control and protect the lives of their offspring is strong. Parents often have a hard time realizing that their children are growing up and will eventually not need them as they did when they were children. Mother still wants to take care of her "baby," or father still thinks that "daddy's girl" needs him for protection. Parents often panic at the very thought of their young being on their own, vulnerable and surrounded by dangers.

Suzy, a junior who wants to be a lawyer, remarks that it is impossible for her to live at home. The hours she keeps and the friends she has are simply unacceptable to her mother. Since there is always a battle when she comes in very late, she and her mother have agreed that Suzy will have to live on her own. Her mother said sadly: "I love you dearly, but I can't live with you if you insist on living as you are. The worry and the tension are simply too much for me." Suzy eventually moved in with a friend. She points out that it is often harder for a female to gain independence, because parents think that they have to give much more protection to a daughter than to a son.

For Jake, a senior pre-med student, the separation from his parents has also been painful. His father is an accomplished surgeon and is really the model that moved Jake to be a doctor. But the father is a very dominating figure and seems to want to control Jake's future. Jake says that being at home is like being in prison, because he is severely restricted in his movements and there are numerous confrontations with his father. Jake feels bad because he has tended to set all kinds of emotional traps for his father and has provoked him into tirades that made Jake feel superior. He feels as though he is trying to make his father into a monster so that he will then have reason to leave home and be on his own. At the same time, Jake is afraid that if he alienates his father, he may risk losing the financial help that he needs to get through medical school. Jake wants to be independent, but he is simply in no position to go it on his own. He often fears that he will not be able to make it if he becomes independent too soon.

Thinking for Oneself

The college years are also an important time for learning independent thinking, for challenging old assumptions, myths, and rules. During these years, we should expect to be taught critical thinking and the skills of clearly expressing ourselves in speech and writing on controversial matters. In college, we are supposed to learn how to analyze, evaluate, problem-solve, discuss, and debate. College is a unique time when we have the leisure and the opportunities to search, question, challenge, and beg to differ. Unfortunately, too many college students find that these years are primarily taken up with merely memorizing content and reciting it back on exams. They often encounter an antiquated approach to education that entails listening to boring lectures where a teacher is "banking in" information, and there is little opportunity for discussion and critique. When this is the case, the student makes little progress in independent thinking and leaves college with simply a new set of facts to replace the old, and neither set has been examined critically.

Without the skills of critical thinking, the young adult, who by nature tends to be idealistic, is easily taken in by slogans, false assumptions, and romantic myths. Young adults generally do not have the life experience or the knowledge to recognize the intellectual "con job" and can be easily taken in if they have not been taught to think for themselves. One thinks of the millions of young Germans who fell victim to the demonic plans of Hitler. Many of them had been taught from the time they were young to conform, obey, and never challenge authority. Most of them did not have the intellectual skills to see through Hitler's inflammatory rhetoric to realize that he was leading them to destruction.

Another example is that of the brilliant young social worker who was taken in by Jim Jones's apparent concern for the poor and the oppressed. She gave up a career to serve the children in Jones's movement, even following him to Guyana. We know how it ended, with this marvelous young woman face down in a field, dead of a poisonous drink she was forced to swallow. These examples are extreme, yet they dramatize how young adults can be duped and taken advantage of if they have not learned to think independently and critically.

The independent thinker is able to disagree and be disagreed with. Education too often passes for agreeing with teachers' points of view or with the views of the textbook. Young adults feel that if they want to be successful in school they must at least pretend to agree with the points of view presented to them. On the contrary, the accomplished teacher will encourage students to challenge the perspective of lectures and texts. This does not mean that students should be encouraged to be disrespectful or disruptive. However, intelligent controversy done in an atmosphere of mutual respect for one another's opinion is at the very heart of what higher education stands for. Fair arguments and constructive criticism are necessary means of intellectual growth. It is only the mentally immature who expect others to agree with their positions.

Young adulthood is the time when one begins to learn to accept relativity. In childhood, things seem simple, absolute, and settled. It is in adolescence that most of us discover the reality of relativity. At first many teens are angry; they feel cheated or that they have been misled by parents and others who gave the impression that there were many firm and final answers available in all areas of human knowledge. The college years lead us to an even more expanded awareness of relativity. Many young adults react by embracing a kind of "total relativity," meaning that it does not really matter what position they take on anything. As one student put it: "I'll have my own opinion on most things, and I let others have theirs. Things are so complicated today that it is hard to know what to think. Who's to know who is right? It really doesn't matter what people think so long as they don't try to force me to accept their positions." Such a position seems to assume that it is really impossible to come to precise knowledge and accurate answers. This is not so much independent thinking as it is isolated and vague thinking.

The Need for Mentors

As young adults separate from parents and start down the road of independent living and thinking, the mentor serves as an important companion. Mentors are people who are older, more experienced, and capable of assisting the young adult.

Mentors have taken their place in the world as independent and mature adults, and are thus capable of helping the "novice adult" prepare for the next steps into personal autonomy after college. The mentor is a person whom the young adult can look up to, not with any sense of the hero-worship of adolescence, but as one who can "walk with" the young adult until the day that such assistance is no longer needed.

Professors and staff members of colleges have a key opportunity to serve as mentors for the young adults in our colleges and universities. Unfortunately, professors are many times so pressured to research and publish that little time is left for such crucial service to the young. But who are better qualified to offer young adults the modeling and the assistance needed during this time than the adults surrounding them on our campuses?

Experimenting with Options

One of the luxuries of college life is that students can make temporary choices, trial options, and not yet have to make long-range commitments. Later on, there will be a time for "playing for keeps," but for now the undergraduate can experiment with different majors, various jobs, and many different kinds of friendships and communities.

Take Debby as an example. She came to college wanting to be a physical therapist like the one who helped her recover from a track injury when she was in high school. She soon discovered-that the science courses necessary in that major were not for her; she simply did not have interest in these subjects. Debby shifted to an English major, thinking that she might be a writer, but soon realized after doing some long pieces of creative writing that she did not have the talent to be a professional writer. Now Debby is majoring in political science and hopes to get into some kind of government work where she can use her ability to work with people. Debby's story is typical of many undergraduates, who are using the college years to search out how they can best use their talents and find the kind of work where they can be successful and happy.

While the undergraduate still has time to experiment with

majors, jobs, and relationships, the big decisions are not too far ahead on the horizon. Major decisions about lifestyle, marriage, and career are just ahead, and the college student knows full well that there is room for just so much experimentation—then it's time to get down to business. All this puts a certain urgency into the life of a young adult, an urgency to which people react in various ways. Some would prefer to have someone else make up their minds for them, and they seek out advisors who will tell them what to do. Others simply escape from the whole process of decision making and distract themselves in pleasurable activities and partying. Still others struggle so much discovering their identity or becoming independent that they don't have the energy to begin making choices about the future. For many, fears float beneath the surface of their lives, telling them that they will end up being clones of their parents. Some fear failure and thus choose courses and jobs that will not be too risky. Others panic at the first setback or failure and simply bracket all decisions "until further notice." But, for the most part, young adults overcome the hesitations and the fears, and begin the long and crucial process of making choices about their future lives.

Being Practical

In making career choices, the idealism of young adults often collides with pragmatism. Many young people would like to choose a career in which they could help others and make the world a better place. But one has to be practical and make a good living. Some young adults would be willing to give several years of their lives in some area of human service. But what happens when they return to the job market several years behind in the race to get ahead in their careers? Our culture simply makes it too risky to sacrifice time and effort for others. And even many of those who are convinced intellectually that they should be counter-cultural end up conforming when it comes down to making a living.

One thinks of Dave, a very bright junior majoring in economics, who is quite critical of how some corporations are insensitive to ecology. He goes about the campus dressed in radical garb, protesting the use of pesticides on crops. At the same time, Dave plans to work this summer for a company that manufactures such pesticides because they pay well. He wants to rebel, but at the same time he has to make the money to get through college. As Dave says, there is not much money to be made in peace marches and demonstrations for saving the environment. Although he participates in many such events, he feels that he still has to be practical about his future.

Since young adults often have little life experience, they put together their dreams for the future more with imagination and fantasy than with the reality of who they are and what they want to accomplish. The media, and perhaps their parents and schools as well, have told them for years to be Number One and that success is largely gauged by the amount of material things they will have. In their imaginations, images of the nice car, the grand home, the splendid furniture, and the exotic vacations become identified with success. To attain all this, one must prepare oneself to get a good job and "to make big bucks." It is incredible how widespread that dream has become for many young adults. But this is a dream that leaves little room for such questions as: What kind of a person do I want to be? What are my best gifts and talents and how can I use them to enrich the lives of others? What can I do to improve my world? How can I leave something behind that will be of value for those who follow me? If these latter questions are posed, the choices regarding majors, careers, and plans for the future will most certainly have a whole new light upon them.

A Young Woman's Dream

Putting together a life's dream is always difficult, but for a young woman today there are added perplexities. Even though many women enter college desiring to have their own careers, they know full well that they will possibly end up supporting the goals of their husbands, and may never be able to carry out their own future plans. If marriage and family are part of the young woman's dream, she will most likely have to pay a large price physically and emotionally to sustain her own career. Like many women today, not only will she have to compete in what is still largely a "man's world," she will also often have to provide the nurturing to her family, and unfairly do the lion's share of the homemaking. If she is able to be "super-mom," she can carry all this off. If not, she will have to make concessions to her own career choices that her husband will probably never have to make. Moreover, many young women today actually have a fear of success, knowing that such success might well be resented by their peers and even by the men they love. Given these dilemmas, it is no wonder that many young women today have a difficult time making choices about majors, careers, and jobs. Nor is it surprising that increasing numbers of young women are wary of the traditional models of marriage and hope to find a mate who will equally share the burdens of homemaking and parenting, and who will allow equal opportunity in the areas of personal growth and career choice.

Intimacy

Erikson points out that one of the key developmental tasks for the young adult is to learn how to be intimate with others. If this task is not taken seriously, the young person faces a future of isolation and loneliness. The capacity of intimacy, according to Erikson, is the ability to commit oneself to relationships and to abide by such commitments even when they call for sacrifice and compromise. Developing this capacity for intimacy is perhaps the most important challenge that the young adult faces during the college years. Success or failure in this area will have many implications later in life in the areas of friendship, marriage, parenting, and career.

In one of the Peanuts cartoons, Charlie Brown says, "I love mankind, it's people I can't get along with." Well, intimacy involves not a general concern for people, but the ability to love and be loved by individual persons. Intimacy, then, is a two-way street. In one direction, it calls for the ability to disclose myself as I am. It requires a good sense of self, a clear sense of identity, and the willingness to allow others to know me, with the confidence that they will accept and love me. The person capable of intimacy can share feelings, questions, doubts, fears, successes with others without fear of being rejected.

In the other direction, the person capable of intimacy can allow others to disclose themselves. This implies a caring, an empathetic attitude to others, a concern for their feelings, opinions, and concerns. We all know the value of such a person, because we are naturally attracted to those who have a genuine interest in us and who are open to listening to our story with concern and care. By the same token, we know how turned off we are by people we meet, let's say on a plane or a bus, who spend hours telling us about themselves, but never show the slightest interest in us or in our concerns. Such an experience is not one of intimacy; rather, it is simply our providing an ear for a self-centered and isolated person. We are usually glad to get free from such an encounter.

Intimacy looks for some degree of commitment, in friendship, love, or partnership of some kind or other. It implies trust that the person will be true to our confidences, will support us when we are in need, and will show up if we are in some kind of difficulty or trial. Nothing angers us and frustrates us more than the situation in which we think we have such a relationship, only to find that we have been betrayed or let down when in need.

Intimacy requires the willingness to make mutual sacrifices. Both partners in an intimate relationship have to be willing to give of themselves, to go the extra mile, to offer time, help, whatever the other partner reasonably requests. Moreover, intimacy requires compromise. That means that there is not the tendency to dominate, manipulate, use, or abuse. Genuine friends participate in a mutuality. There is no winner or loser in conflict, no master or servant in projects and activities.

Of course, the flip side of intimacy is isolation. Here we have reluctance to give of ourselves to others for fear that we will be rejected or that we will lose our freedom. The isolated person is often cynical toward others and cuts them down because they are perceived to be a danger to the isolated person's vulnerable ego. Such a person withdraws, pulls back, avoids closeness because there are simply too many dangers involved or because intimacy will cost too much in terms of self-extension and self-giving.

For many young adults, the first experience of sexual intimacy comes in the college years. For the first time in their lives, they have the freedom and the independence to make their own decisions as to what they can do with their own bodies, their own appetites of sexual pleasure.

Parental control and authority no longer prevail and the old rules don't seem to apply any longer. And yet, many young adults soon discover that sexual intimacy is not simply a matter of sharing a bed with someone. In such beginnings there is always the possibility of being used as an object and then cast aside, of being a momentary conquest, of promising much more than one can actually deliver emotionally and relationally. Sometimes we discover that we have just been another's experiment in romance or physical pleasure, or that we have placed ourselves at risk of disease or an unwanted pregnancy merely to satisfy someone else's passing need for pleasure. We move on, hoping that somewhere and with someone we will discover the kind of genuine intimacy that will involve commitment and fidelity.

The Faith of the Young Adult

The religious dimension of life is not a fringe matter that has nothing to do with the rest of life. One's faith has a great deal to do with self-vision, the drive of independence, personal options, and the question of intimacy. In this section, we will be discussing some of the ways in which faith is related to these developmental tasks of the young adult.

The person of faith has a unique perspective on the question: "Who am I?" The Christian tradition tells us that we are created by God, are in some way reflected images of God, and can, if we so wish, share in the very life of God. The New Testament tells us that we are indeed daughters and sons of this creative and loving parent. They also tell us that the son of this God actually became one of us, and can be considered to be brother in the flesh and devoted friend. This brother, Jesus of Nazareth, showed his followers how to live a human life with integrity. He lived a life of compassion and love for others, particularly for the handicapped and outcasts. Eventually, he was arrested, tried, and was hanged on a cross because his message of love and justice was simply too radical for many of the religious and political leaders of the time to accept. Yet, in his death, this Jesus offered his very life so that each person could find forgiveness and life for all eternity. His own conquering of death in resurrection has given hope to his followers for two thousand years.

The Christian, then, looks at personal identity in a unique fashion. Each person is original; each person has a dignity and a destiny that is extraordinary. We carry a life that is sacred in that it comes from God and is called to be with God even after the apparent end of life in death. This is a radical message, which contradicts the violent destruction of human life that has been so common throughout history, which holds as unacceptable the abuse and oppression of people, the hatred and rejection that comes from racial, sexual, or national prejudice. The Christian insists, "I am somebody," and demands that he or she as well as any other person be treated with dignity, kindness, and love.

Many young adults have been taught that because of their color, their social or financial background, or their handicaps, they are not acceptable. For instance, blacks in the United States were taught for centuries that they were inferior merely because of the color of their skin. As a result of such social prejudice, many black young adults, then and now, have a poor self-image and lack the confidence needed to succeed.

Christian faith denies these fallacies based on prejudice, and teaches all human beings that they are equal in the eyes of God, that they have a right to be treated fairly at home, at work, at school, indeed wherever they may go. Christianity is a religion of confidence, of hope. It encourages its disciples to follow a unique rule of love: to love their God fully, to love themselves, and to love all others and treat all others in the same way that they themselves like to be treated.

As we have seen, trust is an essential element in achieving a healthy and mature self-image. The Christian tradition places a great deal of value in trust. It professes a God who can be trusted implicitly, a God who, from the beginning, has never let people down. The entire Bible, both the Hebrew Scriptures and the New Testament, is the story of this God's fidelity, constant forgiveness, and saving activity. Jesus of Nazareth spoke of a "kingdom" of this God, a reign, or overall prevailing of this God's presence in the world. He clearly demonstrated in his dealings with others that the healing and forgiving power of this God is operative everywhere and in the lives of all who will be receptive to it.

Revealing Experiences If the young adult is to acquire a strong sense of identity, that person needs to trust his or her own experience. In a sense, we *are* our experiences in that we have been shaped and formed by many events and encounters. Catholic theologian Karl Rahner teaches that it is in these very experiences that we can meet God. Rahner does not teach about a God who is off in the heavens, or who is merely a past historical figure who did great things long ago but now dispassionately watches from above. He speaks of a God who dynamically works within people and life, revealing a unique power of love and creativity in everyday activities and experiences. From his perspective, God can be met in a sunset, in a quiet brook or a roaring ocean, in the eyes of a friend or lover, in the silence of our rooms, or in the strains of our favorite song. All this gives us a special reason to trust ourselves, others, and reality itself, for the deeper we delve into human experience, the more likely we are to meet the presence of the divine. Such faith offers good reason for self-esteem and for a deep respect for other people and the everyday events of life. There is so much to experience if one's ears, eyes, and heart are attuned to what is being revealed of God in everyday living.

Thomas Merton (1915-1968), the Trappist monk and author, spent many years in prayer and work, trying to discover his true self, his real identity. When he joined the monastery, he said he was not leaving riches or fame behind. Rather, he was hoping to leave behind all the false selves and masks that had become part of him. He observed that as he gradually peeled all these away and reached in to meet his true identity, he began to meet God there. Merton was convinced that God's image is uniquely imprinted in each person and that the way to encounter that original imprint is to discover the genuine self. As a young adult, after wild years in college and an illegitimate child, Merton had learned that the way to happiness was to face up to himself and his God. After years of struggle to put aside past roles and fears, Merton was able to achieve an extraordinary level of spiritual maturity, and he serves as a mentor for many young people today who strive for an integrated and authentic identity.

Faith and Independence As children, we usually have the faith of our parents. If we have beliefs and belong to a church or congregation, it is usually because all this has been done for us. Children depend on their parents in most matters, and religion is no exception. The faith of the child is simple, unquestioned and unexamined. We believe what we are told to believe because we trust the authority of those who are in charge of us. But, as we have seen earlier, in the teen years we begin to question, challenge, even reject some of these beliefs and affiliations. Yet, because teens are still quite dependent on parents, they are really not in much of a position to put together a faith of their own. Young adults, however, have achieved a relative independence and are encouraged in college to examine critically many of their former religious assumptions and beliefs.

Separating from the faith of our parents can sometimes be a scary affair, especially if we come from a religious background where we have been taught that to depart from a certain set of beliefs can result in punishment, perhaps even in eternal damnation. Take, for example, Eileen who was brought up in a very strict Catholic home and attended parochial schools where she was taught that the Catholic religion was the only true religion. She points out that it was difficult for her to rethink her Catholic faith in college because she really was afraid she would "go to hell" if she doubted or challenged any of the beliefs that she was taught as a child.

In order for her to carry on in her search for her own belief, Eileen had to put aside such fears and indeed rethink the image of a punishing God that she accepted as a child. She writes: "I had always believed that God was an old man in the sky who required that I believe everything that I was told at home and at school. My teachers told me that I would be sent to hell if I missed church, committed certain sins, or even if I had doubts about my faith. In college I had to free myself of this frightening image of God and come to see God as a friend who loves me, protects me, and will forgive me if I make mistakes. I came to see that the mystery of God is much larger than all the metaphors, images, and doctrines that I was given by my church. I now know that there are no simple answers, and that each person must search for the truth and come to believe that which seems to be true. College theology has taught me that there is a variety of approaches to understanding and relating to God. I am still a Catholic, but now I am formulating my own beliefs and my own faith commitment and not merely accepting that of my parents."

Other college students struggle with their beliefs regarding the New Testament. They may have been instructed earlier that the gospels were accurate accounts of what Jesus said and did. Courses in scripture now suggest that much of the New Testament consists of religious myths, sacred stories that reflect the beliefs of early Christian communities, and not historical accounts of Jesus' life.

Michael, a physics major from Denver, was brought up in a Baptist home, where he was taught to accept the Scriptures literally. Before entering college, he had always believed that God directly created everything in six days just as the creation account in Genesis tells us. He was also taught that the theory of evolution was an attempt on the part of "secular humanists" to deny God's power of creation. Michael's science classes convinced him of the truth of evolution, and his course in Scripture introduced him to the "mythical" approach to the Bible. Now he is in the process of rethinking his beliefs both about creation and the interpretation of Scripture.

Young adults react differently to such discoveries about the religious stories they heard as children. Some refuse to accept the critical approach and remain fundamentalists. Others become cynical and write the Scriptures off as mere fairy tales that are of little value. Many students, however, are willing to struggle with the contextual approach to the Scriptures and seek within religious myths the insights of divine revelation.

Many young adults struggle to put together an "owned faith" to which they are able to give a commitment. For most, this is a time of questioning, searching, challenging old assumptions and concepts, and for reexamining the many myths that were taken literally as children. The growing independence of young adults brings them to realize that no one can rightfully be forced to accept religious beliefs. Fear, force, or manipulation should have no place in the sacred realm of accepting God's invitation to friendship. Personal freedom includes religious freedom, or the right that each of us has to make our faith commitment in the privacy of our own hearts and minds. Therefore, the young adult who is gradually gaining personal freedom has the right to search for a faith commitment that is meaningful and authentic. This is no easy task, and for most this requires many years of serious reflection and discernment.

Re-Examining Old Beliefs and Myths In Fowler's terms, young adults are often still moving from a"conventional" faith, one that has been accepted simply because that is what those around them believed when they were younger, to a faith that is more individual and reflective. To do so, of course, means reexamining (and perhaps even rejecting) some beliefs of the past. For Bill, a sophomore who majors in physical education and plans to be a high school coach, the time came when he had to re-examine his image of God. He had been brought up believing in a judging and punishing God who sends sickness and tragedy to people to test their faith, punishes them for sins, or perhaps teaches them a thing or two when they stray. It got to the point that any time something went wrong in Bill's life he attributed the mishap to God, and therefore was becoming very alienated from religion. In college, Bill had the opportunity to rethink all this and he concluded that God is not some kind of a heavenly puppeteer who sends bad things our way. He became convinced that when bad things happen to us, whether they be storms, accidents, hurts, or failures, it is because of the nature of things in themselves, or deliberate choices, or simply due to random happenstance. Bill now sees God as the source of power and strength to survive setbacks, and he is much more comfortable relating to this new image of God.

Other students have to rethink imaging God as a Father. Those who have negative experiences with their fathers at home might tend to project this negativity onto their relationship with God. Some young women who are beginning to realize the inequities of our patriarchal society, and who want to consider also the feminine dimensions of God, do not want to limit God to the image of Father. Indeed, the dominant male language that is so common in the Scriptures and in many church ceremonies is offensive to some young people, both women and men.

Whatever the issue, whether it be interpreting heaven, hell, afterlife, ritual, salvation in other religions, the power of prayer, miracles, or ministry, the young adult stage is a time for many to take stock, to have a religious audit, and see what beliefs they truly own and are willing to profess as true. No easy task this, and for some it is more attractive to escape into a posture of indifference, agnosticism ("I don't know and I don't care"), or to simply drop out of religion until a later time when there might be a need for it. Whatever choice is made, most young adults come through this period of life with a faith perspective that differs from the one they had when they were children or teenagers. They may or may not end with the same belief system and religious affiliation as their parents, but they will be moving to a faith position that is their own. In a quality college situation, they will have had opportunities for looking at many religious alternatives, for thinking critically and precisely about religious matters, and for sharing their religious insights with others in respectful debate.

Faith and Life Options We reflected earlier on how young adulthood is a unique opportunity for thinking over future options concerning marriage, career and lifestyle, and for experimenting with choices without permanent commitment. All this applies as well to one's religious option. The young adult enjoys a new degree of freedom of choice, and perhaps for the first time can make religious choices. There is the area, for instance, of attending church services. At home, services may have been attended because of pressure from the family or from the church or congregation. Once in college, the young person is usually free to make a personal choice in this matter. Some find that once this "heat" is off them, they discontinue church attendance. Others attend only when they are home with their parents in order to avoid controversy or so that their parents will not be offended. Many college-age students seem to need some distance from church in order to decide whether they really want to attend on their own volition. This is also a time to experiment by attending different kinds of ceremonies, searching for one that speaks to them and to their concerns as young people.

One's faith choices can have a bearing on what one picks for a major and a career. This need not be the case if religion is seen as a totally private matter, with no bearing on one's work or everyday life. But for those who view faith holistically, as having a bearing on all aspects of life, faith is a factor in choosing a career.

Young people are generally idealistic and generous. They often want to give of themselves and contribute to their society. If, from their Christian faith, they have learned the value of sacrifice for others, service to the community, and detachment from material things, these values will indeed have a bearing on their career choices. The young person anticipating going into law will have a quite different approach to preparing for this career if the future work is viewed as a "calling," a "vocation," from God to make a unique contribution. This was the case with Daniel O'Meara, a young lawyer in Chicago. At first, Dan was not sure what he was supposed to do as a lawyer, but he felt that this is what he had the talent for and what God wanted him to do with his life. He started off working for several oil companies, where he made a good salary, but spent most of his time securing legal permission to put up display signs. After seven years of this, he was bored, discontented, and still wondering what he should do with his life. Then he became friends with some medical students who were working in clinics among the Mexicans in Chicago. They told him that many of these people needed legal advice, and so Dan quit his job and set up a little legal office over a pharmacy in the Mexican community. It was a costly decision because his salary dropped from $35,000 to $4,000, and he had to move out of his apartment and get rid of his sports car. But Dan says he never has regretted his choice, because the people have been so warm to him and have taught him so much about life. He has learned the value of family, community, generosity and, most important, Dan believes that he is using his talent and his law degree to do what God wants him to do.

Not everyone is called to make the radical decision that Dan made. However, those who believe in the Christian values of compassion, justice, love, and service will make career choices in light of these values. Moreover, those who believe that their personal gifts and talents are indeed given them by a creative and loving God will be inclined to want to use these gifts to help others and improve their society. A commitment to discipleship with Jesus of Nazareth implies a commitment to carrying out his mission of service and sacrifice for others.

New Freedom Soren Kierkegaard once spoke of the "dizziness of freedom," meaning that freedom with all its possible choices for good or evil can sometimes make our heads spin. The young adult, experiencing a great deal of freedom for the first time, can probably relate to this description. Once away from home, there are so many choices about studies, friends, social life, work, and other activities that it is easy to get disoriented. We start to see the dangerous nature of freedom—especially when we "mess up." We begin to realize that there is a distinction between license, where we do as we please, and freedom, where we choose within limits and choose with responsibility. Moreover, there are always risks attached to freedom, for freedom entails making choices without knowing how things will turn out. Karl Rahner tells us that freedom implies the courage to risk a future that is unforeseeable. It is a power of choice that is exciting and at the same time frightening.

Freedom is an essential part of the Christian religion. Many young people are surprised to hear that, because religion is so often associated with restrictions and loss of freedom. Perhaps this is why so many young people shy away from religion during the years when they are attempting to get going on their own. Jesus told his disciples: "So if the Son sets you free, you will indeed be free" (Jn 8:36). He spoke of God as a Spirit that was as free as the wind, moreover Jesus himself seemed to have an incredible inner freedom regarding public opinion and law. Those who attempted to intimidate or frighten him ended up terribly frustrated. Jesus' mission centered on freeing people from fear, low self-esteem, illness, handicaps, and sinful ways. His followers have always displayed a unique sense of freedom, so much so that the apostle Paul could write: "Where the Spirit of the Lord is, there is freedom" (2 Cor 3:17).

Since young adults place such a high value on freedom, they are attracted to a religion that liberates. Christian freedom offers the disciple the freedom from material things, from oppressive laws, from fear of suffering, and even from death. Friendship with Jesus Christ has freed countless people from the prisons of low self-esteem, guilt, and sinful habits. But Christian freedom does not merely liberate people *from* things, it also liberates them *for* something. Christian freedom frees people from whatever holds them down or entraps them so that they can be happy, productive, and faithful to the responsibilities they have toward themselves and others.

Faith and Intimacy

Earlier, we saw how intimacy is one of the chief concerns during the young adult stage of development. The question we want to address here is: How does the Christian faith relate to this area of intimacy that is so crucial for college-age students? We will reflect how the issue of intimacy is reflected in the Christian notions of covenant, community, spirituality, and sexuality.

The New Covenant From the outset, the Christian tradition is concerned with intimacy. Based on and continuing the Hebrew notion of "covenant," Christians believe that they have been called in a unique fashion to share in an intimate relationship with the mystery of God as it is revealed through the life of Jesus Christ. Terms like "the people of God," "the body of Christ," "brothers and sisters in the Lord," and "community," all evidence how much the Christian faith is concerned over close relationships with God and with each other.

Moreover, there is a universal or "catholic" thrust to this desire for unity. Christians do not see themselves caught up in some exclusive covenant that implies, "We are saved and you are not." Rather, genuine Christian faith maintains that all people are created and loved by God and are called to be in intimate union with this God. The Christian message is the "good news" that everyone who sincerely seeks God and lives a good life can share life with God in this life and after death. In this tradition, each person is a neighbor deserving of respect and service. Commitment to this faith provides one with an openness to both God and people, with a profound basis for friendship. Ideally, the gospel life is one of fidelity to our family, friends, and to many others who reach out to us in need.

Christianity is not a religion that is meant to be merely private or personal. From the very beginning, Christians gathered in small communities to share their goods and their beliefs, to celebrate together the "breaking of the bread," and to pray with one another. The word "community" is derived from the two words "common" and "unity." For the early Christians, this meant that they shared a common bond in accepting Jesus as their savior and were unified in their determination to follow his teaching, even if it meant giving up their lives in martyrdom. Today, there is still this unique closeness among those who share the Christian faith. One sees in the base communities in Central and South America a rejuvenation of the Christian value of gathering with brothers and sisters for prayer and support during times of oppression, injustice and violence. In the United States there is a movement once again to see the family as a Christian community, and also to gather in small neighborhood groups for spiritual renewal. On many campuses throughout the world, small communities gather to share their faith, break bread, pray, and plan ways in which they can involve themselves in efforts for peace and social justice. The Christian faith is experienced in an unusual intensity when it is shared with others in friendship.

Spirituality The word spirituality often conjures up images of monks and nuns cut off from the world. Christian spirituality has somehow come to be associated with isolation rather than with intimacy and a deep concern for others. This is unfortunate, because even though solitude and reflection have always been of value for the Christian, their purpose is to help us better appreciate others and to prepare us to be of better service. When Jesus himself awakened early in the morning and went off to pray, or when he went off into the desert for private reflection, it was not to cut himself off from intimacy with others. Rather, when he returned he was recharged and better prepared to be compassionate, forgiving, and loving toward others. Following his lead, disciples of Jesus have always tried to hold two poles in tension in spirituality: the contemplative and the active. Contemplation for the college student might take place in the privacy of a room, on a morning walk on campus, during a private visit to chapel, or even on a stroll through a shopping mall. It is a time to think, a time to commune with one's God and to experience the extraordinary intimacy that is available in prayer.

There is a rich mystical tradition in Christianity that values walking with the Lord in friendship, sharing our successes and failures, and experiencing an extraordinary new power to face the challenges and problems of everyday life. Such contemplation is not merely for saints and "specialists," but for anyone who wishes to share its richness.

The active dimension of Christian spirituality is intended to move us to reach out to others. The reflective and prayerful person is better equipped to be a friend, a lover, a person available to serve those in need. Once we have experienced the loving and saving presence of God within ourselves, we begin to see people and the world around us in a new light. Joseph Grassi, a longtime professor of Scripture, points out that prayer offers students a new level of consciousness, a deep feeling of oneness with other people and with the entire world. Prayer takes one out of isolation and makes us aware of fellowship with those around us and, indeed, with our brothers and sisters around the world. This is the kind of awareness that was observed in the eyes of many of the rock groups and young people who participated in "Live Aid" and who sang together, "We are the world, We are the people." Only a conviction born in serious reflection and prayer could have moved so many to sacrifice for the starving throughout the world.

Sexual Intimacy A commitment to gospel values also affects the way young adults approach sexual intimacy. The Christian tradition has always looked at sexuality as sacred. In the description of creation in Genesis, the very image of God is somehow reflected in our being female and male. In the sacred myth, Yahweh is described as saying: "And now we will make human beings; and they will be like us and resemble us." The author of this great story then goes on to say: "So God created human beings, making them like himself. He created them male and female, blessed them, and said, 'Have many children.'" The revelation underlying this little drama seems to be that in our sexuality we are somehow like God. In the strength, courage, and determination of our masculine side, which renowned psychologist Carl Jung (1875-1961) calls "the animus," we image the powerful presence of the divine. In the compassion, beauty, warmth, and tenderness of our feminine side, the "anima," we reflect the nurturing side of God. Although each of us carries within the self all of these characteristics, both masculine and feminine, we are individualized as one or the other, male or female. It is as though we are one half of a whole, and there is a deep longing within each of us to be united to someone who will complement and complete us as persons.

Sexual intimacy is held sacred by the Christian tradition because it promises completeness, unity, fidelity. To make love, Christian love, is to make a mutual statement of commitment to oneness, to permanence, to a lasting and binding convenant. Sex for the Christian is life-giving, in that the lovers enjoying it are enriched and fulfilled in the knowledge that each has found a partner with whom all aspects of life can be shared. Sex is also life-giving in that it is a way of bringing new life into the world. Sex, therefore, carries with it tremendous responsibilities for commitment to the partner as well as the children that are born from its enjoyment. For the Christian, sex is a profound statement of lasting love as well as a very real participation in the creative process. Christian faith, therefore, prepares one for the deep levels of intimacy that are experienced in marriage.

In this chapter we have been discussing the development that occurs during young adulthood, especially in the areas of self image, independence, life options, and intimacy. We have also attempted to show how Christian faith relates to these areas. In the next chapter, we will deal with the question of how young adults in college might integrate their faith with a commitment to social justice.

QUESTIONS FOR REFLECTION AND DISCUSSION

1. Do you think young women today experience more obstacles to personal development than do young men? Give examples to clarify your answer.

2. How do your religious beliefs and attitudes differ from

those of your parents? Are you able to discuss these differences with your parents?

3. Are there examples of prejudice and discrimination on your campus? If so, give specific examples.

4. Discuss some of the religious beliefs you may have changed since you were a child (e.g., importance of going to church; image of God; fear of hell).

Suggested Readings

Austin, Alexander. *Four Critical Years.* San Francisco: Jossey-Bass Publications, 1979.

Merriam, Sharan, and Trenton Ferro, "Working with Young Adults," in *Handbook of Adult Religious Education*, ed. Nancy T. Foltz. Birmingham, Ala.: Religious Education Press, 1986.

Murphy, David, ed. *What I Believe: Catholic College Students Discuss Their Faith.* Chicago: Thomas More Press, 1985.

Parks, Sharon. *The Critical Years: The Young Adult Search for a Faith to Live By.* San Francisco: Harper & Row, 1986.

Perry, W.G., Jr. "Cognitive and Ethical Growth: The Making of Meaning," in *The Modern American College*, ed. A.W. Chickering. San Francisco: Jossey-Bass, 1981.

Shelton, Charles M. *Adolescent Spirituality: Pastoral Ministry for High School and College Youth.* Chicago: Loyola University Press, 1983.

Chapter Four

Young Adult Faith and Social Justice

As Chapter One pointed out, faith implies a relationship with God, a commitment of the whole person in thought, feeling, and action. A faith that is only intellectual or emotional, a faith without works, is a partial faith. In this chapter, we are going to further discuss the linkage between faith and justice by showing the proper role that colleges should play in developing social consciousness, explaining why faith and justice must be linked in the Christian perspective. Finally, we will discuss young adult attitudes toward involvement in social justice, with reference to some concrete ways in which young people are making a difference in this area.

The Purpose of Higher Education

Institutions of higher education play a significant role in shaping the young people of this country. Each year, well over

12 million students attend over 3000 colleges throughout the United States. These students attend for all kinds of reasons: social life, career preparation, learning, athletics, etc. Ideally, the college years are a time when the whole person is educated, that is, when the potential of each individual to think, feel, and act is activated significantly. The purpose of higher education is to assist people in becoming self-reliant and self-supporting individuals who can think clearly and act judiciously.

One leading educator, Howard R. Bowen, points out that colleges should form "seekers of truth," that is, persons who understand the past and the present, and are open to new ideas for shaping the future. He goes on to say that the truly educated person should be able to think critically, and thus be wary of that which is either dogmatic or faddish. Bowen maintains that higher education has the responsibility to help students think maturely about the ultimates of human existence, and to develop student capacity and motivation to continue learning throughout life. He also holds that colleges should be training the young to be "citizens of the world," and not limited to the local perspective of their neighborhoods and regions. Moreover, college-trained individuals should have a firm moral base that will enable them to relate sensitively to others. This moral base includes a sense of social responsibility as well as a concern for human betterment and service to others.

The ideals of higher education are not easily realized in our colleges and universities. Pressures from business and industry, a shortage of jobs, fierce competition among colleges for students, a materialistic culture, and other factors have moved many institutions of higher learning to become mere vocational training centers, where one goes to "get credits and a degree" in order to "get a job." While it has to be recognized that career selection and training are integral to college, it would seem, given the expense and time required, that much more could be expected of higher education. Colleges have a long tradition of training informed and socially responsible citizens and leaders, people who will shape the future. Yet colleges are often reduced to being either "fast-food places" where one can get a quick pick up of information and credits, or "supermarkets" for gaining degrees.

The American Dream Many educators feel that institutions of higher learning could be in a key position today to offer young people alternative choices to the materialistic "American dream." Many of our other institutions, such as the public schools, and often even the family and churches, have been coopted by a consumer culture that offers the young goals that are self-centered and materialistic. From this perspective, personal success is defined in terms of financial success and the accumulation of material things. As a current bumper sticker puts it, "Whoever dies with the most toys wins." Here the driving force becomes the achievement of what gives personal pleasure and satisfaction. As a result, little time or effort is expended in knowing or caring about the needs of those who are less fortunate, and little or no energy is given toward the betterment of society and the causes of justice.

Young adults who come to college with this "me-centered" mentality often view their time of higher education in a highly pragmatic light. Studies show that too often college can be reduced to mere "partying and credits." For some, unfortunately, college is an unrealistic escape from the world of responsibility into an illusory world of drugs, alcohol, and sexual indulgence. For others, the gaining of a college degree simply represents the acquisition of a license for getting a job. Marks, the cumulative average, and credits can easily become the central concern, and regard for becoming a person of learning and commitment can fade into the background.

It is quite understandable how this pragmatism about college education can occur. The growing cost of everything and a sharp competition for jobs puts a great deal of pressure on the young. This is perhaps the first generation that finds it nearly impossible to equal, much less surpass, the financial level of their parents. Parents of today's college students may have bought a house for less than $20,000 with a low interest rate on the mortgage, and could purchase a car for less than $5000. Today, the same house may sell for more than $100,000, and new cars continue to cause more "sticker shock" each year. Moreover, the cost of a college education has skyrocketed to the point where it can now cost as much as $60,000 to $80,000 to gain an undergraduate diploma. This means that many young adults face extremely difficult financial challenges in the future, and often begin this road of challenge already heavily in debt for college loans. The very thought of what it might cost this generation to educate their own future children is staggering. Such financial pressure can easily distract the young adult, and indeed the colleges themselves, from the more formational and humanistic goals of higher education.

Restoring the Goal of Liberal Education Derek Bok, the president of Harvard University, maintains that colleges should move from their ivory towers and return to their social responsibilities. He points out that one of the roles of higher education is to challenge the unexamined assumptions of students about the world, help them reformulate their understanding of what is going on around them, and assist them in clarifying the part they can play in bettering society.

Higher education's purpose is not to teach people *what* to think but to teach them *how* to think critically. As Bowen points out, it is not enough to merely train compliant workers and self-indulgent consumers. College graduates should have free minds that can inquire, tolerate new ideas, and openly engage in controversy. Education should disturb myths, superstitions, prejudice, discrimination, and ignorance. This is especially true where social analysis is concerned. One of the ideals of higher education is to promote social awareness and critique and to motivate students to want to better the human condition through the confrontation of injustice and oppression.

Passing on Worthy Values One way for higher education to bring students to a keener social awareness would be to return to sound values. In the United States, the exaggerated separation of church and state has rendered much of the public school system gun-shy about dealing with values. This lack of imparting traditional values could be one of the reasons that there is a breakdown of values throughout our culture. One reads of corruption today even in areas where one would expect integrity and honesty; in corporations, government, sports, law enforcement agencies, everywhere from the White House to child-care centers. With such scandal constantly before them, it is understandable why so many of our young frequently become cynical about traditional values, and quickly lose the healthy idealism so necessary for building the future.

Many leading educators believe that the universities are one of the last institutions that can impart sound values to young adults. Industry often seems to have little interest in providing ethical instruction; many families are so broken that they are incapable of passing on sound values; and the churches have many times simply lost contact with the young adult population. On the other hand, colleges still have access to the minds of the young, maintain sufficient academic freedom to deal with ethical values, and have the personnel who can provide sound modeling and mentoring for students in the area of ethical values. Thus, the college is in a position to impart to students the traditional values of honesty, justice, and concern for the less fortunate. Obviously, this would not include either the indoctrination or manipulation of students in the areas of value. Yet, there are pedagogically sound ways for faculty members and administrators to share their values with students, provide exemplary ethical modeling, and assist students in the process of sharing and clarifying values.

Higher Education and Politics Institutions of higher education most certainly have to tread a careful path when it comes to politics. Obviously, they are not expected to endorse political candidates or to use the classroom as a place to influence students along party lines. Granted these cautions, there is one area where universities cannot remain politically neutral, and that is the area of freedom. Universities in the United States stand for democracy and freedom. Consequently, education for peace and justice on a worldwide scale is very much part of their mandate. Quite often, universities claim to be politically neutral, yet they are stockholders in the defense industry or accept lucrative grants of military projects. These in themselves are political statements, and thus make it acceptable for faculty and administrators to take positions regarding public issues. The universities, therefore, rightfully provide a forum for intelligent political discussion. Neutrality in the political arena simply forces colleges to withdraw into an "ivory tower" posture, a posture that impedes the proper training of future leaders of this country.

Young Adults as Victims of Injustice Since colleges are unique institutions primarily concerned with young adults, they are in a position to be sensitive to how students are themselves affected by injustice. Amazing as it may seem, nearly half of the youth in the United States are socially or financially disadvantaged. As Bowen points out, by the year 2000 approximately 30 percent of the youth in the United States will be from minorities and will suffer all the inequity often attached to such a social level. Institutions of higher learning, therefore, cannot settle for merely serving the youth who are better off. Many more creative ways will have to be sought to provide a college education for the disadvantaged. In addition, colleges have the potential to provide effective training programs for training leaders who can serve the many needy young people in this country.

If the universities are searching for reasons to deal with the social problems in this country, they might consider how many of these problems directly affect our young people. Unemployment, racial discrimination, drugs, crime, family violence, war, and many other social problems are attacking the future hopes of many young adults. Dealing with these issues will not only prepare young adults to overcome the problems that attack their future, it will also provide future leaders who are informed, sensitive, and dedicated to human service. Thus, in addition to preparing young adults for future jobs, colleges can also offer students more of a sense of vocation and motivate them to make a contribution to society.

Faith and Social Justice

The ancient letter of James takes a strong stand on the necessary linkage between faith and action. The author writes: "What good is it for someone to say that he has faith if his actions do not prove it? Can that faith save him? Suppose there are brothers or sisters who need clothes and don't have enough to eat. What good is there in your saying to them, 'God bless you! Keep warm and well!' if you don't give them the necessities of life? So it is with faith: if it is alone and includes no actions, then it is dead" (Jas 2:14-17). Such a position stands in stark contrast to those who think that religious commitment is a private matter between a person and God, an area that should not be discussed or brought into the "worldly issues" of politics and social concerns.

Commitment to justice has been an integral part of Judeo-Christian teachings even though, admittedly, it has often been ignored. The prophet Micah summoned his people "to do justice, to love kindness and to walk humbly with our God" (Mic 6:8). And in the Sermon on the Mount, Jesus told his followers: "Blessed are the poor in spirit.... Blessed are those who hunger and thirst for justice.... You are the salt of the earth.... You are the light of the world" (Mt 5:1-16). Also in Jesus' well-known parable of the last judgment he says: "I was hungry and you gave me to eat, thirsty and you gave me to drink.... As often as you did it for one of these the least of my brothers, you did it for me" (Mt 25: 35-40). It would seem from these teachings that faith is actually constituted by a certain social concern that reaches out to the needy and the oppressed. From this perspective, the quality of one's faith can be measured by the degree of commitment to justice toward others.

Some Basic Christian Principles In their document on the American economy, the Catholic bishops of the United States, enunciate certain basic principles which underly their conviction that faith must do justice. First of all, there is the principle of human dignity, based on the religious belief that each person somehow comes from God, is a reflection of the image of God, and is therefore indeed to be valued. To put it simply, Christians believe that human life is sacred. Second, human persons are social by nature and their human dignity is both realized in and protected in community. The bishops thus point out that all members of the community ought to be concerned about matters of injustice and oppression against their neighbors. Next, all people have a right to participate in the economic and political life of the community. All persons, therefore, have a right to life, food, clothing, shelter, rest, medical care, education, and employment. Believers, therefore, have a responsibility to see to it that these rights are preserved and protected. This leads logically to the next principle, that each of us has an obligation to look after those who are poor and vulnerable in our midst. Indeed, this is nothing other than following the example of Jesus himself, who uniquely reached out to the poor and oppressed of his time. All these ideals seriously challenge the apathy that often exists toward world hunger, toward the atrocities going on in the world, and with regard to the one in seven people in this country who suffers from poverty.

A Call to Conversion Jim Wallis, an influential evangelical leader of the social justice movement in this country, maintains that a radical conversion is called for if Christians are to return to gospel living. He points out that we have become both materialistic and militaristic. We have created an economy based on overconsumption and now need an arsenal to protect all this against needy people in this country and abroad. He criticizes the television evangelists who tell people that prosperity is a sign of God's blessing, implying that the poor and oppressed are not so blessed.

Wallis calls for a radical change of heart among Americans, an altering of the spirit of the age as well as the very framework of our society. Such a conversion calls for the recognition of a breakdown in our awareness of being related to others as brothers and sisters, a breakdown which is the root cause of our personal and political alienation. In other words, there is a need to return to a sense of covenant with our neighbors at home and abroad, with the earth and atmosphere that sustains us, and with our God. Wallis speaks as a contemporary prophet, or one who sees the incongruity that exists between our proclaimed beliefs and the reality of our lifestyle, between our faith and our actions.

For Wallis, such a conversion began in his own life when, as a teenager, he saw that his church was little concerned about racism and about the violence of the Vietnam war. The church apparently saw these as "political" matters and saw its role only in terms of "spiritual" matters. For a time, he felt that he had lost his faith because he had separated from his church and chose to join his faith with life in the real world. Like so many of his generation in the 1960s and early 1970s, he viewed the churches as irrelevant to active involvement in social issues.

Eventually, the rebellion of students of that era died out, and many of the young moved back to the mainstream of American life, for the most part bringing their children up as loyal followers of the American dream. For Wallis, however, this was not a satisfying way to go. He returned to the gospels to discover a Jesus who was talking about a whole new order, a new "way," a Jesus who had identified himself with the poor and the dispossessed. The split between his personal faith and social action was over, and he was determined henceforth to make concern for the oppressed and the poor one with his faith in the Lord.

Jesus' call to repentance and conversion, according to many religious thinkers today, is the call for young adults to become the moving force behind a new order in the future. It is a call to promote the breaking in of a kingdom of peace and justice in the world. Such a conversion involves an extremely challenging "turning away" from the materialism, consumerism, and militancy so prevalent in our present-day culture. It is a summons to move away from the "me-ism" and the "Be Number One" mentality of today, and a return to the other-centered and sacrificing posture that was so central in the teaching and lifestyle of Jesus of Nazareth. Strange as it may seem, this is an invitation to genuine freedom; freedom from greed, blind ambition, and the all-consuming pleasure principle; a freedom for pursuing the more satisfying goals of helping others, preserving the environment, and avoiding nuclear holocaust. In truth, many wonder whether indeed there will be a future, if the young adults who will carry the responsibility of shaping the future do not respond to this challenge.

A Christian Vision of the Future The teachings of Christianity envision a future of opportunity for all, not merely for an elite few. Here there is a vision that rejects the present situation where the people of the United States, representing 6 percent of the earth's population, use more than one-third of the earth's material goods and energy. It is a vision that does not accept as just that a minority of people in the United States should control most of the money and power. Here there is discomfort that 8,000,000 people in the United States are seeking work and cannot find it, and that among these unemployed is a disproportionate number of blacks, Hispanics, and young adults. This perspective maintains that it is a contradiction to call oneself Christian, and yet remain comfortable in the face of homelessness, hunger, injustice and violence.

This tradition that faith must do justice goes back to the ancient teachings of the Bible. It returns to moral principles that were mentioned earlier in this chapter and will now be developed in more detail: principles regarding human dignity, our covenant with God and others in the human community, and, finally, our responsibility to share our goods with others, especially with the poor and needy.

Human Dignity The Bible proclaims the dignity of the human person by showing that somehow human life is created and sustained by a Creator God, who is imaged in each individual person. The right to be treated with dignity, then, is inalienable, that is, it cannot be taken away for any reason, whether it be race, nationality, sex, age, class, or religious belief. Indeed, as the Declaration of Independence proclaims, all people have been created equal, at least in the area of human dignity.

Yet, ironically, both the Jewish and Christian religions have not always clearly understood this teaching. Slavery was tolerated among the ancient Jews, in the gospel communities, and indeed in the United States until the last century. Wars have been and still are fought among religious people, and millions are slaughtered with little apparent awareness of human dignity. Racial discrimination is still prevalent on many of the campuses in the United States and throughout the world. Women still find their gender often to be a liability in seeking a profession or in serving their country or their church. Lower classes and the elderly often are being treated like second-class citizens. And one still hears of atrocities committed in the name of religion in places like Northern Ireland and Lebanon.

People of the Covenant Our Jewish-Christian tradition maintains that God invites all persons to share in a covenant relationship. All persons, in one way or another, receive this invitation to walk with God as a friend. Yet, freedom is always to be maintained, and it is up to each individual whether to say yes or no to this calling to partnership with God. A yes, of course, implies agreement to follow God's moral code faithfully and lovingly. This moral code aims to protect human life and dignity, and it prescribes the respect for the just rights of the other members of the human community. There have been many efforts to spell out more specifically what these rights are. Perhaps the most accurate listing of these rights of individuals can be found in the two "Covenants" of the United Nations. The first is called the International Covenant on Economic, Social, and Cultural Rights. Here are some of the main human rights listed in this document:

1. The right of everyone to an adequate standard of living for self and family, including adequate food, clothing and housing
2. The right of everyone to form trade unions and to join the trade union of choice
3. The right of everyone to social security, including social insurance
4. The right to be free from hunger
5. The right of everyone to the enjoyment of the highest

attainable standard of physical and mental health
6. The right of everyone to education.

The second "Covenant" deals with civil and political rights and lists the rights to life, to freedom from torture and degrading treatment, to liberty and security, to leave any country (including one's own), to freedom of thought, conscience, and religion, and to be free from discrimination.

One can easily speak of human rights, but when they are spelled out so specifically, it becomes evident how many persons today are being deprived of their basic human rights. It also becomes clear how much dedicated effort will be required by vast numbers if there is to be equity and justice in our world. Religion does seem to take on an air of irrelevance if it is not linked to concern for the injustice and oppression that is so common in today's society.

Citizens of the World We mentioned earlier that the role of universities is to train citizens of the world. Likewise, churches and other ecclesial bodies are becoming more responsible in educating their members to an awareness that they are part of "the people of God," a worldwide community with many members who do not have their basic human rights recognized. Such awareness is profoundly reflected in the Shakertown Pledge, a series of promises that was made in 1973 by a group of directors of religious retreat centers as an effort to promote interfaith commitment for simple living and global concern. It is an excellent example of the integration of faith and justice and it reads as follows:

The Shakertown Pledge

1. I declare myself to be a world citizen.
2. I commit myself to lead an ecologically sound life.
3. I commit myself to lead a life of creative simplicity and to share my personal wealth with the world's poor.
4. I commit myself to join with others in reshaping institutions in order to bring about a more just global society in which

all people have full access to the needed resources for their physical, emotional, intellectual and spiritual growth.

5. I commit myself to occupational accountability and, in so doing, I will seek to avoid the creation of products which cause harm to others.

6. I affirm the gift of my body, and commit myself to its proper nourishment and physical well-being.

7. I commit myself to examine continually my relation with others and to attempt to relate honestly, morally, and lovingly to those around me.

8. I commit myself to personal renewal through prayer, meditation and study.

9. I commit myself to responsible participation in a community of faith.

This statement reflects a holistic Christian vision that relates faith to life on all levels and is dedicated to justice and peace. It reveals the inspiring vision that has been seen in some Christian communities; in the dedication of the Quakers to world peace; in the heroic efforts that some Christian communities made to maintain the Underground Railroad that rescued so many slaves from bondage in the last century, in the courageous actions of those who demonstrate against nuclear arms, the pollution of the environment, abortion, and many other serious social issues, and in the prophetic statements against the arms race by the Methodists, Roman Catholics, and others.

Sharing Our Goods Deep in the Christian tradition is compassion for the poor and oppressed. Luke writes that God raises up the poor and lowly, and Jesus' first public utterance is the reading from Isaiah: "The Spirit of the Lord is upon me, because he has anointed me to preach the good news to the poor" (1: 51-53; 4:18). Jesus warns the rich against greed and reliance on material things, and tells them how difficult it will be for them to enter into the kingdom of God because of their attachments.

Jesus himself lived a simple lifestyle, and often voices concern for and brings healing to those who are on the fringes of society.

Moreover, the early communities valued the simple lifestyle, and the early community in Jerusalem even held all things in common and made sure that there was none needy among them (Acts 4: 32-34). In today's language, this is called having a "preferential option for the poor," that is, giving first consideration to how our laws and social structures affect the poor. They are to be given first consideration because of the tendency to ignore them as the faceless and voiceless of society.

In order to be empathetic toward the poor and also to be in a position to share with them, many Christians advocate a certain simplicity of lifestyle. In 1979, the Presbyterian church made a statement that adequately describes this kind of a commitment.

> We believe Christ calls us to dissent from our present lifestyles and to make a radical break from the patterns of overindulgence, consumerism, and reckless waste. We are called individually and ecclesiastically to choose a lifestyle which more nearly reflects the simplicity of Jesus' life and allows us to identify with the poor and powerless throughout the earth. Such an altered lifestyle enables us to reconsider what we truly value in life, how we measure success, where we live, what we eat, how we use energy, how we invest our lives and resources, and where we travel. In short, we are challenged to live more simply that all may simply live.

Myths About the Poor In the United States, there are many misconceptions about the poor. First of all, some think that most of the poor are racial minorities. In fact, two-thirds of the poor are white. Second, it is thought that poverty is a minor issue, especially since the poor are seldom visible to the middle and upper classes. In fact, about 33 million Americans live beneath the government's established poverty line, and this number has increased by nearly a third since 1973. Another misconception is that the poor are lazy and refuse to work. Again, the truth of the matter is that many of the poor are working, often two jobs or more, but are paid wages that are insufficient to lift them out of poverty. Many of our poor are physically or mentally unable to work. Of the long term poor, many are minorities and families headed by women. Most of them are working at wages too low to bring them above the poverty line. One in seven Americans lives in poverty, an incredible statistic for a country where there is such abundance.

Changing Unjust Structures John Paul II, in his provocative document on social justice, *The Social Concern of the Church*, points to growing inequities throughout the world. There is an ever-widening gap between the countries in the developed North and the developing South. The Third World has become more and more deprived, and we now have to speak of areas so poor as to be referred to as the "Fourth World." The document speaks of certain economic, financial, and social mechanisms or structures that are manipulated by both the Eastern and Western blocs that continually bring more wealth to these areas, while suffocating the developing nations. Both the capitalistic and communist countries vie for world control; two centers of power stand with guns at each other's heads while they attempt to dominate others economically and politically. Vast amounts of money are spent on weapons to defend these two opposing positions, while millions throughout the world suffer from the lack of the bare essentials.

The pope sums up the situation as follows: "One of the greatest injustices in the contemporary world consists precisely in this: that the ones who possess much are relatively few and those who possess almost nothing are many." He calls for international collaboration, a new sense of interdependence among nations, a realization of the common destiny that people throughout the world share. He urges the peoples of the world to see themselves as members of the human family, who should share a concern about the horrible injustices done to millions of their brothers and sisters.

Young Adults and Social Justice

Young adults in college have varied reactions to the issue of whether or not a Christian should be involved in efforts of social concern. In my own informal surveys and those of others, we have found a wide range of opinions on the matter, ranging from no concern for the matter to an enthusiastic involvement in social service and reform. In the following, we will survey the various approaches we have discovered among young adults with regard to the link between faith and justice.

There are still many young people who have given little or no thought to the matter of social involvement. With regard to religion itself, some are "on leave" for the time being from their church or congregation and thus have given little thought to whether or not they should, in view of their beliefs, take an active role in social issues. Bill, an accounting major from Columbus, Ohio, would be typical of this group. He remarks: "Hey, I'm too busy right now to worry about any more commitments. My studies occupy a lot of my time, I'm holding down a part-time job to help meet my expenses and keep up my car, and what little time I have left is for my social life. Maybe later I'll get involved helping others, but for now I have too many other things to do."

Others are still participating in the religion they were brought up in, but think that their faith life is a private matter between themselves and God. They make a sharp distinction between the secular and the sacred, between the world and spiritual matters, and they seriously question that their ministers should be involved in social issues. Mary is a devout Presbyterian who still holds firmly to the same beliefs of her parents and attends church regularly. Her position is this: "Religious people and especially the clergy should stick to the business of church, prayer and matters of religion. I don't think our pastor should be marching against nuclear weapons or demonstrating for fair housing. He should be in church helping his congregation with their problems. If people want to help others in these justice matters, they should get into politics or social work, not church work. They are mixing apples and oranges; worldly matters with religion." Some young people think that their leaders should not be issuing documents on nuclear disarmament or other justice issues because these are not their areas of competence. Church leaders should stick to theology, preaching and pastoral work. That is what they were trained to do.

Other young adults we have spoken to are of the opinion that they are living good Christian lives by being nice to others, not cheating or stealing, and by working hard at their studies. When we meet these people, we have to admit that they usually are very good people who indeed do make their own contributions to life. From their point of view, it is not necessary to go beyond "being a good person" and get involved in social issues.

As I pointed out earlier, a common feeling toward world problems such as hunger, oppression, the danger of nuclear war, and destruction of the environment is one of helplessness. I talk to so many young adults like Janet, a nursing student, who simply feels overwhelmed by the enormity of all these crises, and doubts whether her efforts could really make any difference. She says: "All my life I was sheltered from poverty and violence. I have never even known a poor person or been in any of the bad areas of town. I don't really understand the reasons for all the social problems in this country and throughout the world. How could I possibly do anything to solve these enormous problems?"

Opposition to the Poor Some young adults have strong feelings against the less fortunate. They have been brought up in a consumer society that views success in terms of material success and possessions, and think that the "have-nots" are in fact "losers," people who are too lazy to work and get ahead. Young adults often have been taught that if you work hard and do your best you will achieve the American dream, and they have seen this borne out in their own families, who through hard work have achieved considerable success and live comfortable lives.

Jake, a business major from Pittsburgh, shares these views. He comments: "Look, there is just so much to go around in this world, and I want my piece of the pie. I intend to get my degree, get a job making big bucks, and someday I'll be on the top of the pile. As the ad says, 'Be all that you can be.' I'm going to be on the top of the ladder—the Chairman of the Board." Jake's views are seen as rather common according to a recent survey at UCLA, which revealed that young people today are increasingly more interested in getting ahead than they are in changing the world.

Others feel so pressured by the economy and by the drive to get ahead that they are wary of taking time out to help others. Amie, typical of this group, says, "Of course, I am as idealistic as any other young adult and I would like to help others. However, I feel like I am in a race against many others to succeed and there are so many pressures on me. I doubt if I will ever be able to afford what my parents have. They bought houses and cars when they were much cheaper. If I take time out to get involved with social justice, that will be just so much time lost in the race to get ahead. Sure, I would like to help others, but I don't want to end up poor myself as a result of my generosity."

Finally, there are those who take a rather fatalistic view of social problems. Glenn, who is working to be a dental surgeon, and who is engaged to be married after graduation, believes that poverty and injustice have always been a part of society and there is not much that can be done about it. He grants that there is a lot more corruption today than in the past and he feels rather cynical about the crime that seems to appear on all levels of society, from athletics to politics. Basically, he thinks there is little or nothing that can be done about all this mess in the world. He believes, and this belief is shared by many young adults, that there will be a nuclear war within the next ten or twenty years. Glenn really fears that it will all come to an end before he has had a chance to achieve his goals in life.

Getting Involved It is common today to compare this college generation with that of the 1960s and early 1970s when there was much more social activism and political involvement on campuses. While it is true that things are much quieter in colleges these days, it would be simplistic to say that this generation is apathetic and only interested in partying and sports. There is a growing interest in social involvement on many campuses. Robert Coles, a child psychiatrist and social critic who teaches a course at Harvard University on social activism (which the students have dubbed "Guilt 33"), estimates that more than half the student body at Harvard contributes some time to community service. He points out that the young usually have an idealistic and generous nature. The problem lies not in the young, but in schools, families, and communities, where openheartedness is not nurtured and indeed is often discouraged. It is Cole's conviction that it is crucial that we help our young to get involved in the social, political, and racial problems of today. Such activity, he believes, will actually help young adults become better educated, not only intellectually, but also spiritually and morally.

While it is true that fewer young people are involved in social issues today than twenty years ago, those who are involved seem to have a better grasp of the issues than did many of the activists of the previous generation. Alixe Glenn, a former spokesperson for the Peace Corps, claims that today's youth are "realistic idealists." They are not satisfied with slogans and emotional marches. Rather, they want to get the facts on the issues, understand the complexities of the problems, and know specifically how they can make a difference before they get involved. Young people today are "from Missouri," in that they are usually reluctant to get involved in any cause until they have had a chance to look at it from several sides and make up their own minds. Families and schools have produced a much more critical generation of young people, many of whom have an eye out for the uninformed crusader. Persuasion, inspiration, and dialogue are much more effective ways of getting the young involved today than are sermons and exhortations.

Kristin, who recently changed majors so that she could make a contribution to world peace, is typical of those who want to know the facts before they make decisions for involvement. Her first major was biology and, like so many others, she changed majors several times trying to figure out what to do with her life. Several of her teachers made her aware of the serious tensions throughout the world, and she decided that somehow she would like to do something to bring peace to the world. She changed her major to history so that she could find out what was really going on in her world and took on a minor in peace studies. Now Kristin feels that she is getting somewhere because she is beginning to understand the complexities of the issues and see the kind of job in government where she will be able to put her knowledge to good use. She points out that seeking peace for others has brought a great sense of peace to her own life.

Getting Experience Besides wanting to know the facts and understand the issues, young adults today often say that they need to get some experience before they can get motivated. Many of them have had very little opportunity to do any social service or get involved in issues. They often have negative stereotypes that they have gained from the media. They see students in other countries battling the police and choking from tear gas. Or, they have the image of being uncomfortable among the poor and are afraid that they will feel stupid and out of place. Many have never met a needy person, nor have they known adult role models who are involved in social action.

Once, when we suggested that our students help at a local soup kitchen they resisted because they thought they would be embarrassed in such a place. Most of those who agreed to come along had a positive experience. The soup kitchen was not some "greasy spoon"; rather it was a neat and clean restaurant that politely served meals to the guests who came in for something to eat. The students quickly saw that the operation was being run by professionals who were dealing with the guests respectfully and in an atmosphere of hospitality. The students simply served as waitresses and waiters and felt comfortable engaging in some conversation with the people who came in. They discovered that the customers were people like themselves, and they especially enjoyed the children who were warm and friendly to them. The students learned a great deal that night. They learned that their stereotypes were not accurate. Moreover, they saw that there were concrete ways through which they could make a difference in helping others. When we reflected on all this in class, it was quite evident that everyone felt changed, even inspired by the situation, and they were eager to return in the future to be of help.

There are many other discoveries made on the part of students who take the plunge and get involved in social action. Some have remarked that the interaction with all kinds of different people broadened their views and gave them deeper insights into what is going on in the world. Others felt that their feeling of helplessness in the face of social problems disappeared because they found that they were not expected to solve huge problems, but were being called on to make a small but important contribution. Still others felt a sense of satisfaction in going out of their limited world of home and college and extending themselves to the less fortunate. Giving to others was a refreshing change from merely taking from others and looking out only for themselves. Many also remarked that they always gained a great deal from those that they served, observing the deep faith and incomparable hope that often exists among the needy. They discovered that there are other values in life than what a person owns and wears.

Several factors can contribute to the success of such experiences in social action. First of all, young adults usually want to be assured that they are not making a long-time commitment in agreeing to such activities. Young adults are at a stage of life where they want to experiment and establish their independence and freedom and often resist getting tied down to anything for a long period of time. They should thus be assured that these social actions are open-ended and that they can try doing various services for others without making anything other than a temporary agreement.

Another useful factor here is providing well-informed leaders who will truly teach the young adults valuable lessons and skills for social action. It is also important that these leaders provide a community of peers who can listen to each other's feelings and stories of social service, and offer mutual support. Times of serious reflection are crucial here so that the members of the group can share their insights and difficulties. Social action can often be confusing and even frustrating, and it is invaluable to have a community of others who know what you are experiencing and can offer empathy and concern.

Outstanding Examples

In 1988, the presidents of more than 60 colleges across the United States were asked to name outstanding leaders on their campuses. The names submitted, not surprisingly, were of women and men who were dynamic people both on and off the campus. Most of them were not only involved with their studies and at least part-time jobs, they were also struggling to make a contribution to the society around them. These are some of the leaders who were cited:

1. Patricia Accera, a theology and theatre arts major from Marquette University in Milwaukee. Patricia has been active in her parish, in campus ministry, and she has found a great deal of satisfaction teaching drama to handicapped children. She believes that "Christianity is more than a religion; it's a way of life, a lifestyle."

2. Tabatha Jill Conway, a journalism major at Texas Southern University in Houston. Tabatha works as an intern for a black newspaper in Houston and soon plans to enter law school. She wants to be a role model for the young black people in her area. She says, "I want to offer free legal assistance to the poor. Both of my parents were poor growing up. A lot of kids with whom I went to high school have turned to drugs. Black people need positive examples before them; they need to be motivated."

3. Michael Faber, a student of gerontology from Madonna College in Michigan. Mike feels a strong calling to work with the elderly. He says, "I want to do counseling, especially with the terminally ill. All Christian churches are ignoring the elderly, an important part of their memberships. The population of the aging is going to continue to grow constantly and steadily. There are very few people to meet these needs.... That's why, with the Lord's help, I can make a difference."

4. Barbara Costa, from Barry University in Miami, whose par-

ents fled from Cuba in 1962. She says that she tries to give of herself as much as possible and her achievements show this. For two years she tutored underprivileged Haitian children in the poorest community in South Florida. She organized a fundraiser for a home for unwed mothers, helped establish Miami's first Hunger Clean-up in 1987, and is working to set up an undergraduate peace studies program at her college. She says, "I believe the Lord has given me an awareness of the needs of others and a way in which I may apply my talents to help others. My faith service extends into all areas of my life."

5. Stephen Peters, from Loyola Marymount University in Los Angeles, who has reached out to help others as far away as the Dominican Republic and Belize. He maintains that he has learned a great deal from the poor. He states, "In other countries, I have worked with people who have no material possessions. Though truly poor by American standards, I find them to be immensely rich by the standards of Christianity. I have shared with them my knowledge in the area of health and medicine, while they shared with me their faith in Christ. The gifts I receive while giving is the main reason I remain so involved."

6. Finally, another student from Loyola Marymount, Julianne Barry, has worked for two years with 42 youngsters in an orphanage in Tecate, Mexico. She has also collected truckloads of food, clothes and many other items for these needy children, and she organized a drive to raise $150,000 for the orphanage. Amazingly, Julianne has also found time to work with the handicapped in Los Angeles and to coach and counsel troubled youth at a downtown juvenile hall. She and her fiance, Chris North, will soon marry and spend two years working at the orphanage in Mexico.

Anyone who wants to stereotype the present younger generation as the "me" generation has to take a careful look at these students and at thousands more across the country who are making great sacrifices to serve the needs of others.

Seeking Advice Sharon Parks has done extensive research into the area of the faith of young adults. She maintains that even though college students struggle for autonomy and independence, they still maintain a dependence on others for guidance and assistance. As was mentioned in the previous chapter, it is important during the college years for young adults to have mentors, guides, coaches who can offer insight and support. Mentors are usually close enough in age to the college student to be able to identify with the young adult experience and can "invite out" the potentials that stir within the young adult through support, encouragement and role-modeling. Parks laments the fact that fewer professors function in this all-important role of mentor for the emerging leaders of the future. She points out that professors often become mere technicians of knowledge, and that young adults therefore lack guides in the search for ultimate reality and in the struggle to put together a personal vocational vision.

If the young are to find ways to integrate faith with life, religious commitment with action, it would seem crucial that our campuses provide mentors from faculty, staff, and graduate students. If, as Derek Bok observes, one of the purposes of universities is to develop a sense of social responsibility in the young, it appears crucial that these institutions hire people who themselves have such a sense and who are capable of then mentoring students. It is appropriate also to reward our university personnel who themselves are involved in social action and who provide leadership in this area for the young. Criteria for tenure and promotion usually include service to the community, but often this is not taken nearly as seriously as are the areas of publishing and teaching.

Role Models Outside the Universities Though professors can effectively serve as mentors for the young in the area of social concern, few educators have the time or the skills to be professionally involved in social action. Therefore, the universities often must look beyond themselves to individuals who can provide expertise and role-modeling to young adults. Invitations to such individuals to appear on campuses for workshops and lectures could dramatically raise the social awareness among students. One thinks of the impact that Jesse Jackson has had among many young people in this country, assisting them in understanding the plight of the disadvantaged, and in making the young more aware of how they can make a difference through their efforts. Or one thinks of Morris Dees, the executive director and co-founder of the Southern Poverty Law Center, who has put his own life on the line in the struggle to combat the Ku Klux Klan and racial violence in the south. In 1987, Dees won a civil case against the Klan for the murder of a 19-year-old black man, and the Klan was devastated by having its money and property awarded to the tough-minded and courageous mother of the victim.

Others come to mind as outstanding role models for college-age students. There is Rose Cologne, who retired from the Penn State University faculty over 18 years ago and, instead of merely tending her roses, organized advocacy for better prison conditions and started a Volunteer Service Center on Penn State's campus and other programs that have spread nationwide to give thousands of young adults opportunities to serve the needy and improve their communities. There is Hazel Whitsett of Denver, Colorado, who helped found Denver's Northeast Women's Center to provide hope in a community which had virtually no social services. She prepared dozens of grant proposals and even used her own retirement money to provide assistance to women with welfare problems, educational needs, or counseling needs in the areas of jobs, sexual assault, and teen pregnancy. The more of these people who appear on our campuses, the more our students will see that there are indeed other life goals than being financially successful.

The Dorothy Day House It is becoming more common on campuses to establish a center for social concern. Such a facility can provide leadership, information, and a community for those interested in servicing the needs of others. On our campus at Xavier University, the center was named after Dorothy Day, one of the great leaders of our times in the peace and justice movement. This center provides information on a number of ways in which students can get opportunities to serve. For instance, a group of students assist once a month at a local soup kitchen that provides meals and conversation to needy citizens of the inner city. Other students help with "Restoc" a project that fixes up old buildings and provides comfortable housing for low-income families. Others counsel and tutor the handicapped and disadvantaged children in the area. Some participate in the Adopt-a-Grandparent Program, while others serve as Big Brothers and Big Sisters. Whatever their involvement, the students find at Dorothy Day House a place where they can reflect with others who want to serve, and where they can find support and assistance in helping others. The center, like others on campuses throughout the United States, provide space and personnel that can indeed assist college-age students in the crucial task of linking faith with action for justice and peace.

The college years serve as a crucial preparation for the future. In this chapter, we have pointed out that colleges and universities have a responsibility to offer students the insight and skills necessary for improving the future of society, and have stressed that in the Christian tradition there is a definite link between faith and a concern for peace and justice. We have seen how many young adults struggle with connecting their faith life, often viewed as quite personal and private, to some involvement in social issues. Finally, we have pointed out a number of students who have successfully worked their way through this struggle and who are prepared to offer their services to others.

QUESTIONS FOR REFLECTION AND DISCUSSION

1. Comment on your views of Derek Bok's position that higher education should prepare the young to help change society for the better.

2. Some surveys indicate that young adults today are more concerned with material gain than they are with serving others. Does your first-hand experience with your peers move you to agree or disagree with these surveys?

3. Does your institution of learning provide opportunities for serving the needy? If so, what percentage of the students do you think take advantage of these opportunities?

4. What is your opinion on whether or not religious leaders should take positions on issues of peace and justice?

5. Reflect on some service which you have rendered to someone in need, and comment on how these actions affected you.

Suggested Readings

Bellah, Robert N., *et al. Habits of the Heart: Individualism and Commitment in American Life*. Berkeley and Los Angeles: University of California Press, 1985.

Bok, Derek. *Beyond the Ivory Tower: Social Responsibilities of the Modern University*. Cambridge, Mass.: Harvard University Press, 1982.

Bowen, Howard. *The State of the Nation and the Agenda of Higher Education*. San Francisco: Jossey-Bass Publishers, 1982.

Dulles, Avery. "The Meaning of Faith Considered in Relationship to Justice," in *The Faith That Does Justice*," ed. John Haughey. Mahwah, N.J.: Paulist Press, 1971.

Freire, Paulo. *Education for Critical Consciousness*. New York: Seabury Press, 1973.

Johnson, David, ed. *Justice and Peace Education: Models for College and University Faculties*. Maryknoll, N.Y.: Orbis Books, 1986.

Warren, Michael. *Youth, Gospel, Liberation*. New York: Harper & Row, 1987.

Winter, Gibson. *Liberating Creation: Foundation of Religious Social Ethics*. New York: Crossroad, 1981.

PART TWO

RELIGION

CHAPTER FIVE

Why Bother About Religion?

Since many young people and adults do not get too excited about religion (to put it mildly), we would like to use this chapter not to artificially induce excitement, but to consider and comment on what seem to be some of the main reasons why religion is a turn-off for so many people today. We are basing our remarks on what we authors have encountered in our college classrooms and adult education programs. We hope not only to describe the difficulties people have with religion, but to listen to them and learn from such problems. In our comments on these difficulties, we do not intend to present answers that will close the case, but rather to offer some reflections that might generate new insights and make clear why we are convinced that religion is a matter that matters.

But before we begin, what do we mean by "religion"? That question will be answered in greater detail in the following chapter. For the moment, let us offer a loose, working definition: Religion is what comes about when people have some kind of an experience of what can be called "Ultimate Reality" or "Something More" or "God," and when they come together with other people in order to enkindle, maintain, and live that experience. More technically, religion is the social expression of transcendent experience, people coming together to express and live out their religious faith. For a variety of reasons, many people today are not at all certain that they should be numbered among such "religious" groups. In what follows, we will try to spell out some of their reasons.

Criticisms of Religion

When one thinks of critics of religion, one thinks of atheists. Certainly some of the most hard-hitting objections to religion and to religious people have come from hard-thinking atheists. Such critics have confronted believers with either the lack of logic and silliness in their reasons for believing, or they have soberingly reminded believers that, according to the data available to human experience, and according to the accepted rules of human reasoning, it is impossible to prove, to be really sure, that God exists.

This is the sincere, candid opinion of Rick, a junior majoring in journalism: "I want there to be solid, hard evidence for whatever it is that serves as the basis for my life. To be honest with you, I can't find such evidence for the existence of God. To be honest with myself, therefore, I just can't believe in God. I guess you'd call me an atheist."

One must listen carefully to the claims of atheists that religious belief is based on insufficient evidence or faulty reasoning. All too easily, religious people tend to dismiss atheists as "insincere" or "self-seeking materialists" not worthy to be taken seriously. Such a response may be too facile; it may be nourished by an unconscious fear that the atheists' criticisms might, at least in part, be correct. Also, as one of the best known Catholic theologians of this century, Karl Rahner, has reminded his fellow Christians, there are many so-called atheists whose lives are in closer conformity to the way Jesus lived than are the lives of many Christians.

Still, especially from our experience with young people, we don't think that the major reason for lack of interest in religion today comes from the atheistic critique. Nowadays, the real problem with religion has to do not so much with atheism as with indifference or disgust. The reason why many contemporaries don't want to bother with religion is not so much because they think "You can't prove the existence of God," but because they feel "Even if God exists, so what?" The hard-core atheistic argument has lost, it seems, much of its strength.

Not only in matters religious, but in general, people today no longer insist that "You have to prove it before I'll accept it." They no longer demand irrefutable evidence and absolute certainty. Hard-nosed empiricism ("The facts, nothing but the facts") and ironclad rationalism ("Only what is logical is true") it seems, have had their heyday. Perhaps this is because science itself, which in its earlier days claimed to be based only on empirical evidence, has changed. Scientists today, such as Werner Heisenberg, David Boehm, Loren Eiseley, and Thomas Lewis, are much more willing, even happy, to admit that science can never have absolute certainty, that there is something about the subject matter of physics and biology that will always be more than the human mind can comprehend, and that therefore scientific theories and laws are never simply a matter of raw, empirical objectivity.

Also, people today seem to be much more aware that if we base our lives only on what our heads tell us, we will probably lead stunted lives. The heart is also important. And, as the French philosopher Blaise Pascal (1623-1662) reminds us, the heart has reasons that reason cannot fully understand. In other words, feelings are just as important as logical reasoning. While we have to follow what our reason indicates, we also have to be open to and trust what our feelings tell us. If that weren't true, no one would ever allow themselves to fall in love. Love is a matter of both the head and the heart.

For all these reasons, therefore, many people in general today don't seem as concerned about "proving" or "knowing for sure" before they believe in God. The reason why they don't believe lies elsewhere. It's more a matter of not being able to see any real advantage to affirming the reality of God; or they see certain psychological or social disadvantages. Thus, many moderns are ready to admit the existence of an "Ultimate Being." In fact, I hear this from students often: "Sure I recognize the existence of God. Someone or Something had to get this show going. There has to be some Creator." But when I push the issue and ask how this God really figures into their lives, they are often at a loss. They believe, but their belief is more of an intellectual conclusion than a personal commitment. The God that many people recognize today is what historians call a "Deistic God"—the God who created and wound up the clock of creation but who now remains in heaven while the clock ticks away on its own. This is not the kind of God whom one can easily get involved with or who really makes for a difference in one's life.

Or, other people hold to a form of agnosticism (from the Greek word meaning "I don't know"). They just don't know if God exists. God is still a question for them. But—and here is how today's agnostics differ from those of a generation or two ago—it's not a question that bothers them. Whereas people previously agonized over the question of whether or not God exists it's a "so-what" question to many. What difference would it really make to know that God existed or not? Perhaps for an afterlife it would be important. But for this life, today, as we live it right now, the existence or non-existence of God makes no practical difference. Many people today are "comfortable agnostics."

If we try to delve more deeply into the reasons why so many contemporary persons don't want to bother with religion, why they are either indifferent or opposed to it, I think we can come up with two general attitudes: 1) The "ho-hum" attitude, which sees religion as useless; and 2) the "watch-out" attitude, which considers religion to be dangerous. I invite you to think about whether the following observations fit your experience of yourself or of many of your contemporaries.

The "Ho-Hum" Attitude: Religion Is Useless

"What you say about God, about Jesus Christ, about the values of the gospel all makes such good sense. I don't deny it. But it just doesn't grab me in a way in which I can fit it into my life. Or I just don't feel motivated to make the effort to fit it into my life." Such were the sincere comments of Rich, an intelligent, sincere, and outgoing sophomore from Toledo. It's not that he is an opponent of religion. In fact, he would like to make a place in his life for a more active, involved faith. But he just doesn't do it. Or he can't. This, to a great extent, describes the situation of many young people and adults today. They are mired in a bog of indifference or inertia toward religion and religious faith. Is it their fault? Does the problem lie in or outside of themselves?

No doubt, the problem often lies within the person, in selfishness, laziness, fear. But from what we hear from college students, we would suggest that the primary reasons for the widespread ho-hum attitude toward religion in our contemporary society lie outside sincere individuals like Rich and are to be found in: 1) society itself, 2) the message of religion, and 3) religious people. To briefly explain what we mean:

1. In the First World, in societies like those of North America and Europe, many people find life to be so fast-moving and fascinating that they simply don't have time to think seriously about religion. They're on a roller coaster and there just isn't time or opportunity to do much else but hang on, either for dear life or for enjoyment. As Judy, a sophomore pre-med student put it, "I have all I can do just to keep up with my studies and with my twenty-five-hour-a-week part-time job. If I want to keep my 3.8 average in order to get into med school, if I don't want to fall too much into debt, I have to give just about all my time to books and work. Whatever driblets of time are left over, I eagerly collect for my meager social life. If I can get to Sunday Mass (and if I can stay awake through it!), I'm lucky." In the intense pace of her life, Judy may be somewhat of an extreme case; yet the majority of students seem to be swept up in the proverbial "rat race" to the extent that they just don't have the time that a serious pursuit of religious living seems to require.

If young people are not hanging on to the roller coaster for dear life to get ahead (as is Judy), they are doing so for the wholesome fun of it all. Yes, they are busy with work or studies, but they are also having fun. They are living full lives, enjoying friends and activities, and planning for the future. "I find genuine satisfaction in my work," Bob, a junior, told me, "and especially in my friends. My life is full. Sure I have my problems with parents, teachers and grades. But I'm basically busy and happy. Yes, I believe in God and hope that I'll get to heaven if there is one. But I just don't feel the need—nor do I have the time—for getting seriously involved in religion."

"Life is full, life is fun, life is (often) frantic. To squeeze anything else into it, like religion, seems neither possible nor necessary." That expresses the feelings of many honest, ordinary people today.

2. Another reason why many people cannot get excited about religious faith has to do, they say, with the message of religion itself. Given the kind of society we live in today, religion is too impractical. After a semester of "Introduction to Theology," Rick, an older student (about 28) majoring in political science, told me in his usual thoughtful and gentle manner: "What we learned about the message of Jesus and Buddha is great stuff, no doubt. And the example of prayer and meditation, and of active love for one's neighbor provides a noble ideal. It would be great if everyone in the world would love their neighbor as themselves and 'practice compassion toward all sentient beings' [as Buddha put it]. But it just won't work. If you want to get ahead in this world, if you want to be a success in business, if you want to keep the Soviets at bay, you just can't be a 'nice guy' like Jesus and Buddha. We're living in a world of competition, of survival of the fittest, and of innate aggression. Nice guys finish last, or lose their jobs, or are blown away." Rick was not trying to be defiant. He was struggling with a painful question: In the light of the values and givens of our modern world, could he really take the message of Jesus or Buddha seriously? That's a real question. And many people like Rick can't answer it. In the meantime, it's keeping them from a serious pursuit of religion.

3. "Look at the kind of people that go to church every Sunday. I just can't get excited about wanting to be one of them." Coming in a variety of forms, this is one of the criticisms I hear most often. It implies that the people who do call themselves religious and who do participate in organized religion are not doing a very good job of selling religion. In fact, according to what I hear from young people, official churchgoers are providing a goodly bit of negative advertising for religion. This is for two reasons: "They're just like everyone else," students will tell me. "We see no difference between people who go to church every Sunday and those who don't. Why are they going?" Perhaps it is just a matter of routine, of social custom, of wanting to look good. Or, what's worse, young people will comment that religious persons are worse than their non-religious counterparts. This is the criticism of hypocrisy, often illustrated in the "parking lot syndrome": "They spend an hour in church singing God's praises and proclaiming their love of neighbor, and then in the parking lot curse the guy in the blue Pontiac for cutting in front of them."

Perhaps this is a trivial example, but it illustrates the question that many young people place before organized religion: "Where's the beef? What difference does being religious really make? Why don't religious people practice what they preach?" Such questions are more pressing, and more threatening, than any raised by rational atheism.

The "Watch Out" Attitude: Religion Is Dangerous

Another, and perhaps even more challenging, barrage of criticisms of religion comes from a completely different front. Though they reflect widespread attitudes on the part of students and adults, these criticisms have also received a more academic or philosophical elaboration by two of the most influential modern critics of religion: Sigmund Freud (1856-1939) and Karl Marx (1818-1883). According to this perspective, religion is not just useless, it is downright harmful, an obstacle to the already difficult tasks of leading a psychologically healthy life and of building a more just and peaceful world. Simply stated, religion, according to these critics, gets in the way of being human and of improving the world. Religion is both psychologically and sociologically dangerous. Or, in Freud's and Marx's terms: Religion is both a crutch and an opiate.

Religion as a Crutch For Freud, religion is a crutch. "So what's wrong with a crutch?" one might ask. Nothing, when you have a broken leg. A crutch is there to help you do something you normally should be able to do on your own. That, precisely, is Freud's complaint about religion. It gets in the way of people's ability to walk on their own two feet; it gets in the way of their taking responsibility for their own lives, making hard decisions, growing up to a maturity that can handle the knocks of life with strength and resilience. Religion, like crutches, is for people who can't walk on their own and deal with life as it is.

In Freud's trenchant terms, religion is the satisfaction of infantile needs, something that humanity required when it was in the infancy of its history. A little child, Freud explains, naturally needs to see the smiling, loving face of its father or mother looking down into its cradle; otherwise it cannot be secure. But as we grow up, we have to face life without having our parents looking after us. If we never "leave home," if we never venture out on our own, we never really grow up. We remain psychologically immature.

This is exactly what Freud thought religion does. Because people don't want to grow up, because they are too frightened of being on their own and taking responsibility for their lives and their world, they "imagine" or "project" the face of a divine Father in heaven to take the place of the parental face above the cradle. They turn to religion to tell them that they don't have to worry; they don't have to make everything okay—God will. They turn to their priest or minister or rabbi or to their Bible or Koran to be told the way things are, rather than figuring out life and the meaning of the world for themselves.

When something terrible happens, like a fatal sickness, a tragic accident, a natural catastrophe, people will attribute it to and accept it as "God's will," rather than ask just why their baby died of dysentery, or why the plane crashed or why the river keeps flooding. When God has given a divine law, people don't have to figure out right and wrong for themselves; all they have to do is obey. When God is determining everything that happens, people don't have to worry, they just have to trust. When the final, absolute truth about the universe and the meaning of life has been revealed by God, people don't have to search. It's all there, in a sacred book or in an infallible religious leader. Life may be like a scary movie, but because people believe that God is the director, they know there will be a happy ending. They don't have to worry. They can sit back and eat their popcorn. This, basically, is the Freudian criticism of religion.

To listen to young people today, it seems that though they may never have heard of Freud, they find a lot of reasons to agree with him. One such reason was expressed by Patty, a junior biology major. In a class discussion, she was beside herself: "I can't understand it! Our biology teacher, Prof. Hedeen, has spent three weeks laying out the theory of evolution; he explained carefully and clearly the areas where scientists agree and where they still argue. Though we can't be absolutely certain, there is just so much evidence for the beauty and mystery of the way life evolved on this planet. Yesterday, however, Stacey stood up in class and announced that she doesn't believe a word of it—not because there were flaws in the textbook or in the prof's explanation, but because it contradicts the Bible! She has completely closed her mind to modern biology! Her whole outlook on everything is based on one book!"

Such an example may be somewhat extreme. Yet I've heard complaints that go in the same direction about "strict Catholics" and the way they believe that everything the pope (or even their local pastor) says is God's truth. One of the issues that has especially alienated many adults from the Catholic religion is the way the pope has settled the question of population control; with arguments that don't seem to make a lot of sense to the majority of Catholics in the United States, he has simply ruled out any form of artificial birth control. It seems that Catholics aren't being allowed to think for themselves, to weigh the evidence concerning the need to control the earth's population and the various ways of doing so. They are simply being told what to do. "We can't be adults and decide for ourselves, especially in matters as personal and as complicated as sexual relations," a frustrated young mother admitted in an adult education class. "Good Catholics," she went on to say, "are treated as little children."

In the opinion of Mary Kay, a junior active in the university peace and justice program, there is an even more frightening reason to agree with Freud's claim that religion promotes infantile dependency. She came storming into my office one day after just reading a book called *Blessed Assurance: At Home with the Bomb in Amarillo, Texas* (A.G. Mojtabi, Boston: Houghton Mifflin Co., 1986) about the people who work in the nuclear weapons factory in Amarillo, Texas. "Most of them are Christians," she exclaimed, " and they think they are doing God's will by building these weapons of destruction! They believe that God, not humans, is in charge of the end of the world, and that God may well have it in mind to make use of nuclear war to bring this world to an end. If that's the case, when the end comes, these Christian weapons-producers think they will have first seats behind the pearly gates, because they had been God's partners. If that's what religion does to people, we're better off as atheists!"

I tried to calm her by pointing out that this is certainly not the viewpoint of all Christians. Yet I had to admit that there are many Christians who, though they don't go as far as the workers in Amarillo, are not really concerned about nuclear war; and the reason for their lack of concern is their trust in God. They believe that God would simply not allow God's creation to be destroyed in such a senseless fashion. God is in control; they don't have to worry. When I admitted this to Mary Kay, she gave me a Freudian answer: "In leaving the danger of nuclear war in God's hands, they are shirking their own responsibility. They should be working in peace movements rather than praying in their churches."

Though these examples may be extreme, they reflect a fairly widespread sense among young people and adults that religion, at least religion as they know it, is more of an obstacle than an aid to thinking for oneself, taking responsibility for one's life, and getting fully involved in life. Religion for them is a crutch. And many of them are throwing away their crutches.

Religion as Opium Another expression of how religion, in the minds of many, does more harm than good is the way it so easily and so often is used as a means of taking advantage of and manipulating people. "Opium" is the image that Karl Marx used to describe this danger: Like a drug administered by a doctor, religion puts people to sleep or desensitizes them so the doctor can perform all kinds of painful procedures without the patient feeling anything. In this case, however, the procedures are not for the patient's good. Marx also called this "ideology." In general usage, the word signifies the philosophical outlook of an individual or group; in Marx's sense, it indicates the abuse of truth for one's own personal benefit. To tell people that the world is coming to an end tomorrow may be true or false; to tell them this with the intent that they should therefore turn over their wealth to the preacher is ideology. Religion as opium and as ideology are related: Religion is used as a drug in order to take advantage of people. Marx, and many people after him, argued that this is exactly the way religion has been used throughout the history of humanity.

Again, though we have met only a few Marxists among our students, what we often hear from them shows that they are in sympathy with his assessment of religion. Jorge, from Nicaragua, explained to his fellow North American students in a theology class how religion had been used in his country before 1979, under the dictatorship of the Somoza family: "Most of the priests and bishops told the *campesinos* (peasants) that it was God's will that there be poor people, that their true home was in heaven, and that if they suffer in this world, they will receive a greater reward in the next. Many bishops and priests also stressed that it is God's will that we obey the political leaders of our country. The result of such a message, of course, was that the poor remained poor and the rich, rich. No wonder there was such a happy marriage between the government and the church!" Jorge went on to explain how this was basically the same situation in other Latin American countries, especially during the past century and the first half of this one. Religion was used as a "drug" to keep the people inactive and to protect unjust social systems.

Jorge's claims touched off a lively discussion, with the majority of students admitting that he was right. A number of North American students pointed out that you don't have to go to Central America to find such abuses of religion. They felt that many (though certainly not all) of the television preachers in the United States were up to basically the same thing. In their insistence that the Bible is the one and only true message of God, and especially in the highly emotional pitch they give to their preaching style, these preachers induce a "religious high" in which the people's emotions are turned on and their minds are turned off; this is when the basket is passed or the "send your money to" message is announced. It seemed to my students that this, too, was an example of using religion to take advantage of people for one's own financial gain. It's what Marx would call ideology.

At this point in the already animated discussion, two young Catholic women made an even more controversial point. They argued that the claims of popes to have "supreme authority" in the Catholic church had been used in the past to manipulate people and to amass great wealth and power for the papacy; everyone in the class seemed to admit this. But then the young women went on to say that this same papal power is being used today to take advantage of women, to exclude them from the priesthood and positions of authority in the church, and so to keep them in a subservient role. For ages, women have accepted this because they were told that God speaks through the pope. Today, however, many women and men look upon the religious teaching that "women cannot be ordained priests" not as God's will but as another example of how religion is used as an ideology.

There is another way in which religion can be employed to take advantage of people—not as a "drug" but as a "club." In this case, religious beliefs or religious authority are used not so much to keep people subservient or to bilk them of their money, but to use them as a "club" with which to beat up on and dominate other people. This is what the experts term "civil religion," when religion is used to elevate and extol one's own group, country, or religion as the one specially chosen by God. Religion becomes a tool to promote extreme nationalism or ethnocentrism (our race or ethnic group before all others). Because "our" religion is the one chosen by God as the highest religion, all other religions and all other peoples are looked upon as inferior. And if these inferior people don't recognize the truth, then the "superior" religion feels itself permitted or even obliged to force them to "see the light" and to submit to what is clearly God's truth. Religion becomes a club, a weapon used in war; and religious believers become the warriors, the cannon fodder for the generals, politicians, or religious leaders waging these "holy" wars.

This is one of the areas where I hear youth's sharpest criticisms of religion. One of the greatest scandals today is the way religion is being used to foster hostilities, even bloodshed, between peoples and nations. From the past, people who know their history point out the Crusades, in which Christians and Muslims believed they could win a sure place in heaven by killing each other, or the wars between Catholics and Protestants that wracked Europe after the Reformation. Today, the situation does not seem to be much different. People read daily in the newspapers how religion helps sound the call to battle in Northern Ireland (Catholics vs. Protestants), Palestine (Jews vs. Muslims), Sri Lanka (Hindus vs. Buddhists), India (Sikhs vs. Hindus). All of these parties are fighting with the conviction that God (or Allah, or Brahman, or Buddha) is on their side.

In general, wars are difficult to bring to an end. But when they are wars motivated by religion, when people are convinced they are fighting for God's truth, not their own, it becomes almost impossible to bring peace. For many thinking people who are concerned about peace, such a use (or abuse) of religion is one of the greatest obstacles to their wanting to have anything to do with religious faith. That so much blood could be spilled in the name of God leads many people to question whether such a God can really exist.

In distant and recent history, then, religion seems to serve as a crutch and a drug. In the eyes of many, the dangers of religion far outweigh its advantages. Why, then, bother with religion, except to do away with it?

Response to the Critics: Sad But True

The first response that can and must be given to all these criticisms of religion is a simple one: "You're right." Unless one is dishonest or living with her or his head in some kind of religious sand, it is impossible to deny that much of what presents itself as religion has been in the past and still is today either useless or dangerous. It is important that religious people not only admit such problems, but that they feel and deal with them. That's why in a book like this one on faith, religion, and theology, we have to listen carefully and sensitively to the pressing questions and problems that people have with religion. And we have to admit not only that people have such problems, but that there are good reasons for having them. Unless some such admission is made by anyone who wants to study or practice religion today, he or she will not be dealing with religion as it really is, or with people as they really see religion. It would be like trying to sell a product without doing a market inventory. So, religious people should be grateful to critics like Freud and Marx, who have helped them understand not only the religious market but the deficiencies and dangers of the product.

But does simply admitting that there are justifiable problems with religion get us off the hook too easily? Look at the frequency and intensity of these abuses. Look at the terrible harm that religion has caused. It seems that there is not a single religion in history or in the present world that has not fallen prey to such abuses and corruption. Shouldn't this scandalize us? Shouldn't this raise questions about the overall validity of religion?

We don't think so. We can never be indifferent to the way religion can lead to boredom or harm. Certainly, we are naturally scandalized and angered at the way people have used religion to take advantage of others. But that heinous crimes have been committed in the name of religion should not totally surprise us, or lead us to throw out the baby with the dirty bath water. The reason, I think, is to be found in a general and simple truth: whatever is capable of accomplishing great good is just as capable of accomplishing great evil. Whatever can fill us with exhilarating joy can also plunge us into the depths of anguish. The most noble capabilities can also be used for the most disgusting deeds.

The clearest example of what I am talking about is human love. One of the most noble capacities of the human spirit is the ability to love other human beings, to commit ourselves to them, to be faithful to them. Perhaps there is nothing that so overwhelms us with joy, peace and happiness as the experience of loving or being loved by parent, child, friend, or spouse. And yet, as most of us have experienced (or will), human relationships can also be the occasions of crushing pain, disappointment, and horror. Husband and wife, parents and children, friend and friend can cause each other just as much hurt and despair as pleasure and happiness. "You can really hurt the ones you love" is a saying based on sad reality.

If this is the way things are, what should we conclude about human love? Some people, after terrible hurts and broken commitments, have given up on love and relationships. "I'll never trust another guy (or girl) again"—that may be a temporary outburst, or it may be a lifelong decision. And yet the majority of human beings, knowing full well that love can cause so much pain, that it is so difficult to have a healthy relationship, that one out of two marriages in the United States ends up in divorce, still give love and friendship a chance. They still believe that human relationships are worthwhile.

I think that the same thing can be said of religion. Though it is capable of terrible abuses, it is also capable of incredible good. Religion, like human love, is not only worthwhile, it is necessary.

But to say all that is not enough. By itself, such a recognition of religion's potential for bad and for good would too easily give us a way out. Religious people must not only recognize the possible problems and abuses of religion, they must also take precautions against such evils. This is something we will discuss later in this book. It is capsulized in the Latin saying that Martin Luther was fond of: *Religio semper reformanda* (religion is in constant need of reform). Within its organizational structure, every religion needs a team of "quality control experts" (in the past they were called "prophets") whose job it is to be on the lookout for religion's corruption and to call for its reform. Any religion that thinks it is okay the way it is, is ready to fall into abuse or boredom, if it hasn't already. Like any good marriage, religion is never perfect but always has to be worked at, tidied up, put back on track.

While admitting, then, that in every religion there lurks a Mr. Hyde as well as a Dr. Jekyll, the authors of this book are convinced that the true personality of religion is that of Dr. Jekyll. Religion can be more creative and transformative than destructive and static. Again, this is the same belief or trust that most of us share about marriage: although every marriage has the potential for disaster, its true promise is that of happiness and fuller life. Yes, religion has produced a Jim Jones, an Ayatollah Khomeini, a Pope Alexander VI; but it has also brought forth a Mother Teresa, a St. Francis of Assisi, a Mahatma Gandhi.

This chapter has tried to face the problems and dangers of religion honestly. The rest of the book attempts to show that the promise of religion outweighs its dangers, that the risk of religious faith and community is worthwhile and deeply satisfying. In what remains of this chapter, we would like to lay out a few of the foundational planks on which the rest of the book builds, a few of the general reasons why we think that religion today presents the modern woman or man with an option that is not only worthwhile, but maybe even necessary.

The Psychological/Personal Value of Religion

Critics such as Freud ridicule religion for being a means of "need fulfillment." One might simply respond, "What's wrong with that?" All living creatures from amoebas to humans have needs, and these needs naturally must be fulfilled. The pivotal point is not whether religion fulfills needs (let's hope it does) but what kinds of needs are being met. Are they healthy or sick needs? Or, are natural needs being met in a healthy or destructive manner? As adults, we have adult needs (for a support system, for example) and these must be taken care of; but we may also have infantile needs (for being told what to do), which we would do better to leave behind.

With many other religious educators and with a good number of modern-day psychologists, we would like to suggest that religion meets natural, adult needs, the kind of needs which, if not met, can turn us into sick human beings. This is a point that is made more amply in other parts of this book. For the moment, however, let us put it in a very general way: Humans beings, so it seems, have the need to trust that there is an enduring meaning for their individual lives and for the life of humanity as a whole. We have to trust that life—mine, yours, ours—and all that goes into life—loving, hoping, trying to make things better—makes sense, that there is some meaning to it all. We have to be able to feel that when we try to live good lives, that when we try to reach out to our fellow human beings in love and sharing and cooperation, we are doing something that fits the way things really are; we need to feel that we are in harmony with the way life and the universe are made to work.

We're not talking about the hope that there is going to be a great big reward in heaven (though we certainly are not denying the reality of heaven). To do good only in order to be rewarded, to live a moral life on earth only because there's a payoff in heaven, is not exactly an adult form of behavior or a mature morality. What we are claiming is that humans have to trust that when they go out of themselves in love and commitment, they are not wasting their time; they have to be able to trust that through such actions they are contributing to something larger than themselves. If we don't have this basic trust in the meaning of human life, we can't live human life in a full and healthy manner.

Is that really so? Some psychologists (like Freud himself) and philosophers (like Jean Paul Sartre) would say that to be mature, to be an adult in the human species, we have to bravely accept the fact that there is no larger meaning, that we are utterly left to ourselves. Life on this planet is nothing more than a cosmic accident, we are told; that human life evolved on this particular globe was a purely chance occurrence, and, given the second law of thermodynamics, this accident will eventually peter out into nothingness. In the meantime, we have to be brave and create whatever fragments of meaning we can while we strut our brief part on this stage of human existence.

Are such "existentialists" and "realists" right? One cannot say for sure. It does seem, however, that for the majority of human beings, if they are left totally on their own to "create" meaning all by themselves, if they cannot feel themselves part of a larger cosmic picture, if they are nothing more than a cosmic accident, then life becomes either unbearable (and then suicide is a logical option), or it becomes a matter of "me first" and of trying to have as much pleasure as I can for this brief moment (perhaps a more logical choice). But for people who hold up love and commitment and working for the betterment of humanity as part of what it means to be human, there has to be, it seems, a larger picture; there has to be something more going on in this universe. (As other chapters show, in actually living lives of love and commitment, people come to experience that there *is* "something more" going on.)

Please note, we are not saying that this something more pulls all the strings and is there simply to ensure a happy ending. No, people can believe in God and still feel responsible for their lives; they can still feel the necessity of making choices, searching for meaning, dreaming new dreams that will cost sweat and tears and maybe even their lives. Without human action and responsibility the "meaning" of life will *not* be realized; but at the same time, religious people feel that it cannot be *only* a matter of human action and responsibility. Humans have to find and create meaning *for* themselves; but they cannot, so it seems, do it *by* themselves. And this is where human beings feel the natural and healthy need to trust that there is "something more" to human existence, something that is part of human existence, something which, if humans are "in sync" with it, makes it possible to find and create meaning and a fuller life.

Here enters the role of religion. Religions are the means, the telescopes by which humans look beyond, or better, the microscopes by which they look within, to view and try to understand that "something more," that Mystery called by different names, the Mystery with which they want to be in harmony, which helps provide the meaning for human existence, which is the foundation for their basic trust. As it was explained in Part One of this book, humans have this basic trust built into their very nature; it is a sense that there is something more that is part of them and their world. Religions, in a variety of imperfect forms and limited means, help people to identify, picture, and feel what it is they are trusting. Put simply: Religion helps provide and cultivate the sense of meaning that is necessary for living a full, a committed, a hope-filled life in this world.

That is why a number of contemporary psychologists make the bold claim that without some form of religious faith, psychological health is not possible. The Swiss psychiatrist and one-time colleague of Freud, Carl Gustav Jung (1875-1961), made such assertions. From his own experience and from working with his patients, Jung discovered that the deeper meaning necessary for carrying on the struggle of life was "imprinted" within the unconscious depths of every person; but he also discovered that persons cannot contact this deeper meaning within each of them through purely intellectual or rational means. Rather, symbols and myths are necessary; they are the antennae or receivers by which persons come into contact with and hear this mysterious meaning (Jung called it the Self, with a capital S) which is both part of them and yet more than them. And he realized, contrary to his colleague Freud, that it is especially in the religions of the world that humanity finds the most effective assortment of myths and symbols to feel and discover this Mystery. So, even though Jung was sharply critical of organized religion for the way it had literalized and sterilized the power of its symbols and myths, he could make this amazing statement about what makes for psychological health:

> Among all my patients in the second half of life...there has not been one whose problem in the last resort was not that of finding a religious outlook on life. It is safe to say that every one of them fell ill because he had lost that which the living religions of every age had given to their followers, and none of them has really been healed who did not regain his religious outlook.

Another well-known psychiatrist who argued for the psychological necessity of religious experience was Abraham Maslow (although he, too, in his early writings, was extremely critical of organized religion). He identified a "hierarchy of needs" according to which we first have to meet certain physiological needs (such as food, safety, belongingness, self-esteem) before we can fulfill our highest need of "self-actualization." Yet Maslow also came to recognize that we cannot self-actualize ourselves, take on responsibility for ourselves and freely decide who we are to be, unless we fulfill our need for what he termed "core-religious experiences" or "peak experiences."

Through such experiences, according to Maslow, we acquire a sense of the meaning of life and our role in it, of oneness with others and with the world, of self-worth and yet selflessness. Peak experiences provide what he termed "B-cognition," an awareness of "Being" (again, with a capital B), which provides a sense of purpose and value for our lives. Maslow compared our need for B-cognition to our physical need for certain vitamins. Without these vitamins we grow weak or sick. He held that with a "B-deficiency" we will never be able to actualize ourselves as human beings. We need the kind of "peak experiences" that will provide this awareness. For Maslow, such experiences could be found through natural means and settings, like human love, or art, or nature; but they are also available within the religions of the world. He saw his role as a psychologist to enable and encourage people to open themselves to such core-religious or peak experiences.

Maslow's claims are illustrated in the life of the former basketball star, Bill Russell. Russell relates how during his childhood and early high-school years, he was held captive by a poor self-image, caused in part by his family situation and by the way he, as a minority teenager, was treated by both his teachers and the local police. Then one day, as he was walking down the corridors of McClymonds High School in Oakland, California, "it suddenly dawned on me that it was all right to be who I was. The thought just came to me: 'Hey, you're all right. Everything is all right.'" Russell called his realization a "revelation...the closest I've come to a religious experience." And he came to recognize that there was something in the universe—for want of a better word he called it "magic"—that brought about this experience, something that assured him that he was really "all right." If there were not such a "something" in the universe, "how could I explain my revelation?" On the basis of his experience, Russell went on to "actualize" himself in new ways, with a new self-confidence and sense of meaning. (From *Second Wind: The Memoirs of an Opinionated Man*, by Bill Russell and Taylor Branch, New York: Random House, 1979.)

This is not to say that the awareness of Mystery or something more has to come in as abrupt and overwhelming a way as it did for Bill Russell. For most people, the sense of Mystery or God is something that grows gently and comes in a variety of experiences extended over a longer period of time. In any case, what is being claimed here is that such religious experiences, however they come, are essential for the human being's need for meaning, for something to trust. Perhaps the word "essential" is too strong, as if only religious people could be psychologically healthy. Clearly, that is not the case. What we are suggesting is that religion can and must make important contributions to the psychological health and productivity of a person's life. The basic trust in life's meaning that comes from belief in God can bring many more benefits to humanity than the dangers and abuses that are also lurking in the reality called religion. Dr. Jekyll can be stronger than Mr. Hyde.

The Social/Ethical Value of Religion

Nowadays, perhaps the more urgent value, even necessity, of religion and religious faith comes not from the individual but from the social needs and crises that confront humanity. Our contemporary world, it can be said, stands before crises that it has never had to confront before; they are crises that bring about a degree of suffering and destruction that human beings in the past could not even imagine. Today, our world has become not only the so-called global village, in which we are closer together and able to communicate with each other as never before; it has also become a "threatened village" in which the very life of individuals, of the species, and of the planet itself is at stake. These are problems that must be confronted, that must be solved. But to achieve, even to hope for, such a solution, religion, it seems, must make a contribution. To understand why this is so, we first will examine, only briefly, the three crises that make our world a threatened village.

The Socio-Economic Crisis—Injustice and Human Suffering
Most of us are familiar with the appalling statistics on the enormous numbers of people who are suffering today because their most basic human, physical needs are not being met: their needs for food, water, shelter, medical care. Maybe these statistics and this suffering are so familiar to us that we can't hear or see it any more; maybe it's just too big to handle, and so we turn away. For the sake of stirring our feelings, however, let us offer some "conservative" figures that have been assembled by Father Leonardo Boff, who works among the poor in Brazil: He tells us that today (mainly in the Third World), there are 500 million persons who are starving, one billion who are living in absolute poverty, one billion, 500 million persons who have no access to the most basic medical care, 500 million with no work or only occasional work and a per capita income of less that $150 per year, 814 million who are illiterate, two billion with no regular water supply.

Awful as such realities of human poverty and suffering are, why are we calling them a threat? For two basic reasons. The first was voiced crisply and angrily by Patti, a sophomore who was taking a course in liberation theology: "The poor don't have to be poor. Most of them are poor because other people are making or keeping them poor." We realize today that the so-called givens of poverty, lack of drinking water, non-existent or poor schooling, do not need to be "given." Most of these physical sufferings are not natural; rather, they are caused by the way some human beings treat other human beings or use others for their own self-serving purposes. Oppression and injustice are chains that crisscross our globe, nationally and multinationally, and have become a "given" part of socioeconomic and political structures. Forged as they often are in the kilns of racism and sexism, these chains keep vast portions of the world's population in bondage, denying them a voice in political decision making and in determining their own lives. There is a vast "underbelly" of history, people who, in their victimization, produce the labor, the raw materials, the armies that have sustained the course of history. Their suffering is caused by injustice. And injustice is caused by human beings.

The second reason why this situation is so threatening is that today the poor and suffering people of the world are realizing just this, that their suffering is caused by other human beings. They are realizing that it is not natural, it is not God's will that they be poor and have nothing to eat. It is, rather, the will of other human beings. So the previously "silent majority" of oppressed people is no longer silent. Centuries of injustice are irrupting in the consciousness of the suffering people, especially in the so-called Third World, and flowing into the conscience of the First and Second Worlds. At a meeting in 1981, Third World theologians representing the poor and oppressed announced:

> Over against this dramatic picture of poverty, oppression, and the threat of total destruction, a new consciousness has arisen among the downtrodden. This growing consciousness of the tragic reality of the Third World has caused the irruption of exploited classes, marginalized cultures, and humiliated races. They are burst from the underside of history into the world long-dominated by the West. It is an ir-

> ruption expressed in revolutionary struggles, political uprisings, and liberation movements. It is an irruption of religious and ethnic groups looking for affirmation of their authentic identity, of women demanding recognition and equality, of youth protesting dominant systems and values. It is an irruption of all those who struggle for full humanity and for their rightful place in history.

The threat of this socioeconomic crisis, therefore, is not only that millions of people in our world today are victims of injustice, but that they are realizing it, standing up, and calling for change. If the change doesn't come, there is going to be trouble; many of them are, rightly or wrongly, ready to take up arms. The root cause of so many of the conflicts and dangers of war in today's world is not Communism, as some people argue; it is injustice. As third-year student Mary Kay, who had taken a course on the Third World in a peace and justice program, announced before her classmates: "If we want to promote peace, the first thing we should do is not fight Communism but work for justice." Much the same might be said of many (perhaps not all) of the religious conflicts that we mentioned above. If we look closely at the situations in Palestine, Northern Ireland, Sri Lanka, we will find, we suggest, that the underlying problem is not the people's conviction that "my religion is better than yours"; it is, rather, the violation of human or civil rights of one group by another. Religion is used to feed an already raging fire. But as we will try to show in a moment, religion can be used to put out the fire of conflict based on injustice and to light the fires of transformation, creativity, growth, and life.

The Nuclear Crisis—Extinction of All Life There is another crisis, perhaps even more pervasive than that of socioeconomic injustice and unrest; it grips First, Second, and Third Worlds equally. It is the reality that the entire population of the planet could be snuffed out by the pressing of a few buttons by a few political figures. For the first time in its history, the human race is capable of something never before possible: humanocide. Humanity is able to commit communal suicide. We now have the means, the weapons, by which we can destroy not only the lives of millions but also the lives of children still to be born.

Dealing with this nuclear threat, some would say, is the hour's most pressing and most communal issue; it touches and terrorizes all of us. As theologian Gordon Kaufman stated: "...the possibility of nuclear holocaust is the premier issue which our generation must face ... [it is among] the central and defining features of our lives as human beings in the so-called civilized world in the late twentieth century."

The question, of course, is how to deal with this issue. It seems that the politicians and world leaders are getting nowhere. Treaties are made, limited arms reductions are agreed upon, but the overall arms race continues. Not only that: It daily becomes more likely that the "smaller" nations will also acquire nuclear weapons. Then we might have the convergence of the nuclear crisis and the crisis of injustice: will the poor, oppressed people eventually turn to nuclear weapons in their demands for justice?

What can be done to avoid such frightening prospects? Can—must—religion make a contribution?

The Ecological Crisis—The Destruction of Mother Earth There are those who argue that an even more menacing crisis threatens not just human life, but the source of that life. Today, not only is the human species unjustly exploiting and killing off its own, not only is it maddeningly on the brink of humanocide, but it is also strangling mother earth and the ecosystem. The industrial revolution, which has brought such advantages to our species, has also created an altar of consumerism and profiteering on which the life blood of mother earth is poured daily. One of the most forceful of earth-prophets, Father Thomas Berry, states what he holds to be irrefutable facts: "Our industrial economy is closing down the planet in the most basic modes of its functioning. The air, the water, the soil are already in a degraded condition. Forests are dying on every continent. The seas are endangered. Aquatic life forms in lakes and streams and in the seas are contaminated. The rain is acid." For Berry, such ecological destruction should precede every other issue on the international and interreligious agenda:

> For the first time we are determining the destinies of the earth in a comprehensive and irreversible manner. The immediate danger is not *possible* nuclear war but *actual* industrial plundering....The issue of inter-human tensions is secondary to earth-human tensions. If humans will not become functional members of the earth community, how can humans establish functional relationships among themselves?

Again, is there any way of confronting and resolving this ecological crisis? Is there any meaningful contribution that the religions of the world might make?

The Role of Religion in Resolving Crises

No doubt, the socio-economic, the nuclear, and the ecological crises that surround humanity today are, to put it mildly, terrifying. The temptation is to throw up one's hands, feel overwhelmed by the so-called "innate selfishness" of human beings, and declare that nothing can be done. At most, some people will say, we can enjoy a few drinks before the Titanic goes down. There are those who have embraced this option. For them, all they can do during their lifetimes is gather some fleeting pleasures for themselves, perhaps also for a few other people in their circle of family and friends, before the final curtain comes down. Human beings have always been warring with each other, which means that they will, eventually, do so with nuclear weapons. In the meantime, the life-sustaining capacity of the earth is fast dwindling. The Titanic will eventually go down. So for today, open up another beer and turn on the football game.

If people are going to try to fix the Titanic rather than just sip beer on it, if they are going to be able to roll up their sleeves and try to do something about the crises confronting humanity, they must be able to *hope* that a solution is possible, that humanity is *not* caught in selfishness, that there *is* something that will enable them to get out of this mess before the world disappears in a depletion of resources or in a nuclear fireball. People need *basic trust* in the meaning of life, in the existence of something greater than themselves that will help them discover the vision and the strength to recreate and change this world of selfish, warring groups and nations. But as we said earlier, providing basic trust is precisely the official business of the religions of the world. It seems, therefore, that religions do have an important, perhaps a necessary, role to play in today's world.

But more is needed than trust. We also have to have a new vision of how we are to change the world and our way of living with each other. We have to be able to see ourselves and our world differently. Many people, religious and non-religious, are coming to a general agreement as to what that vision must contain. Among experts in the human and the natural sciences and especially among spokespersons in art and literature, we witness a growing consensus (at least in the West) that one of the most important ingredients, if not *the* essential ingredient, in this new vision has to do with a "paradigm shift" in the way we define ourselves, both as individual persons and as nations. In our understanding of what we are and how we are to act, we must move from the present dominant paradigm of *individualism* that sees the components of all reality as primarily individual, separate, dualistic, competitive, and hierarchical to a model of interrelatedness that envisions the world of persons and nations as essentially relational, interdependent, inclusive, cooperative, and holistic.

In other words, we have to redefine and feel ourselves, in our relationships to each other and to this earth, as a living organism whose parts live in each other rather than as a machine assembled from pre-existing components. Or, as Raimundo Panikkar puts it, we have to grow in the sobering awareness that in order to ask the question, "Who am I?" I must ask the question, "Who are you?" I cannot know myself without knowing you. I cannot promote my own welfare, unless I also promote yours. I cannot be myself without being you. We have to feel part of each other; we have to feel responsible for each other. As philosopher Charles Hartshorne has put it: "The 100 percent American, or Russian, or what have you, is an enemy to all of us. We need an element of world citizenship in each person." No one person or one nation can any longer be "Number One." We all have to *be* and *live* and *share* together.

Here is where the religions can lend a helping hand. This paradigm shift, this different way of understanding and feeling what we are as persons and nations, is basically the vision and the message of all the major world religions, for in different ways all the religions call their followers to move from an ego-centered to an other-centered existence. All religions call their followers to love not only God, or the Ultimate, but to love other human beings as well. It is, however, a message the religions have not always applied beyond their own borders. Yet they do all contain a message that tells people that they are "unified" or made "brothers and sisters" in the one God/Reality and must and can live that way. It is a message religions need to announce and the world needs to hear.

There are some scholars who would hold that the contribution of religions to the clarification of values and to the construction of peace in our divided world is not only important but necessary for the future of humanity. Historians Arnold Toynbee and Wilfred Cantwell Smith argue that the ruts of warring selfishness are worn so deeply in the path of human history that humanity will be able to extricate itself from these ruts *only* through the vision, the motivation, the empowerment coming from religious symbols and experience; only through the hope and the self-sacrificing love born of religious experience, these historians maintain, will humans be able to "muster the energy, devotion, vision, resolution, capacity to survive the disappointments that will be necessary—that *are* [already] necessary—for the challenge..." of building a peaceful and just world.

A study of the religions of the world and a study of the present state of our world, therefore, establish two conclusions: 1) The religions of the world, in the original messages of their founders and in their Scriptures, hold up a vision that there is a unifying Force, Presence, God within the universe and that human beings are called and empowered to live in unity, love, and justice. 2) Our contemporary world, given the devastating dangers of the socio-economic, nuclear, and ecological crises, stands in need of hearing and believing and acting upon such a message of transformation and communion.

Again, our conclusion is that religion, despite the very evident dangers it carries, also provides, or can provide, a valuable if not necessary contribution to the future of humanity. To study and be part of religion, therefore, seems to be a worthwhile undertaking.

In this chapter, we have tried to clear away possible obstacles to the study of religion, faith, and theology. We have attempted to look, honestly and realistically, at the principal criticisms of religion that one hears nowadays on the street, in the classroom or living room, at cocktail parties or the local bar, in newspapers and scholarly journals. The clear-cut complaints or the general uneasiness that many people feel about religion seem to sift down to two general attitudes.

The "ho-hum" attitude looks at religion as perhaps nice, but useless or impractical. It's not that people don't believe in God; it's just that they don't see a really important place for God and for religious life in the world as we experience it today. Life in its bustle is both busy and satisfying; or religion, in its demands and ideals, is too impractical; or, religious people are either too dull or hypocritical. There's nothing in religion that really grabs people. Nice, but not much use.

The second general attitude is that religion is dangerous. If in the first attitude, people just shrug their shoulders about religion, in the second they actively avoid or fight against it. From their own experience of religion and from their knowledge of the history of religion, they see it as either a crutch that prevents people from really growing up and taking responsibility for their lives or as a drug that allows people to be manipulated in order to enrich their religious leaders or to beat up on their enemies.

Our first response to these criticisms was to admit both their reality and validity. We are convinced that any study of religion must begin with, or somewhere include, an honest admission of how much harm religion has done and how much it has been abused. This means that such harm and abuse is most likely part of one's own religion. The first step in the study of religion is, one might say, to be suspicious of it. But that, we are convinced, is not the whole picture. By briefly reviewing what we think the psychological-individual and the ethical-social values of religion are, we tried to suggest that the potential of religion for good exceeds its frightening potential for evil.

Questions for Reflection and Discussion

1. Briefly describe the "ho-hum" attitude toward religion. Does it fit any of your own experiences or feelings?

2. What are the criticisms of religions made by Freud and Marx? Do they apply to the religion you know?

3. What is the psychological value of religion? Do you think this is a value needed by all people?

4. What are the major crises facing humanity today? Do you think they are overstated in this chapter?

5. What are the ways religion can help respond to these crises? In your estimation, can the religions play a helpful, a non-helpful, or a necessary role in resolving these crises?

Suggested Readings

Appel, Willa. *Cults in America: Programmed for Paradise.* New York: Holt, Rinehart and Winston, 1983.

Barnes, Michael H. *In the Presence of Mystery: An Introduction to the Story of Human Religiousness.* Mystic, Conn.: Twenty-Third Publications, 1984.

Carmody, Denise Lardner, and John Tully Carmody. *Peace and Justice in the Scriptures of the World Religions.* Mahwah, N.J.: Paulist Press, 1988.

Clift, Wallace R. *Jung and Christianity*. New York: Crossroad, 1982.

Crews, Clyde F. *Ultimate Questions: A Theological Primer*. Mahwah, N.J.: Paulist Press, 1986.

Cox, Harvey. *Religion in the Secular City*. New York: Simon & Schuster, 1984.

Gordon, Haim, and Leonard Grob, eds. *Education for Peace: Testimonies from World Religions*. Maryknoll, N.Y.: Orbis Books, 1987.

Johnson, Roger A., *et al.*, eds. *Critical Issues in Modern Religion*. Englewood Cliffs, NJ: Prentice-Hall, 1989. (2nd edition).

Neusch, Marcel. *The Sources of Modern Atheism: One Hundred Years of Debate over God*. Mahwah, N.J.: Paulist Press, 1982.

Kaufman, Gordon D. *Theology for a Nuclear Age*. Philadelphia: Westminster Press, 1985.

Küng, Hans. *Does God Exist*? New York: Doubleday, 1980 (especially Section C: "The Challenge of Atheism").

Kushner, Harold S. *When Bad Things Happen to Good People*. New York: Schocken Books, 1981.

Lonergan, Anne, and Caroline Richards, eds. *Thomas Berry and the New Cosmology*. Mystic, Conn.: Twenty-Third Publications, 1987.

Maslow, Abraham H. *Religions, Values, and Peak Experiences*. New York: The Viking Press, 1964.

Richey, Russel E., and Donald G. Jones, eds. *American Civil Religion*. New York: Harper & Row, 1974.

Chapter Six

Religion: What Is It?

Trying to define religion is like trying to define love. Just about everyone knows what the word "love" means, but ask fifty people to define love, and the definitions would form not a unified picture, but a quilt of multi-colored, differently shaped patches. Religion, like love, means different things to different people. We receive a multi-colored quilt of answers whenever we ask the following questions on the first day of the first-year college theology course: "What is religion? What causes religion? How can we tell if someone is religious?"

Why is it impossible to come up with a common definition of religion or love? We think the fundamental answer is as simple as it is profound: because both realities deal with something that is essentially *mysterious*—something as real as it is beyond our full comprehension. Whenever a human being experiences or begins to get a sense of God or human love, she or he is never sure "what's going on." In where it comes from, in what it does to us, in how it shakes up our lives—the Mystery of God, like the power of love, is beyond our clear, full understanding. (It shouldn't be surprising that "God" and "love" affect people in the same mysterious way since, at least in the New Testament, God is defined as love. See 1 Jn 4:8.)

Even the so-called experts cannot agree on a common definition of religion. Historians, psychologists, sociologists of religion, philosophers, and theologians argue among themselves concerning the essential content of religion (Does religion have to deal with God?), its central religious activity (ethics or ritual?), its origins (as magic or monotheism [belief in one God]?), and whether religion helps or hinders society (energy or opium). To facilitate discussion and to save you the confusion of all this scholarly bickering, in this book we're going to propose and work with one particular description of religion, a description that not only represents the views of the three authors but reflects a "common opinion" among Christian theologians. It's an opinion that is sufficiently clear and sufficiently rooted in both history and contemporary experience to provide a basis for determining your own view of just what makes religion religion.

The view of religion that follows bears two fundamental characteristics: It understands religion as something basically positive and profitable for humanity and as something that has to do with what in broad terms can be called the "Transcendent" or the "Ultimate" or "God." After reading Chapter Five, you should understand, even if you may not fully agree, why we authors regard religion as something valuable or even necessary for the human project. Why religion has to do with the Transcendent will become clear in what follows.

But what follows is not going to clarify everything. What we are offering is really not a definition, but a *description* of religion. As we said, religion, like love, cannot be pinned down or neatly wrapped up in a box. We will outline a general picture of religion, but you will have to fill in your own colors and details.

Religion Deals With "What Counts Most in Life"

To the question, "What is the essential object or content of religion?" perhaps the simplest answer would be: "Whatever counts most in life." Admittedly, that's a very vague answer. And yet, it does describe what religion, any religion, is about. Paul Tillich, one of the best known Protestant theologians of this century, said the same thing in more formal terms when he suggested that religion is made up of whatever is one's "Ultimate Concern": "Religion is the state of being grasped by an ultimate concern, a concern which qualifies all other concerns as preliminary and which itself contains the answer to the question of the meaning of life." According to Tillich's description, "what counts most" is whatever is most important for understanding and living "the meaning of life."

We all want to live a satisfying, happy, full human life. Religion expresses, puts us in contact with, whatever is most important for doing so. Religion supplies the direction and the energy for living life; it helps clarify where we want to go in life and how to get there. It enables us to get up when we've just been knocked down; it prompts us to get out of bed with zest when all is going well and with fortitude when the chips are down. Religion expresses what has been called "the fundamental option" in one's life, the big goal that helps us sort out all the smaller goals; religion also supplies the fundamental motivation for pursuing that goal. Whatever matters most for us, whatever operates in our mind and feelings when we have to make big decisions (like career or marriage), whatever really makes life worthwhile (or at times, at least bearable), that's what makes up religion for us.

From a psychological perspective, in order to understand how people come to determine "what counts most," we can study the interplay of two ingredients in every religion: *behavior* and *belief*. In every religion, behavior and belief interact in order to demonstrate or reveal what counts most. The interaction is quite simple: each of us decides how we want to behave or live our lives, but in order to do that, we need beliefs or reasons why such a way of life is really the best, why it makes sense. Religion consists of what we want to do in life and why we want to do it. "What" and "why" or "behavior" and "belief" feed into each other and determine each other. In choosing a certain way of life and behavior, we come to feel and discover the reasons why it is worthwhile. Yet we never would have set out on that way of life if we didn't first have some sense of the reasons for doing so.

In more technical terms, we are dealing here with what philosophers call "praxis" and "theory." Life is made up of acting and thinking, of doing and understanding. This is especially true of religion. Our "ultimate concern" is made known to us and takes hold of us through a process of both praxis and theory, of behaving and believing. Which comes first? Which is most important? Where do we really encounter the Ultimate? Do we live according to what we believe? Or do we believe according to the way we live? Do we live a certain way because the reasons for doing so make so much sense? Or do the reasons for living in a certain way make sense because of the life that they produce? What is more fundamental: theory or praxis? behavior or belief? acting or knowing?

It's impossible to answer these questions because, in actuality, neither comes first. This is what we mean by an interplay between the two. In religion, persons come to determine their Ultimate Concern not along a straight line (first this, then that); but rather, in a circle (this then that, that then this). We act or behave in a certain way because we believe there are good reasons for doing so; and we believe in these reasons because we find the way of acting to be satisfying and good. Behavior is determined by belief, and belief by behavior.

This is all still quite abstract. More concretely: John is studying and working hard and devoting all his energies (even on Saturday night when he could be out on a date) to getting ahead and making his first million dollars. This is his basic behavior—to make money; yes, he will go out on dates and enjoy friendships, but only as long as they don't really get in the way of making that first million. His behavior is sustained by the belief, which he may not always articulate clearly to himself, that human happiness consists mainly of material gain. Money is his Ultimate Concern, what counts most. Behavior and belief feed into each other. John will continue to act this way as long as there is positive feedback between behavior and belief. If, however, some friend or teacher is able to get him to question his belief about happiness and material gains, or if his way of life does not, in the long run, really satisfy him, he will have to change both behavior and belief.

Joan is committed to becoming a famous writer. This is her consuming passion, her dominant behavior. She's ready to sacrifice everything in order to attain her goal. Her determination and her behavior are nurtured by the belief that what counts most in life is the sharing of ideas and the creation and communication of truth and beauty; personal immortality consists only of the way we live on in the memories of others. Her immortality is assured if she can write that great novel. Again, behavior and beliefs nurture each other and sustain such a way of life. Writing or experiencing notoriety is Joan's Ultimate Concern.

Betsy has decided to become a doctor and she, too, is totally focused on her goal, renouncing much of her social and family life to keep up her grades and save enough money for medical school. This is her dominant behavior. Her dominant motivation, however, is not to make enough money to buy a house in the suburbs and own a BMW; she wants to be of value to other human beings and for her, medicine is one of the best ways of doing that. Her motivation is rooted in her belief that helping and loving each other is what life is all about, what makes for genuine happiness, and that this is so because there is a force of love called God that created this world. She knows there is such a God because of the satisfaction that her way of life has brought her. Her behavior and her beliefs sustain each other.

These examples are all too "neat"; they leave out a lot. Life and life's decisions for John, Joan, and Betsy are not that easy and firm. Yet, essentially, this is how each of them is living, at least for the moment. For each of them, there is something that "matters most" and this something is the fruit of their behavior and their beliefs. We might say that each of them has a different way of being religious or practicing their religion. This would be according to the "loose" definition of religion.

The Loose Definition of Religion

According to what we can call the "loose" definition of religion given by some experts (Tillich, for example), religion is simply whatever matters most for a person, whatever that Ultimate Concern is. A person's religion, therefore, can consist of money or power or love or beauty or service or sports or cars—or God. Also, for the loose definition, neither does it matter what kind of behavior one's Ultimate Concern leads to. One can be fully committed to loving and serving one's neighbors, or one can be totally taken with one's own welfare, or that of one's group, before all others.

Thus, Tillich could recognize the Nazi Movement of his native Germany as a religion (although he preferred the term "quasi-religion"—"almost-religion"), for it served many Germans during the 1930s and 1940s as their primary commitment, and motivated them to sacrifice even their own lives for the promotion of what they thought was their own "Super-Race." With this loose definition of religion, Communism (working for the perfect society), Humanism (commitment to the welfare of humanity), Scientism (total dedication to the pursuit of knowledge), or Nationalism ("my country, right or wrong, before all else") could all be considered religions.

In this book, we're not following this loose definition, not because it is false, but because it is *too* "loose." It doesn't work well in focusing on what this book wants to deal with. Yes, people have all kinds of things as their Ultimate Concern; but to call all of those things "religion" would make the study of religion practically impossible (the exam material would be all-encompassing!). Also, such a loose definition of religion just doesn't fit what, on both the common-sense and the academic levels, has always been considered religion (at least in Europe and North and South America). To call Communism or stamp-collecting "religion" would, in the long run, generate more confusion than light.

Finally, and more personally, while we might be persuaded to accept all kinds of *beliefs* as religious, most of us, we think, would find a lump in our throats and fear in our hearts if we have to accept all kinds of *behavior* as religious. It is difficult, to say the least, to look upon a movement that exterminated six million Jews as a religion. Behavior that promotes one's own benefit at the cost of others' welfare just can't be called religious. (Well then, one might ask, what about the "religion" of the Crusaders who slaughtered thousands of Muslims? Was it really religion?)

For all these reasons, we're going to stick to the "tight" definition of religion.

The Tight Definition of Religion

According to the stricter notion of religion used by a majority of theologians, philosophers of religion, and anthropologists, before a person's Ultimate Concern can qualify as religious, it has to show certain distinctive qualities. First, the person's beliefs have to recognize that Concern as including something *ultimate, transcendent*, or *divine*. Second, the model of behavior, at least ideally if not actually, has to call persons to *transcend* their own *limited egos* in concern for "other" realities/persons. Both of these distinctive qualities of religious belief and behavior need a little explaining.

We are not saying that all religions have to deal explicitly with God, for, as we shall see, there are some religions (for example, some forms of Buddhism) which do not explicitly mention God, or which propose an Ultimate sharply different from what Christians would call God. We are saying that to constitute a religion, people have to recognize that "what matters most in life" is or includes a level of reality that transcends, or goes beyond, what we normally understand as human or finite. Religions recognize that there is a More, a Something Greater, a Transcendent, a Mystery that is at the foundation or at the center, or at the end of human existence. This Something More can be considered in a myriad of different images and ideas (so different, as we shall see in the next chapter, that one can rightly ask whether this Something More is the same in all religions). It can be viewed as primarily Transcendent (beyond the world); or as primarily Immanent (within the world); it can be viewed as a

Being or as Being-Itself, or as a Reality so mysterious that it can be called a "No-thing." It can be grasped as personal or as beyond personality, as all-powerful or as all-gentle.

In all these different (and sometimes apparently contradictory) ways, religions recognize an ultimate concern that is really "Ultimate." Religious persons, therefore, are people who believe that in order to live a satisfying, full human life, in order to figure out what life is all about and how we are to live it, in order to find the energy and motivation and hope to carry on with the difficult project of human history, human beings happily have to recognize that there is Something More to themselves and to the world and to reality. They want to recognize that Mystery and to live in harmony with It/Him/Her.

In the way this has been stated, it might sound as if this process of "believing" in or recognizing Mystery is basically an intellectual matter. As Part One of this book has made clear, religious belief is (or should be) primarily a matter of experience. In religions, therefore, people do not just recognize, they are not just told about this Something More, they *experience* it, they feel it, it becomes part of their lives. At the heart of all religions, therefore, is an experience, an encounter with Mystery, with what Jews, Christians, and Muslims call God.

Also, according to our general description of religion, as part of such an experience of Something More, religious persons will, in some way, be called out of themselves to search for their welfare and happiness in becoming part of others. In Christianity, this is called love, caring for one's neighbor as one cares for oneself. In some way, and in different degrees, all religions call upon their followers to go outside of themselves in relatedness not just with the Something More but also with other human beings. According to this perspective, religion will promote some form of ego-transcending, other-embracing behavior. Or, to state it negatively: If a religion serves only (or mainly) the welfare of one's own self or one's own group, it is not living up to the authentic ideal of religion.

One might ask whether this description of religion, with its required qualities for religious belief and behavior, is limited and arbitrary. Certainly it is limited; but we don't think it is arbitrary. It is based on the authors' own experience of what religion is and of what they think religion should be. But this description is also based on a study of the major world religions and reflects, in general, the ideals that the religions of the world hold up for themselves. Clearly, our description does not portray what the religions, all too often, have actually been. Despite their contrary track record, most world religions continue to hold as their ideals the beliefs that there is Something More to life than what we are generally aware of and that human beings can best find themselves by transcending themselves.

A final comment on our description of religion: It does not intend to put down or devalue other movements or people who clearly affirm that "what matters most in life" is to be concerned about other people and about improving this world, but who do so without a belief in Something More. In fact, with many Christian theologians, the authors of this book would hold that even from a religious point of view, it is more important to live lives of love and concern for each other than to come to a clear, absolutely correct knowledge about God or the Ultimate. In Christian terms, it is more important to *live God's life* of love and justice than to *believe in God*. Belief that is not part of a life of love and concern for others is worthless.

So, from a theological point of view, people who for whatever reason do not recognize an Ultimate and perhaps call themselves atheists, but who are genuinely trying to love other human beings and work for justice and human rights, such people are already *living God's life*. Theologians like the Roman Catholic Karl Rahner and the Protestant Paul Tillich would say that such people are already "implicitly" or "subconsciously" believing in God because, in order to live a life of love and concern for others, even when it hurts, one must sense that there is a reason to do so. From a religious point of view, the foundation or energy that calls us to love each other is God or the Ultimate; therefore, from a religious point of view, such people are not really atheists. They have a sense of God; implicitly they have experienced God.

Religion and Religions

So far, our description of religion has remained quite abstract. We can make it more concrete and perhaps more meaningful by examining how it fits the actual world of religions.

What follows is a schematic overview of world religions. Such general pictures, because they are general, are also dangerous. Important details and differences are swept under the "general" rug. Also, behind every generalization, there is an individual, personal perspective; so you're getting a general picture of religious history from my white, male, Christian, North American viewpoint. Despite these evident dangers, the advantages of taking a bird's-eye view of anything are also clear. As the cliche has it, we often miss the beauty and the pattern of the forest because we're too preoccupied with individual trees. Unless we take the risk of making general comparisons, we miss the patterns and similarities that seem to exist in the forest of world religions.

The following overview is admittedly and consciously limited. It presents only the so-called world religions. Not included, for limitations of space, are the indigenous or primal religions such as those of Native Americans and Africans.

A helpful way of locating the possible patterns amid the beliefs and behavior of different religions is to explore how each religion would answer three questions: 1) Where are we? Or, what's wrong with the human situation? 2) Where do we want to go? This question reveals the religion's *beliefs* concerning what matters most. 3) How can we get there? This question indicates the ideal *behavior* urged by the religion. The following overview tries to answer these questions. We've listed the various religions according to their places of origin. Notice that although some religions are usually referred to as "Western" (Judaism, Christianity, and Islam), all the major world faiths have their roots in what today is called the East. (The West may pride itself for producing technology. The East has produced religion.)

Belief and Behavior in World Religions

Religion	Where We Are	Where We Want to Go	How to Get there
Middle East			
Judaism Christianity Islam	Alienation from God and each other.	Unity with God and with others.	Faith in God & love of neighbor, according to -Torah -Gospel -Koran.
South Asia			
(India) Hinduism Buddhism	Ignorance of our true nature —Suffering.	Realize our oneness with Brahman, or our selflessness in Nirvana.	Meditation and compassion.
Far East			
(China) Confucianism Taoism	Disharmony in society and nature through disharmonious action.	Harmony between person, world, society	-Confucianism: Tradition Education. -Taoism: Union with the Tao.

The religions that originated in the Middle East, in what today is Palestine and the Arabian peninsula, are sometimes called "the Abrahamic religions." All of them recognize the Jewish Patriarch Abraham as a key figure in their own self-understanding. Among these three traditions, Judaism is the parent religion, whose unity and personality were forged in the escape from slavery in Egypt around 1200 B.C.E. (Before the Common Era). Under the inspiration and vision of Jesus of Nazareth and the leadership of Paul of Tarsus, Christianity developed first as a Jewish sect and then as a distinct religion during the first two centuries of the Common Era (C.E.). The faith and leadership of Muhammad the Prophet gave birth to Islam during the eighth century as a monotheistic religious revival among the polytheistic Arabian tribes and as a reform of Judaism and Christianity.

According to the beliefs of all three Abrahamic religions, human beings are in big trouble and are in need of help or salvation. The trouble, however, is not God's fault but humanity's, the result of the misuse of human freedom, right from the very start of history. This is what the story of the fall of Adam and Eve makes clear. The misuse of freedom has brought about a sense of separation or alienation from God, from other persons, and from one's own true self. Because of this separation, humans continue to act selfishly and so continue to cause more problems. They act selfishly because, in their pride, they think they can handle things totally by themselves, or because, in their fears, they think they must have power or riches if they are going to survive.

But for all three of these religions, this is not the final word on the human condition. As part of their central *beliefs*, they all proclaim a common God (also called Yahweh or Allah) who created humanity as God's children, and who has not abandoned the human family. This has been revealed to the Jews through the patriarchs and prophets; to Christians through Jesus Christ, God's Son; and to Muslims, through Muhammad, the seal of the prophets. For all these religions, God is a God of love and justice who continues to love humanity and to call humans to a new life or *behavior*: one of trusting God and loving each other.

The Indian religions of South Asia predate those of the Middle East. Hinduism, the parent religion, was not founded by any one individual but took gradual form when the ancient Vedic Hymns were composed in India around 1500 B.C.E. During the fifth century B.C.E., when a young Hindu named Siddhartha of the Sakyamuni found himself dissatisfied with the state of his religion and set out on a new search for truth, he soon became known as the Buddha (the Enlightened One), and Buddhism was born. For both these traditions, the basic problem confronting humanity is not one of separation due to sinfulness, but of ignorance: People do not know what they really are, they are caught in *avidya* or ignorance. And because of this ignorance they act selfishly and so cause untold amounts of suffering for themselves and others.

As part of their central beliefs, Hindus and Buddhists hold that where we want to go, or better, what we want to realize, is a state of selfless oneness. For Hindus, our individual "Atman" or self is essentially one with "Brahman" the universal, Ultimate Self; for the Buddhists, our true nature is what they call "Buddha nature," a state of selflessness in which everything is related to and responsible for everything else. For both these religions, the behavior or the way to realize our true nature is essentially through various forms of meditation or yoga (some forms of Hinduism and Buddhism also stress trust in "savior figures" like Krishna or Amida). But meditation won't work unless we are living moral lives, which means not harming other beings. Indeed, the more we realize that our Atman is Brahman or that our true nature is Buddha's nature, the more we will naturally and spontaneously feel compassion for all living beings.

The Far Eastern religions of China, Confucianism and Taoism, are actually quite different from each other. Both of them arose in China around the sixth century B.C.E. when China was devastated by warring factions. The basic problem, as perceived by both religions, is that of disharmony. Things are out of balance, both within society, in the relationship between persons and nations, and within nature, in the relationship between humans and the material world. Human beings are not acting harmoniously, according to the natural, balancing rhythms of nature. The beliefs of both religions, therefore, affirm that there is a natural, dynamic harmony to the world and that there is a balanced relationship amid everything that exists. This harmony and interrelatedness are constantly taking place through an interplay of differences called "yin" and "yang." Differences, therefore, are good, but they have to balance each other. For the Chinese religions, therefore, the entire world and everything in it, including humanity, is basically good.

But how to reaffirm or repossess that goodness? What is the proper way or behavior to regain harmony? Here the Confucianists and Taoists give different, but ultimately complementary, answers (which might be considered "yin/yang" answers). For the Confucianists, the best way to restore harmony is through education, especially by repossessing the wisdom of the past which laid out the order and structure that society is to follow. The Taoists are more mystical and shun such book learning; for them there is the mysterious "Tao," literally, the way of nature, which is part of everything that is. If, through observing nature and through meditation, persons can wake up to the presence and energy of the Tao and feel their oneness with it, they will naturally act harmoniously.

All of the above is merely the frosting on the cake of each religion; the cake itself is much more interesting and complex and calls for further tasting and study. But if there is any value to such an admittedly generalized overview of the world religions, we might conclude from it two things that have a "yin-yang" flavor: 1) There are stark differences among the religions of the world, and therefore statements such as "all religions are the same" are simplistic and dangerous. 2) In and through these differences, all religions are calling their followers to lives of unity, love, cooperation, and harmony based on personal participation in (or realization of) that which is more than and yet part of humanity: God, Allah, Yahweh, Brahman, Nirvana, Tao. Maybe, despite the differences, there are common patterns or ideals within the beliefs and behavior of the different religions. To use a Buddhist image, maybe all of the religions are very different fingers pointing to the same mysterious Moon. Whether there is any truth to that image we will consider more carefully in the next chapter.

After these broad considerations about the nature of religion and the way it expresses "what matters most" for people, we can now take a closer look at just how religions work, how they communicate their beliefs and behavior. The first issue to discuss in this regard is the way religion blends the individual and the community.

Religion: A Blending of Individual and Community

Is there such a thing as a "religious loner?" From students, a rather familiar refrain is: "I certainly believe in God. And I am trying to live a good, moral life. But I don't need religion. I can find God more easily during a walk in the woods on Sunday morning than in a church. Religion for me is very personal, my own business." What these students are proposing is a kind of "rugged religious individualism." They want to be religious by themselves, religious loners. Is that possible?

With all due regard for what may be the understandable reasons why such young people don't want to have anything to do with the religion or church they were brought up in, we would have to differ with them. In doing so, we are not trying to push all forms of religion, but we are suggesting that some form of religion is necessary. To be religious, one needs a religion.

The Anglican theologian John Macquarrie puts the case crisply and provocatively: "...faith belongs in a community of faith. Perhaps there are private faiths and private religions, but these are exceptional and, moreover, defective in so far as they lack the communal dimension that belongs to human existence in its very constitution." Macquarrie is claiming that for an individual's faith and belief in God to be real, it has to be lived out together with other believing people in a community of faith. But a community of faith is what we call "religion." We are suggesting therefore that faith needs religion; without religion, faith isn't real; it can't develop and grow and effectively be part of one's life. This is, for many, a strong statement. It sounds like we're trying to convince people that they "have to go to church."

We propose our case against religious loners and for religious community through the following considerations: Macquarrie mentions one of the most weighty: the "communal dimension that belongs to human existence." That means, simply, that we human beings are social beings; to be human is to be social. "No man is an island," the famous poem by John Donne announces. We need each other in order to be and to become; and that need is not just physical: what we are, how we think, the values we affirm, the way we feel about ourselves is "given" us by other people.

If all this is true in general, it would also be true of what we are as religious persons; if belief in God really matters for us, if it's more than just a Sunday morning trip to church, if it's something we want to incorporate into our lives, then we're going to have to find support and strength and guidance for our religious faith with and from other people. If a young woman wants to be a good swimmer but tries to do so all by herself, if she refuses to train with and learn from others, she'll never make it. The same would apply, it seems, if we want to really live a life based on faith in God.

Another reason why we need others in order to maintain a religious view on life comes from the nature of religious experience. Our bird's eye view of the different world faiths shows that to experience the Ultimate is also to experience our relatedness with other people. *Unity* is a recurring characteristic of what people experience through religion, unity with God, or Brahman, or the Tao, and therefore unity with other people. (Many theologians would hold that we start with the experience of unity/love with others and that leads us to experience unity/love with God.)

It would seem, therefore, that the term "religious loner" is a contradiction in terms. To be religious, to experience God, naturally and necessarily puts us in contact with other people. We search for and encounter the reality of the Ultimate together with others. Our personal faith needs a community of faith.

A third reason why faith must be lived out in a community is somewhat more controversial. If it is true that to experience God or Nirvana is at the same time to experience our relatedness with and love for other human beings, and if love and compassion are not simply a matter of well-wishing, then religious experience will also lead people to do good to others, to help them, to stop their sufferings. This means that it is also an essential part of religious faith to want to—to have to—change this present world of suffering and oppression into a world of greater harmony, love, and justice. As Part One of this book proposed in greater detail, authentic faith must be a faith that works justice. Religious people must be involved in the world, and that means being involved in social and political issues; they must change this world. But this cannot be done if religious people are acting as "loners." To really make a difference for the better in this world, religious people must act together, they must in a certain sense be "organized." As the Roman Catholic theologian Gregory Baum puts it, religions are not only communities of faith and worship, they are also "movements" meant to make a difference in this world. A movement is always a group of people. Again, faith needs a community, or a movement, of faith.

But if we are, in a sense, attempting to get you to "go to church" and be part of a community of faith, we also want to warn you that you'd better be careful once you're there. In describing religion as a community of people living out their convictions about what matters most in life, we want to also insist that the "community" aspect of religion must always be blended and balanced with the "individual" aspect. Religion is always a mixing, a unifying, of community and individual; but in this mixing, the central ingredient, as it were, is the individual's faith and experience. Here we find the heart of religion: the person's own experience of God, the person's own freedom and commitment to live out that experience in a way that he or she deems best.

In the preceding paragraphs, we laid out reasons why the individual's experience cannot really be owned and lived out by one's self. Individual experience must be integrated into a community. But in this integration, the community can never take the place of the individual's experience; it cannot make itself more important than that which takes place in the individual's heart and conscience. As we shall see in the last part of this chapter, the community aspect of religion brings not only necessary advantages, but also unavoidable dangers. These dangers and abuses are all too real on the contemporary religious scene, as we saw in Chapter Five.

So, if faith needs a community of faith, the community must never take the place of or become more important that the individual's faith. There is, in other words, a difficult but creative tension between the individual and the community within all religion. It would be a mistake to try to resolve that tension either by not taking the community seriously or by blindly obeying everything it dictates. If some people can claim that "I can't live within a religion," we are suggesting that "Neither can you live without it." The tension between individual and community that is part of religion can sometimes be painful, but it can also be creative and exciting.

So far we have been saying that faith needs community. We should also add, if only briefly, that from the perspective of sociology, one can also say that community or society needs faith. Sociologists and anthropologists recognize that every society or nation, if it is going to function and grow and respond to challenges, must understand itself within a "larger picture" of meaning and purpose. Not just individuals, but nations also need to believe in something that grounds their self-understanding and nourishes their dreams. A nation/society must understand its own story within the context of a larger story. As sociologists such as Emile Durkheim and Clifford Geertz have pointed out, religions have provided such "social meaning" for tribes and nations. Especially in the past, religions have helped societies understand where they come from, where they can go, why the ideals they hold up are reliable. Every nation, in other words, needs some kind of "faith."

And, if today religion has fallen out of the picture for some people and nations, and no longer provides this faith, some other kind of "faith" will have to take the place of religion and provide a larger picture or story within which the society can understand itself. For the Germans under National Socialism, this larger picture was based on "faith" in the Third Reich. For Marxists, it may come from their "faith" that history operates according to certain innate principles moving it toward a "classless society." For many capitalist countries, the larger picture is tied into an unexpressed belief that technology, science, and free enterprise will bring about the "Great Society." None of these visions can, strictly speaking, be proven. Like religions, they depend to a great extent on faith and trust.

So every society needs something to trust in. Every society needs some form of faith, religious or secular. Community, therefore, needs faith, as faith needs community. This helps us understand the relationship between individual and community that is part of religion. It also explains and justifies the desire of religious people that their religious faith, their vision of what is true and what is needed to improve this world, might make a contribution to the faith or to the "larger picture" that guides their country's political policies. Although it is never to be identified with a political party, religion does have something to say to the world of politics. As a community of faith, religion is also a community of action and involvement in the world.

The Mechanics of Religion—How It Works

Each step in our efforts to understand religion has tried to be more concrete. We began with the general description of religion as dealing with "what matters most for living a satisfying human life" and tried to show how that description applies to various world religions; then we discussed how religion functions through a blending of individual and community experience; religion is a community of people searching for and living out what matters most for them. Now we would like to review how this blending, this dynamic tension, between individual faith and community expression takes place within a religion. How does a religion work? How do individuals receive and express their faith within a community? How does the community guide and sustain its members? What are the mechanics of religion?

From a study of both present-day religion as well as the history of religions, we detect three principal ways in which individual faith finds community support and expression, and so forms religion. Each of these expressions are found, to a greater or lesser degree, in all the world religions. For purposes of easy recall, we can name them *creed, code,* and *ceremony*. All three are necessary for a *community* of faith.

Creed By "creed" we mean the wide variety of ways in which people use ideas, words, and images to express what matters most for them. We said that the heart of religion is a person's own experience of God or Something More, or, in terms of Eastern religions, one's own experience of Enlightenment. Yet part of this experience is the need to express it, to put it into words, pictures, or ideas, to somehow let it "get out" of us into the larger world. As human beings, we don't just have experiences; we express them. In fact, some would argue that "expressing" or speaking the experience is part of "having" it. Why is this? Maybe it has to do with the fact that humans are a marvelous mixing of body and spirit; what we feel with our spirit we have to express with our body. And so it is that when a person has what is called a religious experience (or, in order to have one), that person also has to speak out that experience. Speak it to whom? Well, first of all, to and for themselves, but then, and especially, to others. We have to communicate to others, so that they can see, share, and support what we have experienced. That's natural. That's what gives birth to religious creeds.

Creeds can take a variety of forms. Historians and psychologists of religion tell us that one of the first ways people come to experience and then express a sense of Something More is through stories—symbols and myths. As we will see in Part Three of this book, when people break through to a sense or revelation of the Mystery within and around them, their first impulse is not to write a doctoral dissertation or a philosophical treatise, but to tell a story or reach for a symbol. In what they say and the way they say it, stories are much more powerful means of communication than scholarly studies (or textbooks like this one!). This is true for adults as well as for children. And it is true not only of past, "primitive" times but of our contemporary society. So, in Judaism and Christianity, we find the beautiful and (if we can "feel" them) powerful stories of the creation of the world, the flood, the escape from Egypt, the birth and death of Jesus of Nazareth. Similar stories abound in the religions of Asia—the origin of the universe from the body of a Primal Person, the struggles of Lord Krishna to overcome the evil Serpent, the search of Lord Buddha to find the meaning of existence.

But, as Paul Ricoeur, the philosopher of religion, puts it, "Symbols or stories give rise to thought." And this leads to another form of what we are calling Creed: people think about the meaning of the stories they have grown up with; they want to interpret them for changing times; they want to know whether these stories must be taken literally or symbolically. And so, stories or myths lead to doctrines or beliefs. The meaning of the stories is spelled out in more intellectual, more clearly defined terms. And these "statements" of meaning become for a religion part of their line-up or "system" of beliefs. So the story of the birth, mission, and death of Jesus became the creed about his divinity and humanity. For Hinduism, the story about the origin of the world from "the One" and the return of everything to that One became part of the belief in reincarnation.

Besides story and doctrines, there is a third level of Creed: as history moves on, there is the need to pass on and especially to adapt the stories and doctrine to changing times. The task of understanding and applying the meaning of the stories and doctrines never ends. And so we have the task of *theology*. In trying to understand what the stories and doctrines *meant* in the past in order to better grasp what they *mean* for the present, theologians, too, are part of expressing the community's experience in ideas and words. The role and challenge of theology will be spelled out in Part Three of this book.

What we are saying in all this is that faith, or the experience of Something More, needs creed or belief. Personal faith cannot exist without communal belief. Faith must find expression in belief; the personal experience can't exist by itself but must be "embodied" in some external statement, some belief. Without belief, therefore, faith dwindles and dies. In asserting this necessary bond between faith and belief, however, we must also insist on the difference between them. There is a danger within religion, especially for the leaders of religion, to identify faith (the personal experience of Mystery) with belief or creed (the always limited statement of that experience). Even though the two must always go together, faith cannot be identified with belief.

This means that, although faith has to be expressed in *some* belief, it cannot be pinned down to or limited to *any one* belief. Faith can be expressed in a variety of beliefs. The Mystery of God, for instance, can be called by many names. Also, beliefs may be adjusted or even thrown out, without faith necessarily having to suffer. Just because some Catholics no longer hold to belief in purgatory doesn't mean that their "faith" has diminished; or just because some Christians now address God as Mother (and not only Father), doesn't mean that their faith has been destroyed (indeed, it has probably grown). As necessary as creeds/beliefs are, there is a danger of identifying them with faith, and therefore confining the vitality of the faith experience to the definitions of the belief statement.

Code Religious experience, or the experience of the Ultimate, is expressed within a community not only by means of ideas and words, but also through action. It's an evident connection: if a group of people have come to feel and say that the world and all humanity came from one source, or that God is a God of love and justice, or that Allah is merciful, or that we are all interrelated in our Buddhanature, what do these beliefs mean for our practical, everyday life in society? What does belief in God or in our unity mean for marriage, for raising children, for the way we buy and sell from each other, for the way we distribute the goods of the earth? If what we said earlier about religion as a "movement," as a force that seeks to change and improve the world, is true, then such questions about the "practical payoff" of religious beliefs are all the more pressing.

And so we also find that all religions have elaborated, tightly or loosely, some form of moral guidelines or ethical codes, codes that seek to state what this community of people stands for in the area of human conduct. Such codes are often worked out in a general way such as we have in the ten commandments of Judaism and Christianity, or the eightfold path of Buddhism (which includes more than ethics); these general statements provide enduring, unchanging guidelines. But moral decisions also have to be made in more particular questions or situations, for example, the morality of slavery, of taking interest on loans, of fighting wars; on such issues, there is more flexibility and room for development or change. As was the case with creeds, one must be careful of absolutizing any moral system and simply identifying the experience of faith with a list of dos and don'ts.

Ceremony In every religion, we find that religious experience or the sense of Something More is expressed not only in moral action but also in *ritual* action. That is what we mean by "ceremony." "Ritual" is a little more difficult to describe than "moral." It expresses the natural need that religious people have to celebrate or enact their experiences. In coming together in each others' homes or in designated places such as churches, synagogues, or mosques, believers continue to make use of the stories and symbols that gave rise to their communities. They do this because they need to *remember*. This is what takes place in ritual or in liturgy: enactment, remembrance, and celebration. And through such ritual, the original experience is stirred up, passed on, made real again in the lives of the community's members from generation to generation.

It is difficult to grasp and explain just how ritual or liturgy works. But from looking at the religions of the world, we see that it does. In celebrating the feast of Passover, in re-enacting the meal that their ancestors ate when escaping from Egypt, Jews continue to feel the strength of Yahweh with them. In telling the story of Jesus, and in "breaking bread" around a common table called the Mass or the Lord's Supper, Christians experience Jesus to be "truly present" in their midst. In praying five times a day facing in the direction of Mecca, Muslims remember the example of the Prophet and carry on his faith and mission.

It almost looks like magic (and from the history of religions we can see that ritual all too often was bent into magic and superstition). Yet usually, in the symbols and readings, the music and dance, the eating and drinking that go to make up liturgy and ritual, religious people are expressing and therefore deepening and living their sense and their experience of what for them is Mystery, or God, or Buddhanature.

Individuals become and grow as a community by communally expressing their faith experience in what we have called creed, code, and ceremony. In these external expressions of belief, of ethics, of ritual, we witness the value and the beauty of religion. But it is also here that we encounter the vulnerability of religion.

The Corruptibility and Reformability of Religion

In this final section, we want to look at a fact that is perhaps clearer and more certain than anything we have said so far: Religion needs reform. Again and again in the course of every religion's history, it unhappily and grudgingly finds itself in need of a retuning, overhauling, and sometimes rebuilding. There seem to be two general reasons why reform is an ever-returning visitor to the door of every religion.

First of all, in the immortal words of Bob Dylan, "The times, they are a changin'." History moves on, not always forward and not always for the better, but it moves. The world in which most religions spent their infancy and adolescence is far different from the one in which they must live as adults. And so, like any human being growing up in a different age or moving to a different part of the world, religions have to adjust. This is the first, and quite evident, though not always simple, reason why religions have to change and reform: they have to keep up with the changing times. They have to adjust to the advances in knowledge (historical discoveries or acquaintance with other religions), to the new insights in science (evolution, the "big bang" theory of creation), to new psychological discoveries (the unconscious), to new dangers that threaten our planet's survival (nuclear war, ecological waste), to voices that have just emerged or (more often) were silenced by the materially wealthy and powerful (the voices of women, blacks, indigenous peoples and other oppressed groups).

Adjusting to such new situations is not simply a matter of applying old answers to new questions; it often means having to admit that old answers don't work and that new answers must be found. It frequently means radical reform in a religion's doctrinal or ethical teachings (at one time, the Catholic church condoned slavery). And yet, adjusting to the changing times does not imply that a religion has only to follow the lead of what the world is saying. To understand reform as primarily a matter of bending with the cultural winds would be to de-form rather than re-form a religion; it would be selling religion short. Responding to the changing times will often mean that the religion has to take a stand against certain changes. Abortion on demand, for example, would seem to some religious believers to be something that calls for resistance rather than adjustment.

A recent example of how a religion seeks to reform itself through adjustment to historical-cultural changes would be, for the Catholic church, the Second Vatican Council (1962-1965). It was an effort on the part of the Catholic church to look at the world as it really is—a world stimulated by scientific-technological discoveries, populated by many different and rich cultures and religions, threatened by nuclear war and poverty—and to reform church teaching and liturgy and practice through dialogue with the modern world. Of course, not all Catholics were happy with such reform. An example of the same kind of reform in Judaism was the birth of what today is called Reform Judaism. In the eighteenth and nineteenth centuries, Jews living in Europe, and eventually in the United States, experienced an "Emancipation." Previously they had been forced to live apart from society, often in ghettos, and so they developed a religion that had well-defined limits and did not have to contend much with the outside world. When Jews were admitted into the so-called mainstream of European life, they had to adjust many of their religious attitudes and practices. Reform Judaism was the outcome.

The other reason for the necessity of religious reform is even more recurrent and demanding than the first: Religion corrupts. Though it may be difficult to figure out why it happens, that it does happen is evident to everyone. There is a tendency within every religion to make itself, that is, its creeds, codes, ceremonies, more important than the Sacred Mystery or the Transcendent Experience that it is supposed to foster and serve. And, in doing so, the religion loses touch with the Something More, with the God and the God-experience that forms its heart. Through corruption, religion becomes an outer husk with no inner fruit, or an external system with no life within, or a system that controls and manipulates, rather than helps people.

The ways this cancer of corruption grows within a religion are many. With the help of Gregory Baum, we can diagnose four of the main sicknesses that recurrently affect religion. The virus of each of these sicknesses seems to attack a particular expression of religion, that is, creed, code, ceremony, or the community structure itself.

Idolatry "What's an idol?" is one of those tricky questions by which a teacher can snag a student and force her or him to think. The answer I usually receive is: "a statue of a pagan god." That can be right or wrong. A statue of the divinity is not necessarily an idol, for, strictly speaking, an idol is not something that represents God but something that takes the place of or limits God. Although there are some religions that would not permit any representations of God at all (like Judaism and Islam), still it might be argued that if a statue only represents or symbolizes the Ultimate, it is not really an idol; on the contrary, it can be a means of bringing people to feel more deeply or engagingly the presence of God in their lives. But if a statue, or anything, is meant to stand for, or take the place of, or tie down God, then it is, strictly speaking, an idol.

And that is what we find again and again in the history of all religions, even in Islam and Judaism: the tendency to absolutize or "divinize" elements of religion so that the religion becomes just as important as (if not more important than) the Ultimate Mystery of God. The virus of idolatry infects the body of religion mainly through its creeds or belief system. Religious leaders, for example, (theologians too) invest their teachings, and sometimes even themselves, with a power or authority that is supposed to belong only to God. This usually happens subtly, perhaps without the religious leaders clearly realizing what they are doing. Their word is identified with God's word; or their authority is made to be the only avenue to "sure knowledge" of God's will. In this way, religion itself becomes an idol. Or, in our image from Buddhism, the finger that is supposed to point to the moon takes the place of the moon. This is one of the most frequently found forms of corruption within religion.

Once students are snagged by this definition of an idol and get the point, they often respond with comments or questions that might snag many a religion teacher: "If an idol is something that takes the place of God or limits God, wasn't the Catholic church, or any religion for that matter, an idol, when in the past it said it was the only way to find God and be saved? And what about people who blindly follow religious leaders like the Ayatollah or the pope, and accept their teachings as the only or unquestionable way of knowing for sure what God wants? Isn't that idolatrous? And what about the Bible? Can't it, too, be made into an idol if every word in it is simply and literally identified with God, or if divine truth is not allowed to be found outside the Bible?" However these questions are answered, they are based on a correct understanding of idolatry.

Legalism "Is Mary a good Christian?" Regardless of the appropriateness of such a question, the way it is often answered is a good thermometer of legalism: "Oh yes, she goes to church every Sunday" (or, "Oh no, she doesn't go to church regularly"). Such an answer indicates a mild infection of legalism. This religious sickness manifests itself especially within religious code. It leads religious believers or their leaders to define religion as primarily a matter of obeying the law, the ethical-legal system that the community has agreed upon. A good Christian, therefore, is someone who obeys the law and goes to church every Sunday. Being religious is mainly a question of dos and don'ts, of a certain form of conduct.

But what's wrong with following a certain form of conduct? What's wrong with defining the quality of religious faith by its ethical conduct? "By their fruits you shall know them," Jesus himself said. Right. But a healthy ethical life is different from legalism. For one thing, legalism operates according to the letter, not the spirit, of the law. "Just tell me what to do, put it in writing, and I'll do it." A legalist is much more concerned about obedience than moral decision making; more simply, a legalist wants to be told what to do and fears having to decide for herself or himself. Actually, a legalist wants to make religion and religious faith too easy. Obedience can be easier than the struggle of taking responsibility for oneself. Also, once one has obeyed "the written law," one doesn't have to to worry about anything else. One has followed God's law and has received an admission ticket to heaven.

Legalism corrupts religion, therefore, mainly because it makes religion too easy. In insisting on the letter of the law, it misses the spirit of the law. The purpose of any religious law is to point to an ideal beyond the law. By telling us to do certain things (Respect your neighbor) or not to do certain things (Don't kill your neighbor), a religious law is calling us to act in way that can never be captured in a law (Love your neighbor). You can't call yourself religious without following certain laws; but if that's all you do, you can't call yourself religious either.

Superstition This is a corruption that infects the expression of religion called cult or ritual. If one judges only from externals, it may be difficult to distinguish healthy ritual from debilitating superstition. In ritual or liturgy, we said, religious people make use of symbols and gestures, like a meal, a dance, the pouring of water, or lighting of fire, in order to remember and stir up and celebrate a sense of God's or Mystery's presence. Authentic ritual, therefore, is a coming together of personal faith experience and some external action. In superstition, the external action takes on central importance; everything depends on doing something and doing it right. In ritual or liturgy, one makes use of a symbol in order to express and deepen faith. In superstition or magic (another name for superstition), one "presses a button," as it were, in order to get a certain result. "Do this to get that" might express the attitude behind superstition.

Superstition, therefore, is based on the belief that God or the supernatural powers can be cajoled to grant certain favors through certain actions. As Huston Smith, a historian of religion, has put it, superstition is like ringing a magical bell in order to get the divine bellhop to do our bidding. But note, the very same act can be either authentic ritual or superstitious magic. John wears a medal of Mary, the Mother of Jesus, as a sign of his devotion and desire to imitate her faith; George wears the same medal in the belief that as long as it hangs around his neck, he will never go to hell. Beth confesses her sins to a priest as an expression of her sorrow for having hurt others and a resolve to "clean up her act"; Judy kneels before the priest in the conviction that as long as she enumerates her sins and says her penance, her sins are automatically erased, no matter what she has in mind for tomorrow night. Hassan performs the Islamic fast of Ramadan as an expression of his readiness to follow Allah's will no matter the cost; Said fasts because that way he can be sure Allah will bless his new business adventure.

Ritual is an expression of inner faith; superstition is pressing a divine button. It seems that superstition, like legalism, is an effort to make religion easier or more certain than it is supposed to be, or to use religion for ends that it is not supposed to serve.

Ideology If the other corruptions of religion seemed to attack either creed, code, or ceremony, this one takes hold of religion as a whole, of religion as community. We mentioned this abuse of religion in Chapter Five: It is when religion is turned into a tool to serve one's own benefit, or that of one's group, before all else. The benefit can be one of money, power, or prestige. Religion is used as a means of manipulation. Religious believers are manipulated or drugged, usually by their religious leaders, to contribute to the wealth of others, or to accept their own exploited position as God's will, or to spill their blood in fighting against outsiders who are presented as the enemies of religion. Perhaps this is the most devastating and disgusting corruption of religion, for it transforms one of the essential purposes of religion—to foster the sense of interrelatedness and unity of all persons—into a tool for aggrandizing self and exploiting others. Chapter Five already offered examples of how easily and how often religion is so corrupted.

Just why does all this happen? Why do we so frequently find the weeds of idolatry, legalism, superstition, and ideology in the garden of religion? That question has no neat answer. Paul Tillich attributed such corruptions to what he called "the demonic" element within all religions. But what is the demonic? And how does it work? To venture an answer, it seems that "the demonic" works primarily through the interplay of two human weaknesses: the inordinate desire for security and the inordinate desire for wealth or power. There's nothing wrong with wanting security, but when people seek after security at any cost, and especially when their main reason for embracing religion is to have security, they are looking for "easy" religion and so are exposing themselves to the virus of idolatry, legalism, and superstition; at the same time, they are exposed to being manipulated and exploited by people who are intent on using religion as an ideology. Religion is not meant to give us absolute security; nor is it meant to make us rich and powerful. When it is used for such purposes, it becomes the abode of "the demonic" rather than of "the divine."

And because the demonic has so often dwelt together with the divine in the house of religion, we witness within the history of all the world religions a constant chain of reform movements. "Thank God," one might say, because religion needs reform as any person needs a doctor. As history has shown, religions that do not admit of reform are destined to live on only in museums or history books. History also shows that through reform movements, religion has not only been put back on track and restored to health; it has also been given an even greater degree of life and purpose than it had before becoming sick. It's as if corruption, once it has been healed, can promote even greater health and vitality.

We see this illustrated in some of the great reform movements of religious history. The Jewish prophets from 750-550 B.C.E. rescued the Jewish religion from legalism and indifference to the poor and restored it to a new commitment to working for God's justice among the nations. The Mahayana Reform of Buddhism during the second century B.C.E. to the second century C.E. broke the attempts of the monks to turn Buddhism into an elitist religion and brought forth "mahayana" or "Big-Truck" Buddhism, large enough for the masses of China, Korea, and Japan. And, certainly, the Christian Reformation, under Martin Luther, John Calvin, and others, not only purged Christianity of the countless corruptions of superstition and ideology but stirred up a new commitment to the Gospel in both Catholics and Protestants. No matter how contemptible the corruption a religion may sink into, reform can both heal it and make it more wholesome.

Recognizing the difficulties of defining religion, we attempted to describe it, loosely, as whatever means people use to seek after "what matters most in life." The tighter definition we are using would add that we are really dealing with religion only when people recognize that what matters most in life includes a "transcendent" or "ultimate" dimension that calls people to shift the focus of their lives from concern for oneself to involvement with others. After illustrating this description with examples from some of the world's major religions, we went on to examine the creative tension within all religion between the individual and the community: Individual faith cannot really live and grow without a community of fellow believers, but the community must never take the place of personal faith and responsibility. This led us to examine how this creative tension between individual and community is lived out in the "mechanics" of religion: creed, code, and ceremony. Meant to express the community's faith and vision in symbols and beliefs, in moral commitments and actions, and in ritual remembrance and celebration, these externals of religion can also degenerate into idolatry, legalism, superstition, and ideology. As anyone belonging to a religion well knows, religion is subject to corruption and therefore is in standing need of reform.

If "What matters most?" is a question that interests most human beings, then religion, too, will be a matter worth our study and evaluation. Today, however, there are those who maintain that it is no longer possible to study religion in the singular. The reason is that today no religion can exist in the singular, by itself. To realize its purpose, every individual religion must be in dialogue with other religions. That rather startling statement is the topic of the next chapter.

QUESTIONS FOR REFLECTION AND DISCUSSION

1. What is the "loose definition" of religion? Do you think that money can become a person's religion?
2. What is the "tight definition" of religion? Does one have to believe in God in order to be religious?
3. Be able to discuss the differences in belief and behavior among the major world religions. Do you think these differences are complementary or contradictory?
4. "Personal faith needs a community of faith (religion)." Be able to explain this statement. Do you agree with it?
5. "Every community or society needs faith." What does this mean? Does it make sense to you?
6. What is the purpose of "creed" in religion? What are the different forms it can take?
7. How do "code" and "ceremony" function in religious communities? Give concrete examples.

8. It was said that the inordinate desire for security and for wealth or power are the root causes of corruption in religion. Explain how idolatry, legalism, superstition, and ideology arise from these causes.

SUGGESTED READINGS

Carmody, Denise Lardner, and John Carmody. *Religion: The Great Questions*. New York: Seabury Press, 1983.

Carmody, Denise Lardner. *Women and World Religions* (2nd edition). Englewood Cliffs, N.J.: Prentice Hall, 1989.

Hall, T. William, ed. *Introduction to the Study of Religion*. San Francisco: Harper & Row, 1978.

Johnston, Ronald L. *Religion in Society: A Sociology of Religion*. Englewood Cliffs, N.J.: Prentice-Hall, 1988 (3rd edition).

Küng, Hans, *et al. Christianity and the World Religions: Paths to Dialogue with Islam, Hinduism, and Buddhism*. New York: Doubleday, 1986.

Monk, Robert, *et al. Exploring Religious Meaning*. Englewood Cliffs, N.J.: Prentice Hall, 1980. (2nd edition).

Overberg, Kenneth R. *Roots and Branches: Grounding Religion in Our Human Experience*. Cincinnati: St. Anthony Messenger Press, 1987.

Shinn, Larry D. *Two Sacred Worlds: Experience and Structure in the World's Religions*. Nashville: Abingdon, 1977.

Smith, Huston. *Religions of Man*. New York: Harper & Row, 1965.

Tillich, Paul. *Christianity and the Encounter of the World Religions*. New York: Columbia University Press, 1963.

CHAPTER SEVEN

Religions—Why So Many?

One of the most evident and at the same time (for many) bothersome aspects of religion today is the simple, undeniable fact that there are so many of them. The sketchy chart of religions given in the previous chapter is only part of the picture of the variety of religions. Besides the so-called world religions—Hinduism, Buddhism, Confucianism, Taoism, Judaism, Christianity, and Islam—there are the "ancient religions" of the oral peoples: Native Americans, Eskimos, Africans, Australian Aborigines; and to this list we can add the proliferating new religions of the Universalist church, Scientology, the Hare Krishna movement, Soka Gakkai (in Japan).

When we say "many," we also mean "different." The "manyness" of religions is not like the many different varieties or colors of apples but, rather, like the abundantly different varieties of fruit. Anyone who claims that the many religions of the world are "really the same," just as different varieties of apples are still really apples, has not studied them carefully. The differences between a Catholic Mass and a Native American Vision Quest, or more evidently, between a Jewish circumcision rite and a Christian baptism, are as evident and great as that between an apple and an orange. Both have something by which they can be called fruit, both are beautiful and important in their own context, but both are bewilderingly different.

This exuberant variety of religions perplexes many people. One would think that, given the importance of religion and its role in aiding humankind to figure out "what matters most in life," there would be greater uniformity between religious traditions, if not in packaging, at least in content. After all, if religions are supposed to tell people where they're going and how to get there, the vast variety of religions sure makes it difficult for the human race to get its act together and move in the same direction. Also, for people who believe that there is "one God" or "one Ultimate Reality," it's hard to figure out why this one God would want, or allow, so many different, and often clashing, messages about what Ultimate Reality is and what it wants of us.

But haven't there always been many and different religions throughout the course of history? Certainly. But as we shall explain in a moment, never before have people been so forcefully aware of this multiplicity. Never before have the religions of the world been so close to each other, if not in physical proximity, at least in communication. The religions of the world, in their manyness, are bumping into each other as never before. The knowledge that they have of each other is not simply a knowledge of manyness; it is a recognition of value. An awareness is growing among people throughout the world not just that there are many other varieties of religion but that these religions are worthwhile and good. In religions that are so starkly different, people are finding truth and goodness. That, for many, is not just interesting, it's scary.

Therefore, in a book like this, it is not enough to study the nature and mechanics of religion as we have so far attempted. We also have to look at the plurality of religions, trying to understand why there are so many and, especially, what this manyness might mean for our modern world. Theologians like Raimundo Panikkar, John Hick, and Wilfred Cantwell Smith, among many others, suggest that given this new awareness of each other, the religions of the world stand on the brink of a new age in the religious history of humankind, an age that will be brought forth by taking advantage of the new possibilities for understanding and cooperation. To better grasp those possibilities, we can begin by examining our world's new experience of the plurality and diversity of religions.

Many Religions Here to Stay

The earliest records of human history give witness to a variety of religious beliefs. If today, some 100,000 years after homo sapiens dropped from the tree of evolution, we're still talking about many religions, it would seem that religious diversity is "as it was in the beginning, is now, and ever shall be." The many religions are here to stay. The dream of Christians that some day all the peoples of the world would be converted to Christianity, which would then be the only religion in the world, does not appear to be an entirely realistic hope. After some two thousand years of missionary efforts to convert the world, Christianity has not yet converted and absorbed the other religions (even though the Christian religion is to be found in every corner of the world). Nor, of course, has Christianity fallen to the missionary outreach of Islam or of Buddhism.

In fact, when we study the missionary history of Christianity, it appears that significant numbers of conversions were won only in those situations where the local religions were either not well developed or were in a state of corruption (for example, the Roman or Greek religions), or where Christianity used the power of the sword or the lure of the pocketbook to win converts (amid some of the native religions of Latin America and India). From a historian's perspective, it appears that if a local religion was healthy and meeting the needs of its people, and if the newly arrived missionary religion did not coerce people to conversion, the local religion was not converted to the new. In fact, if we look at the cast of religions that formed during what the philosopher Karl Jaspers calls the "Axial Period" (900 B.C.E to 200 C.E.), those same religions are still going strong: Hinduism, Buddhism, Judaism, Christianity. No one of these religions has proven itself superior or able to absorb the others.

In fact, as we compare the line-up of religions today to that of a millennium ago, there has been an increase rather than a decrease. For Christians, this raises a provocative theological question: if God wants there to be only one true religion, why have there always been so many different faiths, and why is religious diversity still thriving? Might God prefer a cast of many religions rather than a "one man show?"

There is another, and quite evident, reason why many people today are concluding that religious diversity is not only a given, but a happy given of human history. Contemporary people know more about other religions than they ever did. Ours is no longer a world in which Hinduism, Buddhism, and Islam are familiar subjects only for specialists and scholars up in their ivory towers. Today, given the proliferation of knowledge and especially given an earth-girding and earth-shrinking system of communication, people have abundant opportunities to hear and learn about other, previously esoteric, religious paths. Nowadays, one can browse through the religion or philosophy section of any popular book store in the United States and find just as many and just as attractive books on Hinduism or Islam as on Christianity or Judaism. In fact, the Tao Te Ching, the sacred Scripture of Taoism, has been translated more frequently than any other book except the Bible. I will never forget the surprise and the exhilaration in the words of Petie, a junior theology major, who had spent most of the previous evening reading and meditating on the Tao Te Ching: "It's beautiful and inspiring. It enabled me to feel the presence of God in nature!" In general, then, people nowadays are able to take a much closer look at other religions, and often, they like what they see.

Besides the opportunity to read or study, what has brought many people to a great appreciation for other religions is the opportunity to know and become friends with other religious believers. To know another faith through a well written book can be interesting; to know it on the face and in the life of a colleague or friend can be downright inspiring—and challenging. Such friendships are becoming ever more possible for ever more people. In the way people today are traveling, studying, or moving abroad, the major religions of the world are overspilling their traditional boundaries. Modern metropolises like London, Amsterdam, Frankfurt, New York, and San Francisco have become interreligious neighborhoods. And even in small cities like Cincinnati, there are local communities of Muslims, Hindus, and Buddhists that are small but growing.

Jerry, a freshman from a conservative Catholic family, captured what I'm trying to say when he told me of his close friend Rahim, a devout Muslim: "He's one of the most honest people I've ever met, and always ready to help others. He seems as happy and at peace with himself as anyone I know. Most of his values he gets from his religion. There's got to be something to it. After he was over for Sunday dinner last week, my grandmother referred to him as a pagan. That can't be true."

From this contemporary experience of the reality and value of other religions, Christians, both theologians and ordinary believers, are drawing some conclusions: It must be God's will that there are so many religions and God must be present and active within them. As many Christian readers of this book may remember (or have heard from their parents), this was not always the attitude of the Christian churches. In fact, just a generation or two ago, Catholics were often told by their pastors or religion teachers that the Catholic church was the one and only true religion and that if you were not a Catholic you were not going to make it to heaven. Things have changed. The Second Vatican Council clearly taught that God's truth can be found in all the religions of the world and that Catholics must respect these religions. This new and positive attitude toward other faiths is also reflected in the statements of the World Council of Churches and of most of the "mainline" (non-fundamentalist) Protestant churches. Hindus and Buddhists would tell Christians that such a positive view of other religions has always been part of their teachings.

The Necessity of Dialogue

Once it is recognized that the many religions are here to stay and that such is God's will, a further recognition begins to take shape: The many religions cannot simply exist alongside each other; rather, they must talk to, learn from, and cooperate with each other. We're not sure just how or why one draws this further conclusion, but we are sure that many people, especially young adults, are doing so. In college theology courses and in adult education classes, we find that in wrestling with the big questions of life (creation, evil, salvation, human dignity, end of the world), people are not content only with the traditional Christian answers. Or rather, before they can come to their own conclusions on the Christian answers, they feel the need to also hear the viewpoints of other religions. They sense that they cannot really understand their own answers until they have also heard and tried to understand the answers of others.

Theologian-philosopher Raimundo Panikkar writes: "Before I can answer the question 'Who am I?' I must ask and try to answer the question 'Who are you?'" To expand Panikkar's claim, before I can answer the question, "Who is my God?" I must ask, "Who or what is your God?" If I know only my God, my self, my religion, then my knowledge is inadequate. Max Müller, a famous scholar of religions at the beginning of this century, put it more pointedly when giving reasons for studying other faiths: "They who know only one, know none."

Why is this? Why do so many people feel the need to learn about and dialogue with people different from themselves, with people from other religions? Why are college courses on "Eastern Religions" or "Dialogue among World Religions" usually packed? A common-sense response is that once you realize that you and your religion are "one among many," and once you've had the chance to sense the beauty and value in the many others, you naturally feel the desire or simple curiosity to learn from them. Once Jerry felt how much the Islamic religion had helped his friend Rahim to be such a healthy and happy human being, he naturally felt that he, too, might learn something from Islam (which doesn't mean he ceased to be a Christian).

Philosophers tell us that such common-sense intuitions are based on a sound "epistemology" (the science of how we know). Certain philosophers (the "anti-foundationalists") state baldly what many ordinary people feel but may be afraid to admit: that there are no absolute foundations or sources for truth. Human beings, in other words, cannot expect truth to be served them on some kind of a silver platter or in some kind of a golden book that they merely have to receive and read in order to be sure that they have the truth. Truth is not dished out (even by God) in any one, unchanging package. Nor is it found in any one place, unchanging, for all times.

So what are we to do? The conclusion these philosophers draw is that truth is the object of a never-ending search, and the only way we can carry on this search is by conversation, by joining forces, by dialoguing with those who are different from us, by stating what we think is true and listening to the views of others. Truth can be discovered only through conversation among many and different persons, each being as honest as possible, each listening to the others as openly as possible. And if you're a religious person, you believe that God is part of this conversation. So, if conversation is the way to truth, and if God is part of the conversation, then the religions of the world had better start talking to each other.

If all this sounds a little too philosophical, there is also a more immediate, tangible, and pressing reason why people from different religions must dialogue and cooperate with each other: to save this world and the human race. In Chapter Five, we briefly traced the three major crises threatening the welfare, even the existence, of the world as we know it: the socioeconomic crises of hunger, oppression, and increasing revolutions; the nuclear crisis which, with one fell superpower swoop, can destroy all life and future life; and the ecological crisis that is destroying the life-sustaining capabilities of mother earth. Certainly, the religions of the world don't have a magical solution for these problems. But as we suggested in Chapter Five, each religion feels it has something to contribute to making this world a more unified, just, and loving society. If each religion's voice can blend into a religious chorus, singing and working together, if the religions could lay aside their history of bickering and competing and cooperate in dialogue, there would be greater hope for our threatened world. Interreligious dialogue is necessary.

Fortunately, religious leaders of the world are recognizing this need to get out of their own backyards in order to meet their neighbors. For Catholics, the Second Vatican Council stated in no uncertain terms that Catholics are "prudently and lovingly" to dialogue with other believers. For Protestants, the World Council of Churches over the past decades has been calling its member churches to enter into a more authentic conversation and collaboration with followers of "other faiths and ideologies." From the Buddhist side, one of the most alerting calls for interreligious dialogue has come from the World Conference on Religion and Peace, inspired by Buddhist beliefs and by the conviction that the primary purpose of all religions is to promote world peace.

But it is easier to describe the need for dialogue than to actually do it.

The Complexity of Dialogue

Whether it's between two religious communities or between two friends, authentic dialogue isn't easy. To understand why this is so, we need a clearer idea of what "authentic dialogue" means and what it doesn't mean.

1. Dialogue, any real conversation between two people, is not just chit-chat. It is not shooting the breeze or a simple exchange of information. Certainly, exchanging information is important; without it, there would be no learning and understanding. But the information that is passed back and forth in dialogue is considered by both partners to be vitally important. They're talking about matters that touch their lives, values, and commitments. So, in dialogue, the partners seek not simply to lay out their viewpoints but to present them in a way that the other person can really grasp and feel them.

2. This means that dialogue is not a matter of "anything goes." Yes, in the conversation, the partners are to speak what-

ever is on their minds and whatever they believe in. But just because it's stated doesn't mean it's going to be accepted. Some people confuse religious dialogue with "lazy tolerance"—"I'll accept anything you say as long as you mean it and feel it and are sincere." That's too easy. It also indicates a bad case of relativism, a philosophical position that holds that since we can never be absolutely sure about truth, we can't really judge each other; everything is relative. There's no way of saying what is true or false. If you feel it, it's true for you. Such relativism or lazy tolerance is the death of dialogue. Dialogue also has to include disagreement and argument, always in a respectful, careful way. Dialogue means that I may have to tell you where and why I think you are wrong. That isn't easy. But if we don't do it, dialogue becomes mush.

3. The purpose of religious dialogue is not determined by the "baking method": each religion provides a different ingredient, and when we mix them all together and put them in the oven of dialogue, we come up with a new religion. Technically, this is called *syncretism*, which uses dialogue to fashion a new world religion out of the best ingredients of present religions. In authentic dialogue, religious partners are to be changed, perhaps transformed, but they are not to lose their own identities in some kind of common religious pie. The same would apply to ordinary, serious conversation; we are open to being changed through the encounter with another person, but we don't want to be dominated or absorbed by the other. The intent of religious dialogue is not, therefore, to create one, new world religion. Rather, it is to form a new relationship and unity among the existing religions, a unity in which each religion will be changed without being dissolved.

In trying to speak and listen, understand and judge, we run into the complexities and pitfalls of religious dialogue. They are the same complexities, though multiplied a hundredfold, that come up in any conversation in which we try to understand and judge another person. When we consider how utterly different the religions are from each other, when we realize the cultural chasms that extend between religions, and especially when we recognize just how much each one of us is influenced, limited, and, in a sense, prejudiced by our own culture and religion, we have to ask whether it is really possible to leave our own cultural/religious worldview in order to enter into that of another. Isn't that what we have to do in order to understand the religious experiences and beliefs of a Hindu or Buddhist—climb out of our own religious and cultural skins in order to feel and see as the Hindus and Buddhists do? But is that possible? Aren't we always looking at the Hindu through our own religious glasses? When we think we understand them, aren't we reading our own views into their religion?

The problem becomes even more serious when it comes to evaluating or judging another religion. Aren't our judgments about the truth or morality of their practices and beliefs always based on our own experience and culture? What right have we to judge? What is wrong in our culture might make good sense in theirs. For instance, doing homage to a cow might be a clear case of superstition or idolatry for a Christian or Jew, but for a devout Hindu it may be an act of genuine worship of the Godhead present in all beings.

Perhaps we can understand why some anthropologists and theologians argue that the big danger in interreligious dialogue is imperialism. This is a danger that people especially from Europe and the United States have fallen into—they think they are being open to other religions, they think they are making careful, objective judgments, when actually they are imposing their own views and their own values on other religions. When Christians, for instance, accuse Buddhists of being atheists and of not believing in an Ultimate, they are doing so according to their own Christian understanding of what God is. According to the Christian definition, Buddhists are atheists. But what about the Buddhist definition of the Ultimate? (Buddhists refuse to define anything!)

A Common Ground

In order to avoid this kind of imperialistic imposing of the views and values of one religion on those of another, it seems that we need some sort of common ground, "shared property" between all the religions that might serve as the meeting point where they can understand and evaluate each other. This common, shared ground would enable religious persons to get a handle on the differences between them; and it would provide some shared criteria or guidelines by which they could decide whether a particular religious belief or practice is true or false, good or bad. Such a common ground would be something like two total strangers coming from completely different cultural backgrounds, say Chicago and Bombay, who happen to meet and try to talk; they discover that they both speak a common language (English, but with very different accents) and that they both love to collect stamps. Their shared language and interests give them a basis to begin (only begin) to understand and size up each other.

But does such a common ground exist between the religions of the world? If we listen to anthropologists, philosophers, and theologians, the usual answer nowadays seems to be "no." They warn religious people that to chase after or to try to discover a common essence, a common foundation, or a common God within all religions is like trying to grasp a shadow. The shadow is intangible and it is one's own projection! There are no natural bridges stretching across the awesome differences between religions. There is no common language existing within the various religions by which they can understand and evaluate each other. Each religion, like each person, is caught, for better or for worse, in a cultural perspective. One can look beyond one's culture and religion and learn something about other cultures and religions, but never enough to understand them fully and certainly not enough to pass judgment on them.

It's like an American and an English person trying to discuss cricket. The American might think that baseball is the common ground for understanding the two sports. But the differences between baseball and cricket would seem to be greater than any similarities; so, if the American understands cricket on the basis of baseball, that will be using norms for understanding that are not common but, rather, American. The problem is compounded immeasurably, the experts tell us, when we consider the differences between the religions of the world, especially between Eastern and Western traditions. Although it might be argued that the religions are all seeking the welfare of humanity, the differences in their understanding of what that welfare is and how it is grounded in Ultimate Reality are so stark as to exclude any talk about a common essence or a common ground.

To propose such a common ground is, in the image already used, to propose one's own shadow and then to impose it on others. That's what we have called "imperialism." It seems that Christians, perhaps unconsciously and even with good will, have been guilty of such imperialistic imposition on other religions. For instance, in an effort to achieve a more positive attitude towards other faiths, Christian theologians maintain that Christ is not limited to Christianity but is working in all other religions. (Therefore, members of other faiths are called "anonymous Christians.") This does indeed make for a more open attitude toward other faiths, but it ends up making Christ the common ingredient of other religions. Hindus and Buddhists are not exactly happy about such an attitude.

Other Christian theologians try to remedy the situation by explaining that it is not Christ but God who is the common content of all religions—God expressing God's self differently in all the different religions. Again, the intent is to be more open, more positive to other faiths. But even in this approach, when it comes to describing this God present in all religions, it turns out to be the God of the Christian Bible and tradition. As we saw, Hindus have a very different concept of God, and many Buddhists don't even talk about God.

The danger in starting with common ground between religions is that what we propose as common is usually ours. And we end up seeing a reflection of ourselves in other people's cultures and religions. We end up seeing and judging by our perspectives, not theirs. That's imperialism.

What does this all mean? We said that dialogue between religions is necessary but difficult and that some kind of common ground is necessary for mutual understanding. Now we're saying such common ground doesn't exist. Is dialogue at all possible?

A Starting Point: Shared Commitment

As difficult and dangerous as dialogue among religions may be, it also remains, in the feelings and convictions of many religious people, absolutely necessary. And out of the awareness of necessity is born the hope of possibility. What is necessary must, somehow, be possible. That's a hope. It's a hope that appears verified in ordinary experience: Just as individuals have experienced that despite enormous differences of class, race, and culture, it is possible for two people to understand each other, to learn from each other, maybe even to live together in marriage, so, too, it has been the growing experience of many that despite the overwhelming differences between religions, religious believers can speak to and understand each other. Despite what the experts say about the lack of a common ground, communication and cooperation between two utterly different religions does take place.

But it is important to bear in mind what the experts tell us and to learn from them. The dangers of unconsciously but nonetheless imperialistically imposing our ideas on others is an ever-lurking temptation in all dialogue and conversation. We must keep our guard up, right from the start. To enter the dialogue thinking that we already know what we have in common and how we can build on it is naive and a set-up for frustration. There is no pre-established common ground or essence neatly uniting all world religions.

Yet, if it isn't pre-established, maybe it can be constructed, not by any one religion, but by all religions together. This is the lesson to be learned from the critics and the way in which we might respond to them: There is no common ground already established and able to be known before dialogue. But what we can hope for and work for in and through dialogue is the discovery or creation of a meeting place or new space where different religions can come together and understand and cooperate with each other.

According to the American theologian Mark Kline Taylor, there may be no solid common ground between the religions before dialogue, but in dialogue "shaky" common ground can be built up. In this way, what we have in common and what enables us to talk to each other is not pre-packaged and imposed; it is, rather, brought forth and nurtured in the very conversation itself, by everyone involved. It's like a marriage. Good marriages are not, despite what the songs say, "made in heaven"; they are worked at and built up in the daily effort of living together.

But if we have to build up the basis for religious dialogue in the dialogue itself, how do we do this? Where do we start? Let us make a suggestion: A common starting point for dialogue with or study of other religious traditions can be found not in something that is common within each religion but in something that surrounds and confronts them all. We're talking about something that is not a common teaching or practice in all faiths, but that constitutes a common problem and a common challenge for all of them. Again, we are referring to what we have mentioned frequently in these pages and what is evident to all nations and religions: the sufferings that inflict our race and our planet today, the sufferings of hunger and injustice, of the fear of nuclear holocaust, of ecological devastation. These are problems and crises that are cross-cultural and cross-religious; they stare every religion and religious person in the face, whether they are Christians or Muslims or Hindus. They are problems that cry out to everyone, but especially to religious people, for solution.

All religions of the world, it can be said, both have to and want to respond to these common problems. They have to, because if they don't, they will lose meaning for people and will be put on the bookshelf of history marked "no longer relevant." They want to because each religion purports to bring to humanity what is variously called "salvation," "liberation," "moksha" (Hinduism), or "nirvana" (Buddhism). They all claim to be able to resolve the problems that make up the human predicament. Now more than ever, they will want to make their messages heard. Now more than ever, people are ready to hear; for the situation is desperate, especially for those who are trapped in hunger or victimized by war or dwindling resources.

In fact, the situation is so desperate and complex that religious people from different traditions must recognize that no one religion can have all the answers or all the energy and wherewithall to resolve the crises of suffering and injustice. The job is too big for any one religion, culture, nation. We need many different ideas, many different commitments. As we suggested in Chapter Five, peace and justice will be established throughout the world only if religions throughout the world come together to join forces and visions. Here is the common starting point for dialogue. We can call it a dialogue for peace and justice and unity.

In such a dialogue with (or study of) other religions, the first item on the agenda would not be to explain to each other the different beliefs or rituals of each religion, but to identify what are the most pressing human problems facing the religions in their particular context, whether it be in India, Japan, or the United States. Where are people suffering? Where is there conflict? Where are the earth's resources being destroyed? The first step would be to try to identify and understand these problems and then, concretely, to try to do something about them. This would call for people from different religions to work together to feed the hungry, establish potable water supplies, change unjust political systems, reduce conflict. As part of this acting together, the religions would also reflect together and try to explain to each other what it is that motivates them or directs them in addressing these human problems.

In this dialogue or study based on acting and reflecting, it will become clear that each religion has its own way of understanding the causes of the crises and its own way of finding a solution—its own understanding, in other words, of what makes for human welfare or salvation. A dialogue of peace and justice is not necessarily going to be harmonious. It had better not be, for it is precisely in their differences that the religions will learn from each other. If there aren't any real differences in the way the religions understand the human situation, there is really nothing to talk about.

But in this discussion, in the efforts to resolve and unify these differences, what is most important is not that "our team wins." In a dialogue of peace and justice, the primary concern is not to push "our" notion of God; it is not to prove that our "savior" is bigger than yours; nor is it to make sure that our solution for promoting peace and justice wins out over yours. What is most important is that people actually be helped, fed, educated, given medicine, and that war be avoided and the environment saved. Therefore, in the dialogue or study of other religions, what decides between true or false, good or bad, better or worse among the different beliefs and practices is not whether they believe in only one God, or whether they accept Jesus as their only savior, or whether they believe in the infallibility of the pope (as important as all these beliefs may be), but whether a particular religion or religious belief or practice is able to bring about greater peace and justice and unity in this world. That's the bottom-line measuring stick for truth or goodness.

We should add that the best people to decide whether a religious belief or practice can help resolve problems of hunger, oppression, fear of war are not the religious experts, the dignitaries and theologians, but the poor and oppressed themselves, ordinary people struggling to make their world better. Their views on religious truth count most, and must be heard by the experts.

As we have been indicating, a concern for peace and justice, for the welfare of humanity and the planet, can serve as a starting point or framework not only for the actual dialogue between members of different faiths, but also for the study of religions in college courses or adult education classes. Instead of following the standard "comparative religions" approach (in which each religion, its history and beliefs, is studied by itself) a "peace and justice" approach to studying religions would begin with an examination of one or two major problems in our present world—war and peace, social injustice, women's rights, the ecological crisis—and then go on to explore what each religion has to say about such problems and how it would resolve them. One would not expect each religion to have neatly formulated answers for such modern questions; but within each tradition there are those who are trying to "re-read" their sacred Scriptures and traditions in order to respond to these pressing issues.

A course on "War, Peace, and Religions" or on "Ecology and Religions" or on "Women's Rights in World Religions" would not only be more interesting than the "factual" study of comparative religions, it would also provide, as suggested, a framework of concerns by which we can more readily understand and evaluate world religions.

Other Forms of Dialogue

At this point, a word of caution is called for. In emphasizing peace and justice, or the well-being of humanity and the earth, as the basis for dialogue between religions, we certainly don't want to give the impression that this is the only basis for a conversation between different religious believers or that this method excludes other methods of dialogue. On the contrary, there should be no one way for bringing religious people together and urging them to learn from each other. There are different ways for helping religions to hear each other; and the different ways have to feed into and balance each other.

The Federation of Asian Bishops Conference made the same point some years ago when they surveyed the rich variety of religions in Asia and asked how Christians (a tiny minority among the other religions) might enter into a fruitful dialogue with other believers. The bishops recommended three different but complementary forms of dialogue.

1. The Dialogue of Prayer is one in which religious people try to meet on the level of religious experience before they meet on the level of words. They do this by attempting to use each other's forms of prayer or religious practice. This can mean sharing in each other's rituals, as much as possible, in order to see if the sense of the divine or the experience of enlightenment that grounds a particular religion can be felt by someone outside of that religion. From what those who have experimented with such a dialogue of prayer tell us, one of the forms of religious practice that can best be shared between different religions is that of meditation. By meditating together, by experimenting

with each other's different methods of meditation, religious persons have claimed that they can sense that there is something similar, if not the same, that is entering their consciousness through these different ways of meditation. This is sometimes called the "mystical approach" to dialogue. It is the reason why during the past few decades one finds, for example, American Christians doing Zen meditation and Japanese Zen monks visiting Christian monasteries in Europe and the North America.

2. The Asian bishops also spoke about the Dialogue of Study. Here dialogue is supported through the hard but necessary work of studying each other's Scriptures, or trying to understanding each other's doctrines and practices. Such study, of course, does not take place only through books; it requires that persons from different religious paths make the effort to explain and teach each other what is the meaning, for instance, of the Buddhist notion of nirvana, or the Hindu view of the Ultimate as Brahman, or the Muslim teaching on the "tawhid" or unity of God. These are notions and images that are foreign and complex for those outside the tradition. Unless we apply our minds and imaginations to trying to grasp and enter into these beliefs and images, dialogue will not be able to move forward.

3. Finally, the Asian bishops also recommended the Dialogue of Life. This is closer to what we have meant by dialogue based on peace and justice. It is the effort to understand each other by trying to work together in resolving the common problems or sufferings that face us all. Although we have stressed the practicality and the priority of such a dialogue of life, we also must always keep in mind that it must be sustained and nourished by the dialogue of prayer/meditation and the dialogue of hard study. The point we have stressed is that such prayer and meditation will become all the more urgent and fruitful if carried out on the basis of a shared commitment to peace and justice: the dialogue of life.

Ground Rules for Dialogue

In order to successfully pursue an interreligious dialogue based on peace and justice (or on prayer, or on study) a dialogue in which we genuinely hear and are affected by what the other is saying—we have to bring to the dialogue or study certain personal attitudes without which no serious conversation can ever take place. These attitudes make up what we might term basic ground rules for dialogue. They apply for a successful conversation not only between religions but also between any two human beings who really want to understand each other and grow from that understanding. These attitudes are:

Commitment to One's Own Religion In order for a genuine conversation to take place between two people from different religions, it is essential that the people involved have something to say. We're talking about a religious dialogue (not a political or philosophical one), and that means that those involved must be able to speak from their own religious convictions. Religious dialogue requires people who take religion seriously. This doesn't mean they have to have crystal clarity and total commitment for everything they say; but they do have to "stand somewhere," they do have to "hold certain truths," they do have to be involved. If this is not the case, then dialogue becomes what we have called "chit-chat." Or, the study of religions remains purely a "head-trip" (or a "memory-cram") that never arrives at the heart or at real life.

Holding certain truths means, as we already mentioned, promoting those truths. This, too, is a requirement for healthy dialogue. People must not only announce how they see the world or the Ultimate, but try to bring their partners to share that vision. Yes, in dialogue people try to bring others to agree with them. It's not simply a case of "This is my view, you can take or leave it," but rather, "I want you to take it!" To use a word that is barbed and offensive for some people, in dialogue we do try to convert each other, to persuade, convince, win each other over to our way of seeing and living life. But we do so carefully, respectfully, and honestly. If we didn't try to persuade and convert each other, dialogue wouldn't have any "beef." Nor would it be much fun.

What we have just said about dialogue having to be fueled by the firm commitments of all partners is the ideal. Ideals are not always possible. There are also people who, for all kinds of reasons, enter a religious conversation or take up a course in religion without firm personal convictions and commitments. They have not yet found a place to stand, and so they turn to dialogue as part of their own search. In the process of dialogue, such people gain a lot more than they can contribute. That's okay. Yet if all participants in dialogue were in that situation, there wouldn't be much to exchange or to gain.

Openness and Readiness to Change The eagerness one has to persuade or convert one's dialogue partners has to be matched by a willingness to be converted by them. For most of us, this is a more demanding ground rule, for it requires that we admit that our own positions or truths are always limited, and therefore open to either expansion or correction. Even more so, it requires that we take it for granted that the beliefs or practices of another religion, no matter how strange or different from our own, contain truth that we can learn from. We have to start the dialogue, as Raimundo Panikkar admonishes us, with the presumption that the other side has the truth. If we don't, if we look upon our partners as "mistaken" or "inferior," we will never really listen to what they have to say. After the dialogue, it may turn out that we judge their ideas to be false or dangerous; but such judgments have to be conclusions from what we have heard. And to hear properly, we have to presume that our partners speak the truth.

Openness to the truth of what our partners have to say means openness to acting on what they say. And that means openness to changing our own views and our own ways of acting. Unless there is this readiness to admit our own errors or inadequacies and to correct them, we are not really present to the other person in dialogue. If we enter the conversation with a list of non-negotiables, items about which we know we have the final truth and can never change, we are setting up roadblocks to dialogue.

Such openness to the truth of others and to the possibility of having to change our ways should not be difficult for Christians.

After all, they believe in a God "who wants everyone to come to the knowledge of truth and be saved" (I Tim 2: 4), and who therefore makes known divine truth to all peoples in a variety of ways. Christians can therefore expect to find this God in other religions, present and active and perhaps up to "divine tricks" they have never dreamed of. Through other faiths, God may have surprises in store for Christians, surprises that will call them to see things in different ways and to alter or radically change ideas and practices that they have long cherished.

During the last half of the first century B.C.E., when the early Christian community moved from the Jewish culture in which it had been born and raised and began to dialogue with the world of Roman and Greek culture and religions, it had to make changes it never thought were possible: Christians changed the law of their community that insisted that only Jews could be followers of Jesus and that male Christians had to be circumcised. Difficult as it may be for us today to understand, this was an enormous change. And it was the result of dialogue and openness to others. The Christian God is a "God of history," a God delivering surprises around every historical bend and calling people to move and change with the course of history.

Passing Over But if dialogue is going to work, if we are going to be able to understand and evaluate another religious community, we are going to have to somehow leave our own world and enter into theirs. Religion, as we said in Chapter Six, is based on personal experience; it is religious experience that gives rise to the creeds, codes, and ceremonies of a religion. Therefore, if we are going to understand another religion, we have to somehow, to some degree, enter into its core experience. Religious dialogue, as well as the study of other religions, can never be purely an intellectual matter. It has to involve the whole person. We have to dialogue not only with our heads, but also and especially with our hearts and with our hands. We have to "feel" and "practice" the other religious way if we're going to understand it.

This is what some theologians call the process of "passing

over" to another religion. With our imagination, our feelings, our actions we have to pass over to the other tradition's way of seeing the world and the Ultimate; in a sense, and always in a limited way, we have to become Jewish or Hindu or Buddhist or Muslim. And then we are to "pass back" to our own religion and culture to see what we have learned and how we might understand ourselves differently from this experience of having entered another world.

Just how this process might be carried out can take various forms. John Dunne, a theologian at Notre Dame University, tells us that imagination plays a key role in passing over. With our imagination, we can enter into the myths and stories of the other tradition; we can feel these stories and symbols and let them take us where they might, let them lead us to new insights about human nature, about God, about how we can deal with each other. The story of Buddha, for instance, can help us "imagine" what it would be like to live a life in which we enjoy everything but cling to nothing. The Hindu story of Gandhi and the Bhagavad Gita (one of the principal Hindu Scriptures) enables us to imagine the freedom that comes from "acting without seeking the fruits of our actions." Or, the Hindu symbol of salt dispersed in water provides an image of how God is present in all creation.

Another form of passing over consistent with our peace and justice approach is to share some form of social or political involvement with followers of other faiths. To work side by side with Hindus in a soup kitchen; to stand alongside Buddhists in a peace march; to cooperate with Jews in working for justice for refugees from Central America (in the Sanctuary movement, for example), and in doing all this, to feel and come to appreciate how others' religious faith motivates and guides them, this, too, is a way of passing over to other religious manners of being and acting in the world and of understanding God or the Ultimate.

From our own experience and that of our students, we have seen how sharing in the forms of prayer or ritual or social activities of other religions can be powerful ways of passing over. We remember Jeff, a Roman Catholic sophomore from the west side of Cincinnati, telling us how he could feel the presence of God as he partook of a Jewish Seder meal. Or Sue, a pre-law major, who spoke about the indescribable peace and sense of belonging that she experienced after a weekend sesshin (retreat) of doing Zen meditation. The movie *Gandhi* helped many people pass over to Hinduism by allowing them to "feel" how Gandhi's Hindu beliefs in "ahimsa," or nonviolence, enabled him to face the injustice of the British rule and work for the independence of India. As Native Americans tell us, we cannot judge another person until we have actually walked a few miles in her or his moccasins. Passing over is the effort to put on the moccasins of other religions. For most people, the walk is enjoyable, invigorating, and challenging.

No Final Answers This final guideline is implied in our description of the three preceding guidelines. If we are going to be committed to the truth of our own religion in such a way that we do not close our minds to the truth in others, if we are going to have the freedom to actually pass over to the experience and vision of another religion, then we are going to have to enter the dialogue (or the study of other religions) recognizing that no religion has the final answer or the last word for all the others. This means that no believer can enter the dialogue claiming to be part of the superior religion, the one meant to fulfill or absorb or pass final judgment on all the others. If one religious community begins a conversation with another community by claiming (or just thinking) that its God or its revelation or its savior is the standard of truth or the end of the line or the mountain top for all other religions, it destroys the dialogue before it can even get off the ground.

Why do we say this? Because any religious person claiming to have the final word cannot really be open to anything new in other religions. For such a person, if there is any value in another faith, it has to agree with what is already contained in one's own. Such a person is not open to other faiths, not able to change as the result of dialogue; nor is that person free to genuinely pass over to another religion. Those who claim to have

God's final word are religious know-it-alls who can't learn anything more than what they already know.

Does this guideline contradict our first guideline about participants having to be committed to their own religious truth in such a way that they try to "convert" others to that truth? After all, if you try to convince someone else to see things as you do, that implies that you think your view is better than theirs. In response, there is quite a big difference between saying "This is how I understand God's truth and why it is important for you, too," and saying "I have a God-given final word on truth that God wants me to use to evaluate your truth." In the first statement, I'm committed to what I feel is right, but I recognize both the limitations of what I know and my need to listen to what may be the truth that you have discovered about God; there's room for negotiation and correction. In the second statement, I have a final truth given to me directly by God. One can't negotiate or correct a God-given truth; to do so would be unfaithful to God.

So you can see how final words or ultimate truths supposedly given to a religion by God open the door to, or become an excuse for, imperialism. If I have God's final truth, that means I'm bigger and stronger than you (thanks be to God, not to me!). And if you don't accept that final word, I may have to "persuade" you to do so or make sure you don't cause any trouble.

If we make use of these guidelines for dialogue, and if we take concern for peace and justice as our starting point and common ground for our conversation with other believers, dialogue with people of other faiths (or study of other traditions) can be a means of both gaining greater meaning for our own lives and of removing the sufferings and fears that plague our modern world.

But there is one last roadblock to dialogue, one that especially confronts Christians. It has to do with the last guideline concerning no "final answers."

How Is Jesus Unique?

In presenting the four guidelines for dialogue in class, I usually find that most of the Christian students are right with me, until we get to the fourth guideline. There are always some students who ask, sometimes curiously, sometimes angrily, whether this last guideline about "no final answers" crashes head-on with one of the identifying characteristics of what it means to be a Christian. In both their Bible and in what has been standard teaching through the centuries, haven't Christians always held that Jesus is unique, the final word of God, the fullest expression of God's truth for all humankind? Joy, a third-year communications major and member of one of the prominent Baptist churches in Cincinnati, once put me against the wall with a flurry of questions: "The Bible says that Jesus is the one and only Son of God, the one Mediator between God and humanity (1 Tim 2:5), and that there is no other name by which people can be saved except the name of Jesus (Acts 4:12). Christians have always believed that he is the only Savior for everyone. That means that there isn't anyone greater than Jesus, that he is God's final and clearest and fullest Word. For me to dialogue with other religions the way you want me to would mean to deny something that Christians have always believed."

These are serious concerns that demand a serious response. The question of how to understand the uniqueness of Jesus in relation to other religions and other religious figures is an important, delicate, and, we must admit, a controversial issue. In the remainder of this chapter, all we can do is acquaint you with this discussion and invite you to do some thinking of your own. We will briefly review the traditional viewpoints about the uniqueness of Jesus and then present some recent suggestions as to how this uniqueness might be reinterpreted. As theologians put it, this is still a "disputed question." No one should think that he or she has the final answer.

The traditional understanding of how to understand the uniqueness of Jesus in relation to other faiths can be called the exclusivist model. This attitude characterized most of the history of the church, roughly from the fourth to the seventeenth centuries. It viewed Jesus as the one and only Savior and the Christian church as the one and only true religion. Therefore, as the ancient saying put it, "There is no salvation outside the church." Since Jesus is the only Savior and since he is to be found only in the church, everyone outside the church was going to have a rough time knowing God and making it to heaven. Though there have been some exceptions to this attitude, it has characterized the way most Christians look on followers of other faiths; it also provided the motivation for such great missionaries as Francis Xavier, who traveled to foreign lands in order to baptize as many souls as possible so as to save them from hell.

But gradually, as more and more of the "New World" became known to the old world of Europe, and as Christians became aware of the millions of people who through no fault of their own had never known Christ, they had to ask themselves how a God of love could pack off so many people to hell just because they hadn't been born in Europe. There developed a new model for understanding the uniqueness of Jesus and other religions, that of inclusivism. The basic ingredients of this model were formulated in the sixteenth century when the Council of Trent stated that people who had never heard of Jesus and been baptized could still be saved through a "baptism of desire" as long as they followed their consciences and lived moral lives. But it was in the twentieth century, particularly at the Second Vatican Council, that the inclusivist model was elaborated and endorsed as the acceptable, "official" model for Catholics, for approaching other religions. While it holds to Jesus as the only, or at least the clearest, way of finding salvation, it believes that the saving presence of Jesus and his Spirit can operate beyond the visible church and can be found in other religions, even though adherents to those religions do not realize it.

For this inclusivist model, there is much value in other religions, and it calls upon Christians to recognize this value and to dialogue with other believers. But in the end, these other religions are to be included in Christ and his church, for Christ remains the final and the normative expression of God's will for all peoples. The value and the truth found in other faiths is there in order to prepare them for recognizing God's final and full revelation in Jesus. So, while this model affirms the presence of

God in all religions, it insists that this presence is found fully and finally only in Jesus.

In recent years, some Christians and Christian theologians have been raising questions about this inclusivist model, whether it really allows for authentic dialogue and whether it is really consistent with what Jesus thought of himself. They are therefore exploring a new model for understanding the uniqueness of Jesus in relation to other religions. It has been called the pluralist model. These theologians want to continue to affirm the uniqueness and distinctiveness of Jesus as the Savior for all persons; but they want to be open to the possibility that Jesus may not be the only Savior for all persons. They want to recognize the possibility that God may be working in and through other religions and religious figures in a way similar to God's working in Jesus and Christianity. They suggest that Christians may have as much to learn from other religions as other religions can learn from Christianity.

Such a model, which no longer insists on the superiority or the "finality" of Jesus, is indeed quite new for Christian consciousness. Therefore, a Christian should not accept it too easily. In what follows, we will summarize the main reasons why some theologians feel that the pluralist model is still an authentically Christian model for following Jesus and understanding other religions.

First of all, pluralist theologians argue that just because something is startlingly new and seems to contradict previous teachings of the church does not necessarily mean that it is out of line. As we already pointed out, religion in general has to change if it is to stay alive, and Christianity, because it is a living religion, has changed its teachings and practices often. There was a time, for instance, when the church taught that slavery was permissible, that taking interest was not permissible, and that outside the church there was no salvation, so that "Jews and heretics" were bound for hell. On all these issues, there has been a roundabout change. Therefore, change, even drastic change, is not necessarily un-Christian.

But more directly to our point, the pluralist theologians suggest that when we look into the psychology of Christian faith, into what goes on that enables a person to become a follower of Jesus (since that's what "being Christian" essentially means), we find that it is not necessary to see or feel Jesus as the only or final Word of God. What brings persons to decide that it is worth their while to see the world as Jesus of Nazareth did, and to follow his example of loving one's neighbor and working for justice, is the experience and realization that God is really and truly present to them and speaking to them in and through this man of Nazareth. This is what brought the early Christians to call him the Son of God and Savior, the experience of God really present in him and as him; this same experience is what lies (or should lie) at the heart of Christian experience today. But note, it is an experience of God *really* present in Jesus. It is not an experience of God present *only* in Jesus. To say "really," one does not have to say "only."

Also, in experiencing the truth of Jesus' message, and the power and presence of God in that message, Christians feel in the depths of their hearts that this message can be good for all peoples of all times. They want to "go forth and teach all nations." In other words, they experience Jesus' message and meaning to be universal, that is, meaningful for everyone. Universality is essential to the experience Christians have of Jesus. But again, universal does not necessarily mean final or superior. When Christians experience Jesus they know for sure that this is "good news" for everyone. They do not know for sure, nor do they need to know for sure, that this is the only, or the last, or the best good news. The possibility (or reality) that there is other good news does not cancel out my commitment to the good news given to me.

Something similar is true of human relationships. When one decides to make the commitment of marriage, one has to be relatively sure that one's future spouse is really the good and beautiful person one experienced her or him to be. One does not have to know, nor can one know, that one's spouse is the best and most beautiful person in the world; nor does one have to know for sure that she or he was the only good and beautiful person that one could possibly marry. If people had to first be sure that "You're the most beautiful, intelligent, etc. man or woman," or "You're the only person I could marry," before they pronounced their wedding vows, there wouldn't be many people getting (or staying) married.

But all this is from the perspective of human psychology. As my friend Joy would ask, how does it square with what the Bible says? Theologians who follow the pluralist model would want to sharpen that question and ask how it squares with what Jesus said. Admittedly, as we will see in Part Three, it's not always easy to know precisely what Jesus said, since so many of his words were "interpreted" by the gospel writers. Still, most of the experts on the New Testament would agree that the heart of Jesus' message—what he was most concerned about—was not himself but what he called "the kingdom of God." This was Jesus' passion and the focus of his preaching; he wanted people to believe in and start working for the kingdom of God. This kingdom, as the scholars tell us, was both the future kingdom of heaven and a kingdom of love and justice and unity to be realized here on earth. This was what Jesus was all about, preaching and working for this kingdom, especially for those who needed it most: the poor, the sick, the outcasts of society.

After his death and resurrection, the followers of Jesus shifted the focus of their preaching from the kingdom to Jesus; they did so not simply to extol Jesus, but because they felt that preaching about Jesus was the best way to work for the kingdom. Still, the early Christian church became "Jesus-centered." While there were good reasons for this shift, we must remember that Jesus himself was "kingdom-centered." What was most important for him was not that people praised him above all others, but that they believed his message and worked for a society of love and justice. Being a Christian does not consist of insisting that Jesus is "numero uno," but in following Jesus in a life of concern for others. In fact, he said something to this effect when he told people that "Not those who say 'Lord, Lord,' but those who do the will of my heavenly Father" are his followers (Mt 7:21).

For pluralist theologians, this means that being faithful to Jesus today does not require Christians to hold him up as the only or the best or to put down other religious figures like Buddha or Muhammad; rather, being a faithful follower of Jesus means mainly to live his message of love and justice in one's life, to work for the kingdom of God. And if this can be done together with followers of Buddha and Muhammad, so much the better. After all, Jesus also said that "Those who are not against us, are with us." (Lk 9:50).

And yet we also have powerful statements in the Bible that do use the word or idea *only* when speaking of Jesus: "only begotten Son of God...No other name...only mediator between God and humanity...once and for all...." That kind of language, my friend Joy would insist, is pretty clear. To which the pluralist theologians respond, It's clear if taken literally; not so clear if taken in its context. They point out that the language about Jesus in the New Testament is a special kind of language; we do it a great disservice, and end up abusing it, when we try to turn it into a type of language it was not intended to be. According to Krister Stendahl, former dean of the Harvard Divinity School, statements about Jesus such as "only-begotten Son" or "no other name" are examples of what he calls "confessional" or "love language." It's the kind of language people use when they are excited about or in love with someone else; it's meant to express what they feel about that person and how they are committed to him or her. Such language is not meant to provide theological or philosophical definitions of who that person is.

Again, to use the example of marriage: In moments of deep feeling and intimacy, a husband or wife will easily and naturally say, "You are the most beautiful woman (man) in the world." In that situation of closeness, the statement is true; that's what the person feels. But in a philosophy class or a court of law in which one has to state "hard facts," the statement would not be true. Language is used in different contexts for different purposes. Its meaning depends on the way it is being used.

So, when the early Christians proclaimed that Jesus was the only mediator between God and humanity, they were stating how much this man had affected their lives and how he could also affect the lives of others; they were calling others to take Jesus as seriously as they had and to experience the healing and the energy in him that they had encountered. The main thing they wanted to say was that God was really present in Jesus for them and for all people. In their situation of deep feeling and excitement, in order to say really, they used words like "only" and "no other," just as spouses express the reality and depth of their love for each other by saying "only you."

The primary intent of all this "one and only" language about Jesus in the New Testament, therefore, was to say something positive about Jesus, not to say something negative about others. It was to extol Jesus as the presence of God, not to exclude or put down other people in whom God might also be present. Therefore, pluralist theologians conclude, for Christians today to use such statements as "There is salvation in no other name" as a means to put down Buddha or Muhammad is to abuse this language. Again, this means that one can be fully committed to Jesus and at the same time be open to and appreciative of Buddha.

Whether this pluralist model is an acceptable Christian model and whether Christians can understand the uniqueness of Jesus differently than they have in the past are questions that still have to be decided. Perhaps the best way of deciding them is for Christians to engage in dialogue with other religions as openly and honestly as they can. In dialogue, they will know Jesus more clearly.

In this chapter, we have looked at some facts and tried to draw a few conclusions from them. It's a fact that there have always been many religions and that, in all probability, there will continue to be many. We concluded that, from a Christian perspective, such a fact is God's will and that God may well be found, alive and active, in other religions. If this is so, then the religions of the world have to come together to start some serious talk and cooperation among themselves; this is especially urgent in light of the crises facing our modern world, crises that call to the religions for help.

But we recognized that dialogue between the religions is not, as college students might put it, "a piece of cake." It is complex. And it is dangerous, for in dialogue there is always either the unconscious inclination or the very conscious temptation for one religion to impose itself on the others. So we suggested that religions can best talk to and understand each other if they start with a common commitment to peace and justice, and if they follow some basic guidelines calling for both full commitment to one's own religion together with full openness to the possible truth and value in others. By engaging in such dialogue, Christians will find that they are not "demoting Jesus," but that they are being faithful to his vision of openness to and love of others.

If there is any truth to what we have said in this chapter, it means that there is something missing in the rest of this book. For the most part, the following chapters will deal with faith and theology from a Christian perspective. We've had to limit our perspective mainly because one can't do everything in one small book. But that limitation means that this book is essentially incomplete. To study religion, you can't study just one religion. As Max Müller told us, to know only one is to know none. The study of religion beckons one to become part of a dialogue of religions. What we have to say about faith and theology in the rest of these pages is meant to prepare Christian readers for such a dialogue. The next chapter will give you a taste of what that dialogue might be like.

QUESTIONS FOR REFLECTION AND DISCUSSION

1. Why do people nowadays know more about other religions than ever before?

2. Why are many people today coming to the conclusion that the many religions of the world are here to stay and that it is God's will that there be many religions?

3. What are some of the reasons why it seems that today dialogue among world religions is necessary?

4. What is relativism? Syncretism? And why are they opposed to authentic dialogue?

5. What is the danger in speaking about or proposing a common ground among all the different religions of the world?

6. What kind of a common ground (or common starting point) for interreligious dialogue was suggested in this chapter? Do you think it would work?

7. What are the three forms of dialogue proposed by the Asian bishops? Do you think that any one of them is more important than the others?

8. What are the ground rules for dialogue? Are there any that you feel you could not follow?

9. Describe the pluralist model for understanding other religions. Do you think this is an acceptable model for Christians?

SUGGESTED READINGS

Ariarajah, S. Wesley. *The Bible and People of Other Faiths*. Maryknoll, N.Y.: Orbis Books, 1989.

Coward, Harold. *Pluralism: Challenge to World Religions*. Maryknoll, N.Y.: Orbis Books, 1985.

D'Costa, Gavin. *Theology and Religious Pluralism: The Challenge of Other Religions*. London: Basil Blackwell, 1986.

Drummond, Richard Henry. *Toward a New Age in Christian Theology*. Maryknoll, N.Y.: Orbis Books, 1985.

Heim, S. Mark. *Is Christ the Only Way? Christian Faith in a Pluralistic World*. Valley Forge: Judson Press, 1985.

Hick, John. *God Has Many Names*. Philadelphia: The Westminster Press, 1982.

Hick, John, and Paul Knitter, eds. *The Myth of Christian Uniqueness: Toward a Pluralistic Theology of Religions*. Maryknoll, N.Y.: Orbis Books, 1987.

Hillman, Eugene. *Many Paths: A Catholic Approach to Religious Pluralism*. Maryknoll: N.Y.: Orbis Books, 1989.

Knitter, Paul. *No Other Name? A Critical Survey of Christian Attitudes Toward World Religions*. Maryknoll: N.Y.: Orbis Books, 1985.

Lochhead, David. *The Dialogical Imperative: A Christian Reflection on Interfaith Encounter*. Maryknoll, N.Y.: Orbis Books, 1988.

Oxtoby, Willard G. *The Meaning of Other Faiths*. Philadelphia: Westminster Press, 1983.

Panikkar, Raimundo. *Intra-Religious Dialogue*. Mahwah, N.J.: Paulist Press, 1978.

Smith, Wilfred Cantwell. *Toward a World Theology: Faith and the Comparative History of Religion*. Maryknoll, N.Y.: Orbis Books, 1989.

Swidler, Leonard, ed. *Toward a Universal Theology of Religion*. Maryknoll, N.Y.: Orbis Books, 1987.

Second Vatican Council: *Declaration of the Relationship of the Church to Non-Christian Religions*.

World Council of Churches. *Guidelines on Dialogue with People of Living Faiths and Ideologies*. Geneva: WCC, 1979.

CHAPTER EIGHT

Jesus and Buddha: A Conversation

This chapter will be an interlude in the flow of this book's themes. It is meant to give you a "taste of dialogue," a sample of what we were talking about in Chapter Seven: the complexity and the reward of exploring another religious tradition. To provide such a taste, we have to hit the happy medium between biting off too much and too little; we can't get bogged down in detail, but at the same time, we have to be able to feel where religious differences blend and where they clash.

To cover as much ground as possible, in as engaging a manner as possible, we invite you in this chapter to "listen in on" an imaginary conversation between Jesus and Buddha. (In discussing the chapter, you may want also to "butt in on" the conversation.) After all these centuries, they encounter each other for the first time somewhere in today's world, both of them genuinely open to and interested in each other's message, both of them, also, with a keen awareness of and concern about the "mess" our modern world is in.

When we call this an "imaginary" conversation, we don't mean "concocted." The following dialogue is based on what we know of the life-stories and the messages of Buddha and Jesus, and especially on what is actually taking place today in the growing dialogue between Buddhists and Christians throughout the world. We will also let the two religious leaders explain their teachings against the cultural and socio-economic background in which they lived: Palestine between 100 B.C.E. and 100 C.E. and northeast India around 500 B.C.E. Our main concern, however, is not that everything said by Buddha and Jesus in this conversation be historically accurate in every detail, but that it reflect the generally accepted "image" that Buddhists and Christians have of their founders. We are primarily concerned not about the Jesus or Buddha studied by historians but the Jesus or Buddha believed in by their followers. The "real" Jesus or Buddha is to be found not in history books or archaeological digs, but in the lives and faith of Christians and Buddhists.

Different Backgrounds—Similar Concerns

Jesus: I'm delighted that after all these centuries I finally have the chance to meet someone I've heard so much about, and who has helped so many people for so many centuries. I trust this meeting will be not only interesting but helpful for both of us.

Buddha: I, too, am happy and honored to meet you, for I look on you as one of the greatest spiritual masters of all times. Yet I approach this conversation not only out of curiosity and the desire to learn, but also in the hope that we can encourage our followers to work together in doing something about the great suffering that afflicts humans even more terribly, it seems, than when I first experienced the suffering of my people in India some twenty-five centuries ago.

Jesus: Yes, Lord Buddha, I suspect that the more you and I and our followers learn about each other, the better off both we and the world will be.

To introduce myself, the first thing I want to tell you is that I am not a Christian, but a Jew. I was born, raised, and remain a Jew. That means that I was brought up by my parents to believe in and feel the presence of Yahweh, or God. Yahweh, as you may know, is a Creator God who, we believe, brought forth this world out of love and who remains present in the history of all peoples, especially in the history of the Jewish people. So, right from the start, I believed in a God who is active in history. And, especially from the Jewish prophets, I learned that this God was not only a God of love but also of justice, a God who called people to oppose all forms of hatred and oppression. In fact, our Jewish people and religion began when God called us to rebel against the slavery that the pharaohs of Egypt had forced us into.

As I grew up, I came to feel that I had a very special relationship with this God, a relationship that enabled me to call God not just "Father," as my fellow Jews did, but "Abba," the word in my Aramaic language for "Dad." And from this special relationship, I came to realize that I had a special mission. I described that mission as one of announcing and calling people to believe in and work for the kingdom of God, which is a symbol for the kind of life and society that results when people believe in God and love each other and so allow the power of God to flow through them: a society built on respect, shared responsibility, and justice.

I felt a special urgency in letting my fellow Jews know about what God's kingdom really meant, since it seemed to me that many of the religious leaders of my time were not living up to what they were supposed to believe. There was much corruption in my religion. There were also many reform movements; one of the best known was a group called the Pharisees. In their effort to return the Jewish religion to its roots of faithfulness to God, I had much in common with them, though we also had our share of disagreements and even conflict. Still, I felt the Pharisees were not going far enough. I was calling people to an even more intense commitment to God's love and justice.

Buddha: I'm amazed! Even though I was born some four centuries before you in a distant and culturally different part of the world, I see striking similarities between us. In a sense, I, too, am not a Buddhist. I was born a Hindu, and though I moved beyond my native religion, I remained deeply influenced by and indebted to it. "Buddha" is really not my name; it was a title given to me by my followers. I was known as Gautama, my family name. Siddhartha was my given name.

So, my religious background was Hindu. That meant I was brought up to believe in the oneness or unity of all things in this world, a oneness based on the ultimate Brahman, the source of all being. Brahman did not so much create the world out of nothing, but let the world "emanate" or extend out of Brahman's own being. Thus, at the center of every being there is Brahman; as the Hindus put it, Brahman is Atman, which is the word they use for the individual soul or spirit of a person or animal. This means that the Universal Spirit is our own spirit. Or, as the classic Hindu belief has it: *Tat tvam asi*: "That (meaning Brahman) thou art." This makes all people and all living creatures (even cows!), in some sense, divine. So for Hindus, the Ultimate or God is not so much a deity that steps into history in special acts, but a divine energy that is always there, keeping things going as they are. The intent of Hinduism is not so much to bring about God's kingdom but to help people wake up to what they really are.

This is the beauty of Hindu beliefs. But like you, Lord Jesus, I saw gross corruptions in the way my native religion was being practiced. I suppose you can say that we were both religious reformers. In Hinduism then, as in the Judaism of your time, most of the trouble had to do with the religious leaders, the priests or Brahmins. They controlled religious practices and pretty much reduced them to mechanical rituals, which only they could perform and which they had to be paid for. There was also a strict hierarchy in society, developing into the caste system, which kept many people inferior to others and which told them that only after they were reincarnated hundreds of times could they realize their unity with Brahman. You had to be a Brahmin to realize full unity with Brahman; that, of course, excluded women. Given this state of corruption in Hinduism, there were many reformers at my time, too. And I learned a lot from them. But I too felt that more had to be done so that the truth of Hinduism and of all religion could be realized and lived.

Lord Jesus, I think there may be some significant differences in the family or social circumstances of our lives. I was born in a palace, to very well-to-do parents; my father was the equivalent of a feudal lord and he made sure I led a very protected life, with everything I wanted. At sixteen, as was the custom, I was married to a wonderful young woman named Yasodhara, and we had a son. It was in such lavish circumstances that I began to grow restless. On trips outside of our palace, as I confronted the realities of sickness, old age, and death, I realized the suffering that all peoples have to deal with. Something was wrong with my life, with life in general, and I wasn't getting any satisfactory answers from my religion. So, when I was 29, I left my family and palace and went to study with some of the holy men of the time. I spent some six years with them, following a life of study and penance. They helped me, but not enough. I left them to search further.

Jesus: Though I was not born into the rich class and never married, I don't think the other circumstances of your life were that different from mine. I was born in very poor circumstances, yes, and because of political circumstances, my parents and I were for a time refugees in Egypt. But when we returned to Israel when I was still an infant, we settled down into what you might call a middle-class life in Nazareth; my father had a job as a carpenter—he was luckier than the hundreds of unemployed people of the time. In my dissatisfaction with the religious state of affairs, I, too, studied under one of the best known holy men of the time, John the Baptizer. Though I learned much from him, I, too, felt that what he was about was not enough. Like you, I set out on my own when I was about 30 years old.

Buddha: But when you left John the Baptizer, did you have a pretty clear idea of what you wanted to do, that is, of who God or Yahweh was for you, and of what the Kingdom of God meant?

Jesus: Of course, things became clearer as I went along, but yes, when I started preaching after I left John, I had a clear sense of what God my Father was calling me to do.

Buddha: When I left the holy men I had been studying with, I didn't have such clarity. But I did have a sense of how I had to continue my search. I decided to follow what I later called "the Middle Way"—a path between luxurious living (as in my palace), on the one hand, and rigorous penance and religious practices (as with the holy men) on the other. I would be neither too lax nor too rigorous. So I settled myself under a big fig tree near the city of Gaya and began to meditate. I had a sense, an assurance, that here is where my eyes would be opened. And they were. I experienced what I and my followers call Enlightenment. It was a deep spiritual experience in which I realized what reality really is, what I and all creatures really are, and how we are to live our lives. It was an experience of overwhelming peace and happiness, in which I felt myself at one with the world and the entire cosmos, an experience in which I both lost myself and found myself, and felt an immense concern for all living beings. When I rose from my place of Enlightenment, I was resolved to share the experience I had had with others. That's what I did, traveling around India, for the next forty-five years.

Jesus: I traveled throughout Palestine trying to share what I had realized. But I was able to do so for only a few years. I think the difference in the length of our preaching careers has to do with the differences between the social-political situations of our lives. The Palestine of my days was a land torn by unrest, poverty, oppression. There was an occupying army in our midst; we Jews were a subservient colony of the mighty Roman empire. What made matters especially painful was that the Romans were carrying out their program of exploitative taxation and land appropriation through the Jewish aristocracy, which included many from the classes of priests and lawyers. Our fellow Jews were collaborating with our oppressors, and were growing rich in the process! Thus, in the Jewish society of my times, there was an expanding class of poor, sick, unemployed, landless farmers, widows, and children without support. My vision of a kingdom of justice and love and my words of encouragement and "good news" (which is what "gospel" means) were directed especially to these people, which meant that what I had to say was "bad news" for those who were abusing their power and authority. In fact, this is what led to my execution on a cross: I got into trouble with the Roman and Jewish authorities; they accused me of stirring up trouble, of fomenting rebellion. While I would not call myself a rebel—I did not join the Zealots, the violent revolutionaries of the time—still, I called for a more just and a more egalitarian way of living together based on belief in a loving and just God. For this, I was done away with.

Buddha: The image of you on the cross, Lord Jesus, has always been quite difficult for me and my followers to understand; what you have just explained is a great help. The political and social world in which you lived in Palestine was quite different from mine in India five centuries earlier. Mine was a period of unrest and of transition from a splintered tribal system to the formation of republics and empires; this development gave rise to large cities and to a new merchant or middle class. My preaching about the value of personal responsibility and of individual freedom, and my insistence that all people—not just the high class Brahmin priests—can achieve spiritual greatness and be enlightened found ready ears among the merchants who were trying to establish their place in a rigid social system. Kings also looked upon my message of mutual caring as a moral foundation for their new societies. Clearly, my message of the spiritual equality of all classes and both sexes was a severe criticism of the caste system and good news for the poorer classes; still, contrary to your experience, I received substantial support from the well-to-do and political rulers, even though I did not hesitate to warn kings that if they did not rule according to the Truth (or what I called the "Dharma"), they could be deposed.

So I never got into the kind of trouble you did. In fact, after my forty-five years of preaching and traveling around northern India, I died a peaceful death, surrounded by my disciples. The differences between us are clear in the two main images by which we have been remembered through the centuries: you hanging painfully on the cross, and I seated serenely under the meditation tree.

Jesus: Although the differences between the cross and the tree are clear, I don't think these differences are contradictory in the sense that they necessarily exclude each other. They may be complementary; they may help to balance each other. To explore whether that might be so, I think we have to talk about how each of us saw the "big problem" or root cause of humankind's difficulties.

The Main Problem

Jesus: For me, the most pressing problem—what bothered me most as I looked around my world in Palestine—was that there were so many suffering people. As the gospels say of me, I "had pity on the crowds," people wandering around without a sense of direction, feeling helpless in their poverty or sickness or sense of abandonment by society, and even by God. There were many nights when I went out to the desert just to cry and pray about what I saw all around me.

Buddha: Here I think we are in agreement. As I mentioned, what propelled me on to my religious search was the awareness of human suffering. In fact, in my first sermon after I was enlightened, I summarized my whole message in the Four Noble Truths, the first of which is that "dukkha," or suffering, afflicts every person and has to be confronted. In the second Noble Truth I presented my diagnosis. Suffering, I realized, was caused by "tanha," selfish desire. To remove suffering, therefore, the Third Noble Truth states that we have to remove selfish desire. And to do that, according to the Fourth Noble Truth, I invited people to try out the path I was preaching.

But I went on to explain that there is a reason why people get caught in the quicksand of selfishness; and this gets at the root of the human problem. I think it is *ignorance,* what I call "avidya." People don't know what they really are. They think they are separate individuals — each having to achieve happiness for themselves. According to what I saw in my enlightenment, that's wrong. We are not "selves." In fact, that's how I defined human beings; we are "anattas" or "no-selves." By that I meant that we humans are not "islands unto ourselves" or individual billiard balls that bounce into each other; rather, each of us is a pattern of energy that must interact with other patterns in order to stay alive and grow. We are, in other words, part of each other. That's how I saw the whole world, all reality, as an interrelated, always changing pattern of activities, each activity or "person" dependent on all the others. I called this "dependent co-origination"; we originate and live in dependence on each other. Once people can realize that, they can really start living.

Jesus: Well, I certainly agree with you, Lord Buddha, that selfishness is the cause of the mess people get themselves into. But our diagnoses seem to be different. I think the cause of this selfishness is a lack of faith or a lack of experience of God. People don't feel or realize that they are all children of God and that it is by loving this God and each other that they can find true happiness in this life and in the next. Because they don't know or feel this God, they become excessively concerned about themselves and their own security. Everybody wants to be "number one." And here we have the cause of the world's sufferings; the hatred and fighting and oppression that are part of human history are caused by human beings' refusal or inability to reach out of themselves in genuine love for others. So while you summarized your teaching in the Four Noble Truths, I summarized mine in the Two Great Commandments: Love your God with your whole heart, and love your neighbor just as much as you love yourself.

Buddha: I agree that people don't love each other. But I think the reason for this is not a lack of belief in God but an ignorance of what they really are. Once they can see what they really are, they will act differently.

Jesus: Maybe we're not so far apart. I, too, would say that people are selfish and loveless because they don't realize who they are. But I'd add that who they really are are children of God. You would say they are really "no-selves." Might these two ideas be pointing in the same direction? Also, when you say that once people "see" or "understand" rightly, they will act rightly, I'm not so sure. I think people do selfish things even when they know they are selfish. This is because our human nature is weighed down with what can be called "sinful" tendencies. By that I mean that within the heart of each of us there lurks the inclination to be self-centered and to use others for our own benefits. We need help to overcome that inclination, help from God. It's not just a matter of coming to understand things differently.

Buddha: I think you misunderstood me; or I wasn't clear enough. When I say that people will act differently after they are enlightened and understand themselves differently, I'm not talking about a type of intellectual knowledge, the kind you find in school or in books. I'm talking about a seeing or understanding that takes hold of your very being, that gets inside you and energizes you. Maybe what I'm talking about is, in a practical sense, not that different from what you feel to be "God's help." I just wouldn't call it that.

It seems to me that to clarify what we're talking about, we have to discuss what you mean by "faith" and I by "enlightenment"—or, what you mean by "God" and I by "Nirvana."

Solutions: God and Nirvana

Buddha: But before we take up the deeper questions of God and Nirvana, there's an area concerning the practice of religion where, I think, we are in full agreement. Both of us were unhappy about the religions we grew up in; they had become too mechanical, too legalistic, too external. For many Jews and Hindus of our times, religion was something "outside" of themselves; it wasn't something that they owned as their own, something that came out of their own experiences. People were "doing" rather than "feeling." They were obeying rather than responding. Religion for many of your fellow Jews had become mainly a matter of observing rules and regulations rather than feeling the presence of Yahweh. For many of my fellow Hindus, the main business of religion was focused on performing the rituals of sacrifice instead of experiencing their own Enlightenment.

Jesus: So true. I felt that many of the Jewish leaders had turned the practice of following Yahweh into a set of rules and observations; they were using their religion and their authority as a cover-up and tool for their own greed and cooperation with the Romans. I once told them that they had turned my Father's house, the temple, into a trading place and den of thieves. Yes, both of us wanted to bring religion and the experience of religion back to the people, into their own hearts and lives.

Buddha: That was the main intent of my preaching, that people can and must have their own experience of Enlightenment. It didn't matter whether they were high caste or low caste, male or female (most of my contemporaries thought that women were incapable of Enlightenment)—they could all experience Nirvana. "Be lamps unto yourselves. Don't be dependent on books and teachers," I often told them.

Jesus: Yes, but though we agree that religion must be based on a person's own experience, I think we were both calling people to different experiences. You talk about Nirvana; I, about God. This would mean, it seems, that we both had different solutions to the problem of human suffering and selfishness.

For me, what I learned from my Jewish tradition became a living reality: God was actually present in my life. In all that I did and confronted, I felt the power of this God, loving me and calling me to love others; God was living God's life in me; I felt I was the action of God, loving and doing justice. So, I came to realize that if people would wake up to this God, if they would believe in this Father and feel God's love and call to justice, they would automatically feel differently about themselves and about others. Feeling loved, they would love, and that means they would try to promote justice and remove the sufferings of their fellow persons. Faith in God, and the experience of God's empowerment that faith brings, would make it possible to overcome the innate selfishness we all struggle with. What is impossible for humans by themselves would be possible with God: to love other human beings as they love themselves.

Buddha: But just how would this work? It sounds a little like magic. Believe in God and you'll automatically be able to love others? Does the power of God take over the person's life?

Jesus: No, it's definitely a two-way street. I feel that human beings can't get their lives together without God; but neither does God take over and do everything for them. Human beings must respond. In a sense, while humans need God, God also needs humans. This is something we Jews have always believed. Later on, my followers argued about the necessity of faith and good works. God and faith in God may come first, but there also have to be "good works"—human response and effort.

Buddha: So the solution, or, in your terms, the "salvation," you bring to humanity is this faith experience of a loving God who enables us to love and work for justice?

Jesus: To be precise, it's not just the experience. It's the living out of that experience together with other people. Salvation for Christians is to experience *together* this God of love and justice, to form a community of people who genuinely care about each other (my community came to be known as "church"), a community that is also active in this world, trying to transform the world by replacing hatred, oppression, and war with love, justice, and peace. It's an experience that brings forth a confidence that by caring for each other and working for justice, we are building a community that will last beyond our physical death and beyond the life of this planet.

So, "salvation" for me is to bring people to an experience that enables them to act and to trust, even in the face of failure and death. This was the reality and the message of my resurrection: If my disciples follow my example of letting God love and work for justice through them, such a life will bring forth fruits of greater life and happiness for themselves and for others, even when such a life of love demands that they give up their lives. I once told my disciples that only those people who are willing to give up their lives in love will find their lives and really know how to live. When I faced execution, I realized that I had to practice what I preached.

Buddha: I understand much better now. And I can feel the power and truth in your words and example. Still, I would go in a different direction. To be honest with you, I'm very wary about speaking of God. In fact, I'm wary about using a lot of words when it comes to what you call religious experience. I wanted people to have the experience, to resolve their suffering, rather than to do a lot of talking. I once told the parable of the man shot with a poison arrow. As he lay dying on the road, some friends found him and tried to help; but he kept asking them who shot the arrow, where was the person standing, why did the person do it, what kind of arrow, and what kind of poison it was. His friends scolded and reminded him that such questions were not what really mattered. His main concern should be to get the arrow out, stop the pain, and save his life, not to think about a lot of questions. That's my point. I didn't want to occupy my time with questions about the existence of God, who God is, how the world was created, whether there is life after death. I wanted people to have the kind of experience that would enable them to deal with suffering and live fully.

So, although I never denied the existence of God—I wouldn't want to do that—I didn't really talk about God. I didn't want to for two reasons. First, I realized that what I experienced in Enlightenment was something that is beyond all words or definitions; I felt that to name it is to lose it. Second, I saw all too clearly and sadly that once people name and define God, they tend to "own" God, that is, to use the definition of God for their own satisfaction or benefit. How many wars have been fought to defend the right way of believing in God!

Therefore I directed all my energies to helping people to have the experience I had. The "Eightfold Path" that I taught boils down to three recommendations: 1) Take my advice seriously and try it out. 2) Don't harm any living creature; if you do that, following my advice won't work. 3) You've got to meditate, that is, take time every day to stop your normal thinking and to "feel" reality and yourself for what you really are. (We don't have time right now to go into the what and how of meditation.) I felt that if people followed my advice and example they would come, gradually or maybe suddenly, to the experience of Enlightenment. I referred to this experience as Nirvana, which really is a name to say that no name fits: it means "blowing out," as in blowing out a candle. Nirvana is the experience of the blowing out of our selfishness and our desire to possess things. Some of my followers later also called it "Emptiness" or "Nothing," to stress that Nirvana is empty of all neat definition and is "nothing," not a thing that can be pinned down here or there and then defined.

Jesus: But, Lord Buddha, is Nirvana real? Does it exist?

Buddha: People used to ask me that question. My answer is simple: If Nirvana weren't real, Enlightenment wouldn't happen. Nirvana is an experience of reality, of the way things really are, of the way you really are. Nirvana points to the very real experience of the whole world and all reality as a unified and wonderfully interrelated process, and of oneself as an integral part of that process. It's an experience of belonging to, of being part of or simply being identified with, a process or whole that is beautifully interwoven and constantly changing. The experience of Nirvana, which, as I said, may come in a "big dose" or as a growing awareness, enables persons to overcome their concern for themselves, their selfishness, and to feel and act as part of the universe and of all other living beings. As you experience Nirvana, you can "let go" and let yourself flow more easily and creatively with all that happens in your life, the good and the bad. You are enabled both to accept things and to work with them, not against them.

So this is what I would call salvation: to experience the reality of Nirvana. It's an experience of the present moment. I really didn't have much to say about the future, either the future of this world or of an afterlife. For me, "salvation" is all here, right now. The present moment is the only moment that matters. One must be fully present to the "now" of life. I did point out that once one begins the path to Enlightenment, one will also, necessarily and automatically, feel "karuna," a great compassion for all beings. This would be close to the love that you talked about, Lord Jesus. In Enlightenment, one feels oneself to be part of everyone and everything else. One naturally cares for others just as one cares for oneself. It's close to, if not the same thing as, your "love your neighbor as yourself."

Jesus: Except that you leave out what I called the first commandment: to love God. Again, though there are similarities in the practical results of our teachings, Lord Buddha, I see clear and perhaps important differences. When I speak of God, it's because for me the Ultimate is something personal, a Someone rather than a Something. In calling the Ultimate God, I feel that there is a relationship between me and the Ultimate; and this relationship is so personal that I can call the Ultimate "Father" or "Mother." For you, the Ultimate as Nirvana or Emptiness is impersonal; it's more the experience of being part of an all-inclusive energy or process than a relationship with a Someone.

Buddha: I think you're right, Lord Jesus. And because of these contrasts between God and Nirvana, there are other significant differences in how we call our followers to live out their experiences. You call people to open themselves to God's power and grace, admitting that their own powers are insufficient; though I recognize that there is no such thing as an "individual" in the first place, I do stress self-effort and taking responsibility for oneself. Also, you put a great stress on the future, on working for the full coming of what you call God's kingdom in this world and in the next world; my whole focus is on the present, on accepting and dealing with what is now, without thinking or worrying about the future. And then, you seem to stress community much more than I. Though my followers did form what we call the "sangha," or community of Buddhist monks and laypersons, your "church" seems to be more important and more tightly organized than what I had in mind.

Jesus: Yes, the differences are evident and must be taken seriously. And yet...and yet, I feel that they are the kind of differences that enable and require us to talk more rather than part paths.

Buddha: I definitely have the same feeling. Allow me to try to say what I think is the fundamental reason for this feeling. Even though there are such clear differences in what you say about God and what I say about Nirvana, I have the suspicion that they are both speaking about the same Mystery. Now I know that to appeal to "Mystery" is the kind of thing we Buddhists like to do. We have the saying that all the words we use are but "fingers pointing to the moon." The moon is never to be identified with the fingers pointing to it. So I think that "God" and

"Nirvana" are fingers pointing to the moon of Mystery. Of course, when I say "mystery" I don't mean something that is beyond or removed from our lives (as the moon is removed from the earth). I'm talking about something that is closer to ourselves than we are to ourselves. I'm talking about something in which, as one of your followers put it, we live and move and have our being.

Jesus: Yes, that makes sense. Both my Jewish tradition, as well as my own experience, tell me that no word, image, or idea can ever capture the full reality of Yahweh. That's what you remind me and my followers of when you don't want to use the name God or when you hesitate to refer to Mystery as personal; you are telling us that our words or names are never the full reality and therefore should not be made into definitions. Mystery is always more than what we mean by "Father" or "Spirit" or "Creator." But at the same time, I think I have a reminder for you: that most of us do need "fingers" to point to the moon! Words and names and symbols are important; even Nirvana or Emptiness are "ideas." Such symbols for Mystery can be very helpful, even necessary, for enabling people to have and live out the kinds of experiences we ourselves have had and want to share with others. The important point is not to make any of our words or symbols into absolute or one-and-only ways of talking about Mystery. Might we agree on this?

Buddha: I think we can. I also see another area where you have an important reminder for me: In your recognition of what you call God's grace, or what some of my followers have termed "other-power" in distinction to "self-power," you help me realize that although it is essential that we make our own efforts and have the experience of Nirvana or Mystery *for* ourselves, still we really can't do it *by* ourselves. We have to do it, but we can't do it alone—something like that. The power that we find in ourselves has to be a power that is greater than ourselves, and a power that others help us discover. I think I was talking about something similar when I spoke of the "dharma" as the power of truth that I wanted to awaken in people. It's a power that is both our own and yet more than our own. Does that make sense?

Jesus: To me, it certainly does. Just as a moment ago, I found myself talking a bit like a Buddhist, now you sound a little like a Christian! There's another area where you have pushed me to a clearer insight. With your stress on the present moment, you are reminding me and my followers that there is a danger in becoming so concerned about the future that we miss the potential of the present. I would say we miss the presence of God in the moment. This is a real danger. How often do people become so wrapped up in their "plans" for the future, in the way things will have to be tomorrow, that they lose touch with all that's going on in the present? With your insistence that we have to be fully immersed in the present moment, you are telling us that the future is really not separated from the present, that the future must grow out of what is happening now. Only if our plans for the future are based on and make use of the present will they work. We have to be fully attuned to the present, even those aspects of the present that we don't like, if we are going to make the future better. Does that make sense to you, Lord Buddha?

Buddha: I wouldn't use words that distinguish present and future, but I see your point. And I feel that in this regard you have a reminder for me and my followers. In stressing that there is only this present moment and that we have to accept and live fully in it, Buddhists can end up with what we might call a "passive acceptance." Now that I think about it, in stressing that we must accept the moment, I intended an "active acceptance," a living in the moment that will enable us to act with it and to change with it. We must change and the moment must change. If living in the moment simply means accepting the status quo and not doing something about the sufferings that people are enduring, that wouldn't be Buddhism at all. I think your concern about the future helps us Buddhists recognize this and guard against passivity and lack of real involvement in this world.

Changing This World

Jesus: This brings us to a more general area of possible agreement between us. Don't both of us, after all is said and done, want our followers to bring this world closer to what I called "the kingdom of God," that is, a world of greater unity, cooperation, peace, and justice? Excuse me for putting it that way. I fear that even raising this question might be an imposition of Christian viewpoints on you Buddhists. Still, I think that on this point there is a basis for agreement between us.

Buddha: I see what you're saying, and I think I agree. I realize that even though both of us have our differences about God and Nirvana, we are both in fundamental agreement concerning what happens to persons, how they live their lives after they experience God or Nirvana. When persons start to realize and feel who God is or what Nirvana is, they sense a deep-running peace together with a love or compassion for their fellow beings. I stressed this in my teachings, and my followers stressed it even more when they developed the ideal of the "Bodhisattva." They pointed out that I was a Bodhisattva and that every follower of Buddha must strive to be a Bodhisattva.

Jesus: Lord Buddha, you forgot that I don't speak your language. What's a Bodhisattva?

Buddha: Sorry. Bodhisattvas are persons who, after they attain Nirvana, don't keep it for themselves but return to the real and messy world to share it with others. I told the story of four men lost in the desert, dying of thirst. They come upon an oasis surrounded by a high wall. All of them scale the wall and behold green trees, fruit, and, especially, flowing water. Three of them jump over and drink and splash. One returns to the desert to let his companions know of what he found. That person is a Bodhisattva, a true Buddhist.

So, Lord Jesus, both of us insisted that one can't experience God or Nirvana without loving or having compassion for others. In this we agree. And I suppose that one can't really love or have compassion for one's neighbor without trying to help them meet all their needs. That certainly means to feed them if they're starving or to free them if they're being oppressed. And in doing that, we have to change and improve this world. So, yes, we would both agree on this.

Jesus: Lord Buddha, excuse me if I sound like I'm criticizing you, but it seems to me that, as you admitted a little while ago, you have not stressed sufficiently the need to get involved in this world and to act to change it for the better. You spoke earlier about the danger of passivity, of just going along with the flow of things. I think I may have been a little more aware of that danger than you were. Like the Jewish prophets who preceded me, I stressed the need of taking history seriously, of *acting* in history, of loving one's fellows and working for justice where there is suffering, slavery, and oppression. My followers and I genuinely believe and hope that this world can be different. Or, I should say, that's the hope I want my followers to have.

Buddha: Lord Jesus, don't worry about criticizing me. Our conversations wouldn't be worthwhile, or very interesting, if we couldn't speak honestly and point out what we think each other's weaknesses are. And here, I do think you're right. We Buddhists, like our fellow Hindus, have perhaps not always been sufficiently concerned about this world and this history. But let me point out that such concern has not been entirely lacking. And, as some of my followers today are trying to point out to their fellow Buddhists and to you Christians (excuse me if I call you a Christian!), maybe we Buddhists go about our involvement in the world and our efforts to improve it in a different way, or from a different basis, than you do. If I may put it this way, you enter the historical process from the front door; we go through the back. What I mean is that, yes, I said that history was not real, for the only thing that really exists is this present moment, not the past or future. In a sense, therefore, history doesn't exist. But can you see that once one is freed from having to worry about what one did in the past or what one has to do in the future, once one doesn't have to worry about where history is going, then one is freed to really focus on this moment, and that means that one is really freed to *act* in history?

By freeing my followers from desiring to change history in a certain way, I am enabling them to engage in history with full freedom and spontaneous creativity. You stress the need for planning for the future: You call it the kingdom of God and your program of action is one of love and justice. That's fine. But I would remind you of another kind of danger, that of clearly-drawn plans. When we have "clear" plans and an "urgent" program, we easily become attached to our plans and programs and so lose our flexibility and openness. And, if I may offer you a gentle criticism, Christians have all too often forced their fixed plans on others. I stress the need for not being attached to any one plan, for not worrying about the future, for being fully responsive to the moment, fully in tune with reality, and then acting as one feels fit.

Jesus: I think I see what you mean. Your criticisms are, as they say today, "right on." Again, I feel we are trying to attain a similar goal but by different means.

Buddha: Yes, but the means are not only different; they are complementary. What you just said gave me the idea of putting what I'm trying to express in a different way. You stress *action* and *love*, the need to be involved in this world, to do God's will of loving and working for justice. I stress *quiet* and *wisdom*, the need to meditate and to see the way things really are so as to be in tune with them—in your terms, to be in tune with God's will.

Jesus: Yes, I see precisely what you mean. Action and quiet, or love and wisdom, are brother and sister, two sides of the same coin. They need each other. When Christians stress the need to act and change the world, we have an important reminder for you Buddhists, namely, that there's a real danger of getting so wrapped up in meditation and religion that one forgets one's fellow beings. But then you Buddhists remind us Christians that unless all our actions and plans to change the world are coming out of a deep experience of wisdom, of union with what we call God, then all our actions are either going to be misdirected by our own self-seeking or they are going to peter out for lack of sustained energy.

Buddha: Yes, action must be rooted in wisdom. And wisdom must flow into action. To truly help the world, you must be one with God or tuned to Nirvana. But if you are not trying to love others and change the world, you do not really know God or Nirvana. This, I think, is what we are telling each other, and what our followers would do well to understand!

Different Roles?

Jesus: Looking back over what we have talked about so far, it seems that we have reached a sort of agreement-in-difference concerning our teachings. By that I mean not an agreement *despite* our differences, but an agreement *because of* our differences, an agreement that comes out of and affirms our differences.

Buddha: Yes, you might call it a "unity of opposites." But this deals with what you and I taught. I wonder if such agreement-in-difference is possible in regard to what our followers have said about us, in regard to the role that you and I have come to play for Christians and Buddhists through the centuries. I guess what I'm asking is this: If there is a working compatibility between what we taught, is there a similar compatibility between who we are and the roles we play for our followers?

Jesus: I think you are raising some rather touchy questions, perhaps more touchy for our followers than for us. The problem you're getting at is this: In view of the way you and I have been defined by our followers, or, in view of the "titles" given to each of us, it seems that we exclude each other. At least, we are in competition. My followers call me Lord, Christ (which means Messiah), Savior of the World, Word of God, only-begotten Son of God.

Buddha: And among my disciples I am known as the Supremely Enlightened One (Buddha), the One Who Has Arrived (Tathagata), the Lord of the World (Bhagavad), the Leader of the Caravan. Yes, it seems that there might be some tension here.

Jesus: But let's look at how these titles came about and what they mean. You may not realize, as many Christians do not realize, but I myself never used most of the titles that I now have; they were given to me by my followers, after my death. When I point this out, I am not saying that I'm against these titles or that I wouldn't have used them myself if my situation had been similar to that of my followers in the first generation of the Christian community. You can say that these titles were given to me later because they were the result of a process my followers had to go through before they could understand who I really was. I had to first finish my life and mission, and that includes my death, before they could realize what I meant for them; this was especially the case when they felt my presence among them even after I died. So you see, it was by experiencing how I had affected their lives, before and especially after my death, that my followers came to realize who I really was *for them*: Lord, Savior, Son of God.

Because I gave them the ability to live their lives with a sense of peace and purpose that they did not have before, or because through me they were saved from their state of hopelessness and oppression, they called me Savior. Because in me, they found the one who as Jews they had been waiting for, they called me Messiah or Christ. Because in me they felt the presence of God as never before, because in seeing me, they saw God, they called me the Son of God; in my humanity they encountered divinity. They knew that in me, humanity and divinity were somehow reconciled. I was, in other words, their Lord, the focus of their lives, where they found meaning, direction, energy, and hope.

Buddha: A similar process took place during and especially after my life. At first, my disciples insisted that I was only a teacher, but an extremely important teacher, whom all peoples had to take seriously if they were to be enlightened. And so they called me Buddha, the Enlightened One, or Arhat, the worthy one. But already, some 200 years after my death, because of the role I continued to play in their lives, my followers were already giving me titles or attributes that raised me above other mortals and, in a sense, glorified me. In what is called the "Mahayana" tradition of Buddhism, I am not only a supreme teacher, I am also called a Savior, the one who continues to help to Enlightenment anyone who turns to me. All of these titles, like the ones you bear, express how people experienced me, what I meant for them, how I enabled them to live their lives with a meaning and purpose they didn't have before. But notice, Lord Jesus, I never was given the title "Son of God." The reason for this is that my followers simply don't talk about God as you and your disciples do.

Jesus: Even though these titles are different in that they are saying different things about us, I think there is one way in which they are saying the same thing. They are all declaring that you and I have profoundly affected and transformed the lives of those who follow us and that we continue to do so even today. In a very real sense, we both are still present to people today. This is something that is particularly important for me and my followers: I do live on with and in them; I am present in their gatherings and in their individual lives; they can trust me and feel me living in them. This is what belief in my resurrection is all about: I continue to live in the "body" of my followers and the church. St. Paul, one of my most enthusiastic disciples, could even say, "I don't live any more; Christ lives in me!"

Buddha: My followers certainly never said that I rose from the dead. That's something that, it seems to me, is very unique to you and Christianity. But it's interesting that they did come to say that I was still present in their lives even after I died. This was the case especially among the Mahayana Buddhists who came to say that I had three different "bodies." They were using the word "body" in a broad sense, as a way of being present. On the basis of their ongoing experience as Buddhists, they came to realize that besides the physical body that I had when I was alive and by which I was present to anyone who could see or hear me, I also could be said to have an "essence body," by which I was fully present to or identified with the Absolute, which we Buddhists refer to as Nirvana, Emptiness, Dharma. But I also had what they called an "enjoyment body," by which I continue to be present to anyone who turns to me in faith and trust. Again, it's a symbolic way of saying that I continue to be part of their lives. And I really love that expression of your friend, St. Paul. It's quite similar, I think, to some of my followers, who say that when they are enlightened, they become Buddhas and that they realize their "Buddha-nature," which is the potential of all human beings.

Jesus: These similarities are very interesting and we have to take them seriously. But I think there is a further, stark difference in what our followers said about us after our deaths. It has to do with what you just said about your followers becoming Buddha. When my disciples called me Son of God or Savior they also put important adjectives before those titles: they announced that I was the "only-begotten" Son of God and the "once and for all" Savior. Even though they certainly believed that all people are the daughters and sons of God, for them, I was a special child of God, in a relationship that could not be repeated in any other human being. I'm sorry, but this conviction that I am unique as the Son of God is an essential part of Christianity.

Buddha: You're right, Lord Jesus. There are clear differences here. Even though my followers did say some very "superlative" things about me, they did come to recognize that I was not the only Buddha. There can be others; there should be others. I was Gautama the Buddha. Later, among the Mahayana Buddhists, other Buddhas were identified: Amida Buddha, who vowed to help all suffering people before he entered the fullness of Nirvana; Avalokitesvara, who began as a Bodhisattva attendant to Amida and later became an omnipresent being; Maitreya Buddha, who has not yet come and is still to appear in this world. The purpose of all these Buddhas is to lead others to become Bodhisattvas, enlightened helpers of others. So, while you are the only Son of God, I am but one of many Buddhas.

But you know, Lord Jesus, I'm comfortable with our differences on this point. And maybe you can be, too. I have no problem with your followers proclaiming that you are the "only" Son of God or Savior. For me, that means that there is something "unique" in you; you have something to say and make clear to all peoples that can't be found elsewhere. There is no other Son or Daughter of God like you, if I may use your Christian terms. But at the same time, I would hope that you can accept me as a "Buddha," as someone who also has something vitally important to tell all people, something that we feel can be told through many different Buddhas. Your insistence on "unique Son of God" and our insistence on "many Buddhas" do not have to absolutely contradict each other, different though they really are.

Jesus: That's something my followers will want to think

about more carefully. I'm sure they will.

But in the meantime, what is not only worthwhile but necessary is to affirm and to build on what we have realized today: that the messages that you and I have brought to this world, different though they may be, can both make a difference in this world if people would really live these messages. If only there were more Christians in this world who experienced the presence of a God of love in their lives and who were therefore working for greater love and justice among all peoples. And if only there were more Buddhists who experienced the interrelatedness of Nirvana and so were living lives of compassion for all beings. The world would definitely be better.

Buddha: And what today's conversation makes clear for me is that we can help each other to spread our messages more clearly and broadly. If we can learn from each other, the world will learn more from both of us. I hope our followers can see that.

In the meantime, Lord Jesus, after this long conversation, may I invite you to taste some delicious tea used by my followers in Japan.

Jesus: I'd be delighted. But you have to try this loaf of my favorite Italian bread!

Questions for Reflection and Discussion

1. What are some of the similarities and differences in the life and historical context of Jesus and Buddha?

2. How do Buddha and Jesus differ in their diagnosis of the main cause of humanity's suffering?

3. What are the principal differences between Jesus' experience of God and Buddha's experience of Nirvana?

4. Why did Buddha not want to talk about God?

5. What might Jesus and Christians learn from Buddha's experience of Nirvana? And what might Buddha and Buddhists learn from Jesus' experience of God?

6. Regarding how to respond to the world, Jesus stressed action and love, while Buddha stressed quiet and wisdom. How are these attitudes different? And how are they complementary?

7. Why/how were different titles or roles attributed to Jesus and Buddha after their deaths? Compare some of these titles.

8. Jesus is said to be the *only* Savior or Son of God. How does this compare to Buddha's titles? And is it an obstacle to dialogue between Christians and Buddhists?

SUGGESTED READINGS

Abe, Masao. *Zen and Western Thought*. Honolulu: University of Hawaii Press, 1985.

Amore, Roy. *Two Masters, One Message: The Lives and Teachings of Gautama and Jesus*. Nashville: Abingdon, 1978.

Berrigan, Daniel, and Thich Nhat Hanh. *The Raft Is Not the Shore: Conversations Toward a Buddhist/Christian Awareness*. Boston: Beacon Press, 1975.

Cobb, John B., Jr. *Beyond Dialogue: Toward a Mutual Transformation of Christianity and Buddhism*. Philadelphia: Fortress Press, 1982.

Corless, Roger, and Paul Knitter, eds. *Buddhist Emptiness and the Christian Trinity*. Mahwah, N.J.: Paulist Press, 1990.

Drummond, Richard. *Gautama the Buddha: An Essay in Religious Understanding*. Grand Rapids, Mich.: Eerdmans, 1974.

Dumoulin, Heinrich. *Christianity Meets Buddhism*. LaSalle, Ill.: Open Court Publishing Co., 1974.

Dunne, Carrin. *Buddha and Jesus: Conversations*. Springfield, Ill.: Templegate, 1975.

Eusden, John Dykstra. *Zen and Christian: The Journey Between*. New York: Crossroad, 1981.

Ingram, Paul O. and Frederick J. Streng, eds. *Buddhist-Christian Dialogue: Mutual Renewal and Transformation*. Honolulu: University of Hawaii Press, 1986.

Fernando, Anthony. *Buddhism Made Plain: An Introduction for Christians and Jews*. Maryknoll, N.Y.: Orbis Books, 1985.

Johnston, William. *The Still Point: Reflections on Zen and Christian Mysticism*. San Francisco: Harper & Row, 1971.

____. *Christian Zen*. San Francisco: Harper & Row, 1971.

Merton, Thomas. *Zen and the Birds of Appetite*. New York: New Directions, 1968.

Pieris, Aloysius. *Love Meets Wisdom: A Christian Experience of Buddhism*. Maryknoll, N.Y.: Orbis Books, 1988.

Swearer, Donald K. *Dialogue: the Key to Understanding Other Religions*. Philadelphia: Westminster Press, 1977.

Williams, Jay G. *Yeshua Buddha*. Wheaton, Ill.: Theosophical Publishing House, 1978.

Part Three

THEOLOGY

CHAPTER NINE

What Is Theology?

Theology is both a process and a product. Usually people think of theology only as the latter, as the inherited "baggage" of a religion, that collection of traditional beliefs, rules, and practices that has been passed on from an older generation to a younger. Theology, however, is much more than that. It is also the *process* of reflecting critically upon the way people of a particular religious tradition should live out their faith. It involves seriously examining the origin, development, and meaning of the various elements that have made up a religious tradition (its beliefs, its code of morality, its rituals and practices) as well as asking how that tradition needs to be expressed and re-shaped in our contemporary situation.

Theology, of course, is also the product of this process of thinking seriously about one's religious tradition. As *product,* theology is the *formulation* in words of the meaning, truth, and significance of a particular religious tradition for human living.

The two aspects, process and product, are integrally related and necessary. When theology is simply the product of the past, handed on to us without any real connection to the questions we confront today, it is like a musty book written in a foreign language, uninteresting and lifeless. But when theology has no root in the past tradition, it is like the mayfly that lives for only a few hours, fragile and insignificant.

According to the definition we are proposing here, "theology" is much broader than the origin of the word or its traditional meaning might suggest. The term comes from two Greek words: *theos*, meaning God, and *logos*, meaning word. Originally, then, "theology" meant words about God or the gods. It also meant a "study of the god/gods," since the words people spoke about the gods came after a careful, rational inquiry into the nature and operation of their world. "Theology," however, like the word "religion," is a Western term. In its traditional meaning, it may well describe the content of the most basic reflections of the Western religious traditions—Judaism, Christianity, and Islam. It is, however, inadequate in describing the content of the critical reflections of Eastern religious traditions that do not speak directly of God or gods, such as Theravada and Zen Buddhism or Taoism. Although this section of the book is principally concerned with Christian theology, it is important to remember that "theology" is not confined, in principle, to the Christian world. Theology, broadly conceived, consists in the rational reflection upon and the systematic expression of the meaning of any religious tradition. In this sense, there can be a Buddhist theology as well as a Jewish, Christian, or Muslim theology.

Insofar as theology involves careful study and investigation, it needs to be distinguished from religious belief or conviction. Thinking theologically is not the same thing as believing. Thinking theologically involves careful and critical reflection upon what it is that one believes. It entails questioning; sometimes it includes serious doubt about what one has previously believed. Theological reflection, however, is a natural consequence of mature faith. Whereas belief may exist without theology, mature faith cannot. As the Christian saints Augustine (354-430) and

Anselm of Canterbury (1033-1109) insisted, mature faith seeks understanding. It is part of the natural process of growing out of childlike faith into adult faith to ask questions about the meaning and relevance of one's religious tradition. To do this in a serious way is to "theologize."

Although professional theologians devote their entire working lives to answering questions about the truth and meaning of their particular religious traditions in a coherent and critically rigorous way, all persons of mature faith engage in theological reflection at some time or other. This personal "theologizing" is different from the work of professional theologians, but it is no less a form of theological thinking. A few examples may illustrate what is meant by this process of personal theological reflection.

Lois, a first-year finance major, was very disturbed by the recent death of her younger brother, who had been suffering for some time from leukemia. Lois's Lutheran parents had taught her that God is good and loving, and she had believed it, at least until now. Now, however, all kinds of difficult and disturbing questions welled up within her. How could a good and loving God permit her innocent, lovable brother to die so young? What had he done to deserve this? In confronting these questions, in struggling to make sense of her brother's tragic death in light of her religious beliefs, Lois was engaged in the process of theological reflection.

Mark, a senior physics major, had been raised in a solid, conventional Roman Catholic home. Although not a churchgoer, Mark considered himself a good Christian. He tried to be a person of integrity, honesty, and decency; he did his best to treat others the way he wanted to be treated. Mark's father was a captain in the army, and Mark was proud of his father's distinguished military career. He thought that he could follow in his father's footsteps to a certain degree and still pursue his own interest in physics by seeking a job in the research and development branch of a major defense contractor. In his final semester of college, however, Mark read *The Challenge of Peace*, the 1983 pastoral statement of the National Conference of Catholic Bishops on the problem of war and peace in the modern world. The pastoral letter called the arms race one of the greatest curses on the human race and it supported immediate, bilateral agreements to halt the testing, production, and deployment of new nuclear weapons systems. Mark's intended job would be precisely to design such weapons systems. What ought he to do? By embarking on this career, would he betray his Christian upbringing? What kind of moral authority did the bishops' pastoral have for him as a Roman Catholic? Mark's wrestling with these questions in the light of his religious upbringing and his understanding of the Bible is another example of theologizing.

This element of intelligent, critical inquiry explains why theology exists as an academic discipline in universities as well as in seminaries. In this setting, theology makes its judgments and defends its conclusions by employing tools used in other disciplines (philosophy, psychology, sociology, historical analysis), and by proposing arguments that generally can pass as reasonable. Theology, however, is noticeably different from other disciplines, especially hard sciences such as chemistry, biology, and physics, in that the Ultimate or Mystery upon which it reflects is not subject to scrutiny by means of the scientific method. The sciences presuppose that reality is what we can perceive with our five senses. They demand that for any statement about our world to be regarded as fact, we must be able to verify it empirically or be able to reproduce the phenomenon in a laboratory. Supernatural phenomena, that is, things or events that go beyond the natural realm of our sense experience, are, therefore, not capable of being verified as "real" by the sciences. For this reason it has become increasingly difficult since the seventeenth century for people living in scientific cultures to acknowledge the reality of God or a transcendent Mystery. Fundamental or philosophical theology, one type of theology often found in universities, deals with this problem. More will be said about it later in this chapter.

Theology's purpose, however, is not exhausted in understanding the basic content of a religious tradition. It also includes explaining the significance of that religious tradition for human living. Like the human sciences generally, theology is concerned not only with *understanding* the various facets of human culture (in this case, religion), but also with *enriching* human existence by bringing the results of that understanding to bear upon the questions or problems we confront in life.

Let's take a look at one basic question, to which theology has given an enriching answer: Is our world to be regarded as a hostile prison from which death frees us or as an indifferent environment, which has more or less accidentally brought forth the human species together with many others? Christian theology answers this question with a firm "no." As Protestant theologian Gordon Kaufman reminds us, the Western theological tradition has generally used the image of God as *Creator* to transform feelings of the world as a hostile or indifferent place into a sense of the world as home. Belief in a kind and gracious Creator God has made the created world appear to be permeated by love and a sense of purpose, in short, a home appropriate for human beings, in which genuine human fulfillment is possible. Theology therefore does not merely describe a religious tradition; it also highlights the relevance of that tradition for living life well.

Insofar as theology involves both understanding the way people have given living witness of their religious traditions and expressing their significance for human existence, theology can be said to have two focal points. The religious tradition itself is the one point; human life as we experience it is the other. A religious tradition usually includes a body of literature regarded as sacred (called Scripture), commentaries upon Scripture by significant figures in the history of the religion, rituals, moral norms, and religious practices. Although all of them are part of religion, Scripture holds a special place. This is clear, for example, in the special reverence Jews have for the Tanak (Torah, Prophets, and other writings that make up the Hebrew Scriptures), Christians for the Bible, and Muslims for the Koran.

The other focal point, human experience, is no less important to theology. Theology has value and relevance only insofar as it shows how its religious tradition helps people to make sense of life and enables them to transform themselves and their world for the better. As we have seen in the case of Lois and Mark, theological questions arise out of everyday human experiences whether we want them to or not. Theology, in its systematic and professional form, tries to relate the whole of one's religious tradition in a concrete way to life as we experience it. Simply repeating the religious convictions of a past age is not theology. Theology's character and purpose can be made clearer by taking a concrete example. Let us turn to consider the case of Christian theology.

The Focal Points of Christian Theology

Christian theology can be defined both as the *process* of understanding Christian faith and as the *product* of reflection upon Christian faith's significance for human existence. The two focal points of Christian theology are the Christian *tradition* (the Christian message as expressed in the Bible and in the practices and norms of the church) and human *experiences*. Christian theology seeks to bring the insights of the Christian perspective to bear upon the questions and problems we have. Our experiences, in turn, raise questions and offer insights that sometimes challenge, at other times confirm the insights and values expressed in the New Testament and tradition.

The rise of feminism and the experience of the equality of women, for example, has challenged the patriarchy inherent in church and society. On the other hand, the experience of outrage at the pollution of our environment and the wanton destruction of animals by hunters or medical researchers has confirmed the Christian conviction, rooted in the book of Genesis, that everything God created is good, inherently valuable, and therefore to be respected. Contemporary theology is this process by which our understanding of the Christian tradition is critically related to our understanding of ourselves and our experiences.

Throughout the history of the Christian churches, the focus upon Scripture has been a constant in theological reflection. Since the final formation of the Bible (in the second to fourth centuries of the Common Era), Christians have always referred their convictions, practices, moral norms, and beliefs back to the

Bible's witness, especially back to that portion Christians refer to as the New Testament. The Bible has been viewed by Christians as the ultimate repository of Christian revelation, that is, the primary source for defining what we should think of God and each other and how we should act with regard to both. Although the Bible contains a variety of contrasting points of view, and although it has been interpreted quite differently at different times and in different places, the Bible has consistently served as a norm guiding Christian reflections about the meaning of life and the shape it should have. It is a central source of theological reflection.

The variable in Christian theology has been human experience. Although human beings at all times have pondered the meaning of existence and have had experiences common to all (the desire for food, shelter, comfort; the experiences of joy and suffering), the way in which people have understood their experiences varies according to the contexts in which they live. Recognition that our environment, culture, and place in history affect our thoughts and feelings is a recent discovery. Along with this discovery came the additional recognition in the nineteenth century that theology *should* change in the course of time since people, their experiences, and their self-understanding all change as well. In the past two centuries, this *historically conscious* approach to reality has been supplanting the traditional *classicist* approach, which affirms the truth of the past as certain and unchangeable for every future time and culture.

But even before the dawning awareness of our cultural and historical conditioning, the products of theological reflection have shown the influence of the place and time in which they were created. The Christian doctrine of redemption can serve as an example. For at least seven centuries, from the fourth through the eleventh centuries, the dominant conception of redemption was this: By sinning—turning away from God toward the devil—our original ancestors willingly handed themselves over to the power of the devil. The devil thus had the right to keep human beings in its power, in effect to keep them as its slaves. The only way God could release humanity from captivity to the devil was by paying a ransom. That ransom was the death of God's son, Jesus the Christ. This conception of redemption integrates the common medieval belief in the existence of devils and human sinfulness with awareness of the social fact of slavery. In the late antique and early medieval worlds, people could be released from servitude only if their freedom was bought or if their owners permitted it. This social-political experience of paying the required price to obtain freedom from slavery was applied to the Christian concept of redemption.

In the late eleventh century, St. Anselm of Canterbury (1033-1109) proposed an alternative theory about the nature of redemption. He rejected the devil-ransom theory with the argument that the devil has no rights over God; consequently, God is not obliged to pay the devil a ransom for the release of humankind. According to Anselm, what is fundamentally wrong about the original sin is that dishonor was done to God. Instead of showing gratitude to the God who had created them and showered them with the many gifts of the earth, Adam and Eve showed disregard for God by disobeying God's commands. Moreover, their sin of disobedience was infinitely heinous for it involved the dishonoring of an infinite superior (God) by inferiors (human beings). The only way to right the relationship between God and humanity was to make appropriate satisfaction to God for their sin. Due to the infinite magnitude of the sin, humans could not make restitution. Yet they were the only ones who ought to make restitution, since they had dishonored God. The solution was to have a God-man, namely the Christ, make the necessary satisfaction for humanity. As God, his action (freely choosing to die for our sake) had infinite value; as human, his action came from the required party, namely, the human race that had dishonored God. This satisfaction theory of redemption, which dominated theology in the late medieval and early modern periods, reflects the influence of feudalism with its concepts of honor and satisfaction, and its notion that the gravity of a crime increases with the stature of the person offended or victimized. In short, the experiences Christians had of their world shaped the way they understood and expressed their religious tradition.

Today, many Christians of the Third World are expressing the meaning of Christian redemption in a new way. Their experience of abject poverty and dehumanizing exploitation at the hands of the wealthy has encouraged them to conceive of the salvation that Christ brings in terms of liberation from oppression. They have come to recognize that the biblical story of the suffering Jesus is reflected and repeated in their own life as a suffering people. This recognition, together with their growing awareness of the social injustice committed against them, has caused these Christians to take Jesus' "inaugural address" with new seriousness: "The Spirit of the Lord has been given to me, for he has anointed me. He has sent me to bring the good news to the poor, to proclaim liberty to captives and to the blind new sight, to set the downtrodden free, to proclaim the Lord's year of favor" (Lk 4:18). Salvation has come to include freedom from oppression and the fulfillment of material, as well as spiritual, needs.

What is new in recent Christian theology is not simply the recognition that the content of faith has always been expressed in terms meaningful to its particular context and culture, but also the honest admission that our present experiences may challenge the continuing validity of these traditional descriptions of faith's content. Since the nineteenth century, the relation between Christian tradition and human experience in theological work has undergone a significant transformation. The earlier, classicist approach claimed that past tradition, as understood by the majority of Christians, provided the definitive answers to all the questions raised by our experiences. This point of view has been giving way to the historically conscious approach that acknowledges the equal footing of our present experiences in offering possible answers to the fundamental questions about the origin, purpose, and meaning of authentic human existence. This newer approach also recognizes that there are important aspects of the Christian tradition that have been forgotten or ignored by the majority of Christians in past ages.

This modern, historically conscious approach has qualified the authority Bible and tradition formerly possessed. From this perspective, neither the Bible nor the church's traditional teachings are seen to be *unquestionable* norms that must be taken at face value if one is to live an authentically Christian life. This change in attitude toward the past tradition is one of the major results of the eighteenth-century Enlightenment, a philosophical movement whose essence the German philosopher Immanuel Kant (1724-1804) described as daring to think for oneself. A hallmark of Western intellectual culture since the Enlightenment is the conviction that believing something simply on the authority of church or state is no longer acceptable. Rather, every assertion must pass the scrutiny of human reason if it is to be regarded as acceptable and credible. Present judgments of reason may be found wanting in the future, but they comprise the only common tool that all human beings today can use in order to determine what is true and good. The question of how we know whether a theological statement is true arises with greater urgency in this modern context. Previously, most Christians would have replied: If the Bible says it is so, I know it is true. But, for increasing numbers of Christians, such an answer is no longer persuasive.

Contemporary theologians, wanting to be faithful to the Bible and Christian tradition, yet responsive to the demands of modern rationality, offer two criteria by which we can judge the truth of theological statements. First, for a statement to be an expression of *Christian* theology, it must be *appropriate* to the Christian tradition. That means the theological claim must have a sound basis in the Bible and in the tradition of the church. More precisely, it requires that the statement be in agreement not with some marginal theme or isolated passages from Scripture, but that it be in basic continuity with the fundamental themes and essential thrust of Scripture and the Christian tradition. Second, for the statement to be judged *true,* it must be *adequate* to human experience. Minimally, that means the theological statement must be credible; it must "make sense" in the judgment of our intellectual faculties. In a broader sense, this criterion of adequacy requires a theological concept or statement to reflect or agree with what we have experienced to be the case about living fully as human beings. If a theology fails the first criterion, it cannot be considered Christian; if it fails the second criterion, it cannot be regarded as meaningful or true. Christian theology, therefore, needs always to answer to this dual "examining board" if it is to be able to communicate Christian truth effectively to people who live in an ever-changing world.

The preceding discussion may have left the impression that professional theologians do their work as individuals independent of the rest of the church. Such a situation, if permitted, would not only compromise the quality of the work of individual theologians, but also make it difficult for people to know whether a theologian's statements were an authentic expression of the mind of the church as a whole. The collaboration and criticism of colleagues is necessary to the doing of good theology, for only in such a dialogue with others can a person avoid mistaking one's idiosyncratic opinions for generally valid truths. But, even as a group, theologians do not operate in a wholly autonomous fashion.

Theologians are bound by a double obligation: to express and explain their church's official teachings accurately and responsibly, yet creatively to help shape their church's mind on current and future issues. This means that theologians must be in constant, fruitful dialogue with the leaders as well as with the rest of the church. Due to the different responsibilities exercised by theologian, leader (e.g., bishop), and typical member of a church, creative tension often exists between theologians and the congregation at large, on the one hand, and those charged with the primary leadership function in the Christian community, on the other. Nonetheless, all of these parties should be involved in the process of theologizing since all have something important to contribute to the life of the church.

Types of Christian Theology

There are numerous categories into which theology has been divided over the centuries: doctrinal theology, moral theology, sacramental theology, biblical theology, systematic theology, historical theology, to name only a few. The vast number of different names or types is understandably bewildering, if not overwhelming, as one first approaches the study of theology. Why are there so many theologies? How are they different? Which do I, as a person being introduced to the theological discipline, need to know? The following sketch is intended to give enough shape to the theological landscape so as to provide a coherent picture of the general "lay of the land" without describing all the contours.

The following overview is adapted from the proposals of two contemporary Christian theologians, David Tracy (a Roman Catholic) and Schubert Ogden (a Protestant). Their approaches are not the only intelligible ones for distinguishing the various types of theology, but they have particular clarity and elegance. Tracy and Ogden suggest that theology can be divided into different types on the basis of the questions with which they are primarily concerned. Tracy conceives of three major questions: 1) Is the Christian tradition true? 2) What does it mean? 3) What current situation or problem of religious and ethical import must Christians be committed to transform? These three questions yield fundamental theology, systematic theology, and practical theology, respectively. Ogden, on the other hand, formulates three different questions: 1) What has been the decisive character of the Christian witness of faith for human existence? 2) What is it today? and 3) What should the Christian witness of faith now become in order to be decisive for human existence? These three questions yield historical, systematic, and practical theology, respectively. The overlap is apparent.

Combining and adapting their suggestions, we can distinguish four major types of Christian theology. 1) Fundamental theology is primarily concerned with critically examining our human experience so as to answer the question about the reality of God. This type of theology has also been known as philosophical theology, because it has used the philosophical discipline to defend and to explain the Christian affirmation of God's existence. 2) Historical theology is the type that asks the question about the meaning the Christian tradition had for human living in the past. It includes within it biblical studies, since the Bible constitutes the most important element in the formation of the Christian tradition. 3) Systematic theology is the one most Christians immediately identify with the word "theology." It embodies the attempt to identify and to express the present meaning of the Christian tradition for human existence. 4) Practical theology involves creative proposals for what the Christian witness of faith should become in order to create a more loving, just, and peaceful world. We will take a closer look at each of these four types of theology in turn.

Fundamental Theology Fundamental theology is appropriately named. It deals with God, the foundation of Christian faith. Specifically, fundamental theology is the process and product of reflection upon the question: Does God exist? This question has stimulated the thinking of people for many centuries. In the medieval Christian world, fundamental theology took the form of offering rational "proofs" for the existence of God. Perhaps the most famous are the five proofs offered by Thomas Aquinas (1225-1274) in his encyclopedia of theology, the *Summa Theologiae*. Aquinas candidly admitted that God's existence is not self-evident to everyone. He therefore set out to demonstrate God's existence by observing the world and seeing what its nature and activity implied about the reality of a supreme being. What Aquinas noticed was neither original nor mystifying. He noticed that every change in the world is the result of some source of change, and that every effect results from a prior cause.

We might come to repeat his line of questioning today simply by making our own observations of the natural world. For example, we might engage in this series of questions and answers: Why do trees change color? Because of change in climate. Why does climate change? Because of the earth's position relative to the sun and other factors. Why does the earth change position? And so on. Aquinas reasoned that the cause of a given change is itself the result of some previous source of change until we must conclude that ultimately there is a source of change that is itself unchanged. Aquinas said that this unchanged source of change is what Christians (and others) call God. This type of reasoning about God is known as a *cosmological* argument. It is so named because it begins with observed facts about the cosmos and argues from them to God as the most plausible explanation for these facts.

Aquinas also proposed a *teleological* argument in support of God's existence. This is an argument from order or design. Aquinas observed, as had others before him, that some things that lack intelligence, such as the planets, act always in the same way. This regular and consistent activity seemed to suggest that these things were acting for a particular end or purpose. Aquinas reasoned that whatever lacks intelligence cannot move purposefully, unless it is directed by some being endowed with knowledge and intelligence. He concluded that God is that intelligent being by whom all natural things are directed in an orderly fashion.

The various traditional arguments for the existence of God have come under attack since the Enlightenment. Some philosophers suggest that an infinite regress of finite causes is not impossible. And scientists have pointed out that the world is not as orderly as people once thought. There is relativity and randomness in our world as well as order. Consequently, fundamental theologians have sought to identify other facts that might suggest the reality of God.

One fact upon which contemporary fundamental theologians have focused is the human experience or feeling that life is somehow worthwhile. Despite all the suffering and evil that we have experienced personally or have observed, many, if not most of us, continue to believe that our lives have purpose and that being alive is good. Fundamental theologians are asking why we feel that way. Scientifically, we cannot prove that life is worthwhile. Theologians have suggested that the source of our confidence about the meaningfulness of life is God, whom we have sensed unconsciously or subconsciously as giving life purpose, meaning, and dignity.

Peter Berger, a sociologist, offers the following example. A child wakes up in the night from a bad dream. Surrounded by darkness and feeling alone and threatened, the child cries out for her mother. The mother enters the room, picks up her daughter, and holds her close. She speaks or sings to the child, and the content of this communication is "Don't be afraid, everything is all right." If all goes well, the little girl will be reassured. With her trust in reality restored, she will return to sleep. Berger observes that this common scene raises a far from ordinary question, which immediately introduces a religious dimension: Is the mother lying to the child? Can the world be accepted as a comfortable home? *Is* everything all right? We can deny that the mother is lying to her daughter, says Berger, only if there is some truth in the religious interpretation of human existence. Why? Because the reassurance the mother offers her daughter implies a statement about reality as such. It suggests that life or the source of life can be trusted.

Schubert Ogden claims that religion's basic function is to provide reassurance when our basic trust in (the meaning and goodness of) reality has been shaken; and the possibility of being reassured implies that we already knew that life or its source could be trusted. This source of life that Christians trust is God. Fundamental theologians reflect upon these and similar experiences in order to answer the question about the reality of God.

Historical Theology Historical theology seeks to reconstruct and understand the process by which the Christian tradition was formed. Specifically, it examines the factors, cultural as well as religious, that contributed to the formulation of Christian doctrines and practices. In addition, it describes the ways in which human activity and culture have been influenced by this past Christian witness. Historical theology shares with secular history the same tools and the same means for determining what the past record was and what its significance is. Like history itself, historical theology is not content with merely exhibiting the past for its own sake. Rather, it also seeks to enrich life today by demonstrating the continuing viability of past insights and by showing where and to what extent we need to go beyond past understandings of the Christian faith.

One very important branch of historical theology is biblical studies. Insofar as the history of Christian theology has been in large part the history of scriptural interpretation, this branch of historical theology rightfully holds a preeminent place in the Christian churches. The truly *historical* study of Scripture, however, is a recent development. The French priest Richard Simon (1638-1712), who published *A Critical History of the Old Testament* in 1678, is generally regarded as the founder of the critical study of the Hebrew Scriptures. His *Critical History of the Text of the New Testament* (1689) and subsequent publications established him also as the first person to employ critical methods in a study of the origin of the traditional form of the New Testament text. Although critical historical study of the Hebrew Scriptures was well underway in the eighteenth century, it was not until the nineteenth century that a consistently historical approach to the Greek Scriptures was adopted. In this regard, two German scholars, David Friedrich Strauss (1808-1874) and Ferdinand Christian Baur (1792-1860), provided decisive impetus. Strauss' *The Life of Jesus Critically Examined* (1835) shocked most nineteenth-century Christians with its suggestion that all the supernatural events of Jesus' life reported in the gospels were nothing but myths created unconsciously by the early Christian community. Although Strauss's work was promptly and roundly denounced, it caused Christian theologians to take a more careful and a more critical, historical look at the gospels. Baur's work did a similar service for the study of the pastoral as well as the Pauline letters of the New Testament. More will be said about the historical-critical study of the Bible in the next chapter.

Systematic Theology The specific task of systematic theology is to express the understanding of Christian faith today as it is embodied in contemporary Christian witness. Systematic theology attempts to fulfill this task in a critical and systematic way, by relating the various Christian doctrines to one another and by drawing out their implications for the way Christians ought to live. The former task includes what is often referred to as doctrinal theology, the presentation and explanation of the meaning of the various Christian doctrines, and sacramental theology, the explication of the Christian sacraments. The latter task includes what has been traditionally referred to as moral theology. That is, systematic theology comprises not only "theory" or a contemporary presentation of Christian faith (its beliefs, doctrines, sacraments), but also "practice," or an explication of appropriate ethical behavior.

Since human beings and human culture change over time, it is not surprising that systematic theology in every age formulates the meaning of Christian faith in new ways. Sometimes systematic theologians identify certain past beliefs, once held to be essential to being Christian, as no longer essential. Yet, insofar as they are convinced that the essence of the Christian tradition contains important insights into the nature of God, our world, and ourselves, systematic theologians find themselves obliged to express the meaning of these insights in terms that are appropriate and credible to people in *this* particular age and culture.

Systematic theology holds a central place in the life of the Christian churches because, as Schubert Ogden argues, it has established the general method of the other theological disciplines. This method is one of critically relating our human experiences to the Christian tradition, allowing the latter to throw light upon the former and allowing the former to confirm or to challenge the latter. The method and character of systematic theology will become clearer when we turn to specific examples of it in Chapters Eleven and Twelve.

Practical Theology Practical theology, the fourth major type of Christian theology, has undergone a significant transformation in the past century. Formerly, it was conceived primarily as reflection upon and instruction in the best techniques for educating others about Christian faith and for ministering to them. It was thought to be the official domain of the ordained ministry. So conceived, practical theology consisted primarily of *homiletics* and *catechetics*, that is, the art of preaching and the art of teaching others the principles of the Christian faith.

More recently, practical theology has been more broadly conceived. It now includes serious reflection not only upon how to preach the faith, but also upon how to live the faith in the current situation of global social injustice. Practical theology today attempts to answer the question: How should Christians today think and act in light of the gross inequality in resources, standard of living, etc. between the First and Third Worlds, and in light of the rising expectations of the poor of the earth? How are Christians to live a faith that does justice? The older approach to practical theology has been appropriately named "pastoral," for it is primarily concerned with the spiritual needs of those within the church. The more recent approach extends this concern to the total needs (spiritual and material) of society as a whole. Insofar as both approaches involve active ministry and Christian mission, they both fit in the category of practical theology. Liberation theology, one example of practical theology, will be discussed in more detail in Chapter Twelve.

The Different Emphases of the Four Types of Theology

It may seem by now that the four types of Christian theology overlap and, as a result, one can no longer see how each type is distinctive. It is certainly the case that they overlap. All four types involve the process of reflection upon the meaning of Christian faith and the Christian tradition for human living. Each type, however, can be differentiated from the others by the emphasis each gives to the two sources of theology (religious tradition and human experience), and by the tools each uses to aid its reflection.

Fundamental theology lays heavy stress upon human experience. It asks the fundamental question, whether Christian theology is possible at all. That is, is there anything in our human experiences that might suggest that God is real? Fundamental theology makes use of contemporary philosophy, especially that form of philosophical reflection known as "transcendental analysis." In general terms, transcendental analysis examines the conditions of the possibility of human experience and human knowledge. In fundamental theology, transcendental analysis means, among other things, examining the conditions of the possibility of our experiencing life as good and worthwhile. More will be said about this type of analysis in Chapter Eleven.

Historical theology, on the other hand, attends primarily to the religious tradition, that is, to the ways in which Christian faith has been understood and expressed in the past. Its chief tools are historical criticism and *hermeneutics*, the theory of how texts are to be interpreted. We shall see an example of historical theology at work in the next chapter, specifically with regard to the historical-critical interpretation of biblical texts.

Systematic theology, instead of emphasizing one theological source more than the other, pays close attention to the way in which the two sources (the Christian tradition and human experience) are to be related to each other. To aid these reflections, systematic theology makes use of both contemporary philosophy and hermeneutics. We will learn more about systematic theology in Chapters Eleven and Twelve.

Practical theology, which emphasizes human experience just as fundamental theology does, can be differentiated from it in that practical theology presupposes the reality of God and asks instead: What would God have us do in this current situation to realize our Christian mission? Perhaps more pointedly: In light of the human experience of dehumanizing social and political oppression, what ought Christians to do? Practical theology uses critical social theory to aid its reflections. Critical social theory includes political science, economic analysis, and sociology. We shall explore this type of theology more carefully in Chapter Twelve.

The next three chapters will give flesh to the skeleton of theology outlined here.

Questions for Reflection and Discussion

1. What is theology in the broad sense and how is it different from belief? Can you describe an example of "theologizing" from your own personal experience?

2. What are theology's two "focal points" or sources? How does one's social or cultural situation affect one's understanding of the Christian tradition? To illustrate your answer, explain what "redemption" might mean to a twentieth-century Christian.

3. How has the Enlightenment changed theology? Specifically, how has it helped to shape the criteria used for judging the truth of a theological statement?

4. How are the four major types of Christian theology related? Identify specifically what they have in common and how they differ.

SUGGESTED READINGS

Berger, Peter. *A Rumor of Angels*. Garden City, N.Y.: Doubleday, 1969.

Kaufman, Gordon D. *An Essay on Theological Method*. Missoula, Mont.: Scholars Press, 1975.

Ogden, Schubert M. *On Theology*. San Francisco: Harper & Row, 1986.

____.*The Reality of God and Other Essays*. New York: Harper & Row, 1966.

Tracy, David, and John B. Cobb, Jr. *Talking About God: Doing Theology in the Context of Modern Pluralism*. New York: Seabury Press, 1983.

CHAPTER TEN

Approaches to Scripture and Tradition

Whether we like it or not, and whether we acknowledge it or not, we all stand within a cultural tradition. Tradition forms our presuppositions and shapes our ideas about the world, ourselves, and others. This is, on the whole, a very good thing. It is, in fact, necessary to our full functioning as human individuals and social beings. Tradition gives us concepts, ideals, and values with which we can fashion meaningful lives for ourselves. Instead of having to reinvent the wheel or to repeat the mistakes of our ancestors, we can take their past achievements and insights and build upon them for a better future. Tradition often teaches us what we don't know by instinct.

As the historian of religions Huston Smith has observed, no cultural institution has proved stronger than religion for transmitting the wisdom of the past. Religion, he notes, has sometimes been prophetic; it has always been "conservative." That is, religion tends to conserve and pass on to new generations insights and values believed to be important for conducting our relationships with one another and for establishing a relationship with ultimate reality. Religious tradition, however, is not always a good thing. When it attempts to stifle all development and every attempt at rethinking one's cultural or religious heritage, tradition becomes something that is impoverishing rather than enriching. Part of the Christian religious tradition came into this sort of bad repute in some intellectual circles in the eighteenth and nineteenth centuries. To many scientists and philosophers, religious tradition seemed to be little more than a collection of outdated ideas and superstitious practices, passed on from primitive, unenlightened peoples and used by the powerful to keep the uneducated masses under control. Some of this skepticism about the value and relevance of religious tradition has carried down into our own century.

But even if we were to deny the relevance of religious tradition, we could hardly disavow its influence, even in secular Western culture. Barbara Sproul, a religious researcher, gives an example from the Jewish and Christian traditions that makes this point. She claims that many Westerners, whether or not they are conventionally religious, show that they are heirs of the Jewish and Christian traditions by holding the view that people are sacred and by believing that human beings are superior to other creatures. In the biblical account of creation recorded in Genesis, the idea that people are sacred is expressed in the statement that God created human beings in God's image; the idea that humans are superior to other creatures is expressed in the privilege of naming the other animals that God gave to Adam and in God's command to Adam and Eve to have dominion over "the fish of the sea, the birds of the air, and all the living things that move on the earth" (Gen 1:28). Sproul points out that declared unbelievers often dispense with the overtly religious language that says that people are made in "God's image," yet they still cherish the *consequence* of this religious claim insofar as they believe that people have inalienable rights, as if people really were created by God, as if people really are sacred.

Religious tradition indeed exerts a powerful influence on

people of every culture. The Jewish, Christian, and Muslim traditions have powerfully influenced Western culture, to the point that even those contemporary people who do not honor a "sabbath" (a special day dedicated to prayer and worship of God) still structure their lives by reference to a special time of leisure from normal work, which originally came into our culture from these religious traditions. These same traditions have helped to shape our moral principles, civil laws, intellectual pursuits, and art. The focus of this chapter will be on the Christian tradition and its function in theology.

Scripture: Historical Perspectives on Its Place In the Life of the Church

The Christian tradition is composed of many elements, such as doctrines, sacraments, practices, and forms of worship. In its two-thousand-year history, the tradition has found many diverse expressions. It is embodied today in three major branches of Christianity: Roman Catholicism, Eastern Orthodoxy, and Protestantism. Although each major branch has developed the tradition in a distinctive way, the Bible is common to each as an important source of Christian belief and practice. In fact, the Bible has served as the primary source of the doctrines and practices that have been developed in the Christian churches.

Since the sixteenth century until quite recently, it was common to contrast the Protestant approach to Scripture with the Roman Catholic and the Orthodox approaches. The Protestant approach insisted that Scripture alone was the authoritative norm for Christian belief and practice, whereas the Roman Catholic and Orthodox approaches placed tradition alongside Scripture as a source of knowledge about the Christian life. Tradition was understood to include the doctrines and practices that the church had derived from its interpretation of Scripture or from reflection upon its common faith in the course of the centuries. The contrast in approaches was most sharply drawn in the sixteenth century by Martin Luther and other reformers of the Western church. A brief look at the sixteenth century context may clarify the reasons for the development of this contrast.

The Sixteenth-Century Reformation Martin Luther (1483-1546), originally a monk and priest in the Roman church, proposed the primacy of Scripture over the church's traditions because he felt that certain traditions then current were contrary to the gospel of Christ. One tradition in particular aroused his criticism, namely, the selling of indulgences. At least since the time of the Crusades, indulgences had been a practice in the Western church that allowed sinners to reduce the length of punishment required of them for sins they had committed. Originally, one was "indulged" in this way for having performed some worthy act that promoted the Christian cause, for example, joining a Crusader army, working to help the sick and the orphaned, or making special religious pilgrimages. By the end of the fifteenth century, the benefits of an indulgence could be transferred to one's dead relatives. And, by the second decade of the sixteenth century, indulgences were being sold as a way to finance the building of St. Peter's basilica in Rome.

Luther was distressed by reports from members of his congregation about the claims some indulgence-sellers were making in order to hawk their spiritual wares. Johann Tetzel, a particularly aggressive salesman, allegedly claimed that one could have raped the mother of Jesus and still have punishment for the sin remitted if he purchased an indulgence certificate. And for those Christians who wanted to help their dead relatives in purgatory, Tetzel offered an enticing jingle: As soon as the coin in my big box rings, a soul from purgatory springs! Luther found this practice objectionable because it seemed to suggest that a person could buy God's forgiveness; in short, that one could merit or earn God's favor and grace.

This directly contradicted Luther's understanding of how people become righteous in God's eyes. Through his study of the Bible as a professor of Scripture at the University of Wittenberg, Luther had come to realize that people become righteous or holy in God's eyes not by what they do, but simply by the gracious gift of God. God's grace—not human merits; faith, not good works—makes people pleasing to God and worthy of God's love. Indulgence-selling opposed this message of the New Testament, especially as it was formulated by St. Paul. Luther concluded that if the pope approved this traditional practice, then both he and the tradition were to be rejected. On October 31, 1517, Luther posted in Wittenberg his Ninety-Five Theses, which raised serious questions about the practice of indulgences and the propriety of the pope's support of this tradition. Thus began the Protestant Reformation.

Other reformers, such as John Calvin (1509-1564) in Geneva and Ulrich Zwingli (1484-1531) in Zurich, supported Luther's insistence upon the primacy of Scripture over the traditions of the church. They identified a number of traditional practices (lenten fasts, mandatory celibacy of priests) and traditional doctrines (purgatory, transubstantiation of bread and wine during the consecration of Mass) that did not seem to have a clear basis in Scripture. From this they concluded that these practices and doctrines were not entitled to a sure place in the life of the church.

The Roman church had two responses to the sixteenth-century Protestant reformers. It formulated these responses at the Council of Trent (1545-1563), which convened 28 years after Luther's appeal for a general council. On the one hand, the Roman church insisted that the truths and rules of Christ's gospel are contained in the written books of Scripture *and* in "the unwritten traditions" that were handed down from Christ or from the apostles under the direction of the Holy Spirit. By refusing to say that Christian truth was contained partly in Scripture and partly in unwritten tradition, the council seemed to reject the view that tradition supplements Scripture with a new body of revealed information. Still, the council wanted to make clear that there are two legitimate sources of knowledge about Christian life and practice, not one. On the other hand, the Roman church claimed that since the meaning of Scripture was not always self-evident, no one should presume to interpret Scripture according to his or her own conceptions. Rather, everyone should understand Scripture in the sense professed by the church. The "church" was identified primarily with the bishops, especially the bishop of Rome (the pope). Consequently, the bishops' judgments about the meaning of Scripture came to form part of the church's tradition. In this way, the Roman church made tradition, in addition to the words of Scripture, a source of Christian truth.

The Protestant reformers, of course, rejected this Roman response. In his *Institutes of the Christian Religion,* Calvin denied that the power of judging the truth and certainty of Scripture rested with the church. And, to the Roman Catholics who asked how they could be sure that Scripture had sprung from God unless they had recourse to a decree of the church, Calvin replied that Scripture itself gave clear evidence of its divine source and its truth. In Calvin's opinion, Scripture provides us with the spectacles we need in order to see God clearly.

Although all the major reformers agreed with Calvin that Scripture was true and its meaning clear, they did not always agree on what that "clear meaning" of Scripture actually was. The debate that took place between Luther and Zwingli at Marburg in 1529 provided a glimpse into the Protestant future. The two reformers had come to the German city in order to discuss, and if possible to reconcile, their divergent understandings of the eucharist. Each man came equipped only with a Bible; each cited passages from the Christian Scriptures that supported his own view; each declared the other to have interpreted Scripture incorrectly.

Citing a text from Matthew's gospel, Luther insisted that Jesus' words "Take, eat; this is my body" and "Drink of this cup, all of you; for this is my blood" meant that the body and blood of Christ was really present with, in, and under the forms of bread and wine in the eucharist. Zwingli, citing a text from John's gospel, replied that material things, such as bread and wine, were incapable of making present something spiritual (Christ's risen body and blood). The bread and wine were nothing more than a mere sign or tangible reminder of Christ, whose bodily presence could now be found only in heaven. The split between Luther and Zwingli over what the Bible meant and how it was to be applied to the Christian life was repeated over and over again between other Protestants in subsequent centuries. Thus, the Reformation appeal to Scripture alone eventually yielded not only Lutherans and Reformed Christians, but also Radical Protestants, Puritans, Baptists, Congregationalists, and hosts of other Protestant Christians.

The Situation Since the Reformation When Roman Catholics and Protestants were not engaged in polemical attacks on each other, they could recognize and admit that they had much in common. Both declared their fidelity to the word of God. Protestants stated that they admitted nothing into the church *beyond* what is in Scripture, while Catholics declared that they admitted nothing *contrary* to Scripture. Between the sixteenth and twentieth centuries, the Roman Catholic church came to reaffirm the centrality of the Bible in its communal life. Especially since Vatican Council II (1962-1965), the general Roman Catholic laity joined theologians in carefully studying the Bible and turning to it with greater frequency as a source of spiritual enrichment. Protestant Christians, for their part, felt freer in admitting that many of the practices and doctrines in their own church could not be found explicitly in the Bible. Moreover, many came to acknowledge that this was not, of itself, a persuasive reason for discarding those practices or doctrines. Already in the sixteenth century, Luther and Zwingli upheld the tradition of infant baptism even though it did not seem to have a strong basis in Scripture. And all the major sixteenth-century Protestant reformers, like most of their descendants, accepted the doctrinal decisions of the councils of the fourth and fifth centuries. These early councils had defined two doctrines believed to be essential to Christianity, but which were not found explicitly in the Bible, namely, the trinity and the two natures of Christ.

In the twentieth century, there is less dispute among Roman Catholic, Orthodox, and Protestant Christians about the status of Scripture and the church's tradition than there has ever been. The attempt not only to tolerate, but to understand and appreciate the positions of other Christians has found expression in the ecumenical movement. The Roman Catholic church, in its *Decree on Ecumenism* at Vatican Council II, not only admitted that it bore some of the blame for the divisions with Eastern and Protestant Christians, but also conceded that the other Christian communions were capable of providing access to the community of salvation. The World Council of Churches (an ecumenical organization that includes most Protestant and Eastern Orthodox bodies) and the Roman Catholic church, each in its own way, are committed to working for greater understanding among Christians and for the possible unity of the churches.

There is, however, another movement today that cuts across all denominational lines. It needs to be addressed when we think about the role of Scripture and tradition in theology. That phenomenon is fundamentalism. A number of Christian churches today have been torn apart by strident division within their ranks between strict fundamentalists and non-fundamentalists. This division, however, is not an isolated phenomenon. It is present, even if to a lesser degree, in a large number of Christian communities. The division, whatever its specific form, is rooted in very different presuppositions about the nature of the Bible.

Contrasting Presuppositions About the Bible

Fundamentalism is generally characterized by two convictions. First, the Bible is the only necessary source for knowledge about God, Christ, and the Christian life. Second, the Bible is always without error, or is literally true. For some biblical fundamentalists, inerrancy (the quality of being free from error) is believed to extend to the historical and quasi-scientific statements in the Bible. In order to understand why some Christians are fundamentalists while most are not, it is necessary to take a look at their respective understandings of the nature of the Bible.

The two basic fundamentalist convictions mentioned above are based upon the unquestioned presupposition that the Bible is God's direct, *divine* word to humanity. Fundamentalists believe that the Bible is not only a book inspired by God (most other Christians believe this as well), but also a book written specifically and exactly according to God's direction. In this view, the human authors of the different biblical books are nothing more than instruments used by God; their human perceptions and speculations are not believed significantly to have affected the shape of the biblical texts or to have influenced their content.

Those Christians who are not fundamentalists, on the other hand, have a different understanding of the nature of the Bible. Without necessarily denying the divine inspiration of the Bible, they see the book more as a *human* record of people's (specifically the Hebrews' and early Christians') experience of God's activity in their lives. In this view, the human authors of the different biblical books have given shape to the biblical texts under the influence not only of God's Spirit, but also under the influence of their communities and cultures. They have shaped the biblical texts to reflect the beliefs and serve the needs of their religious communities. This means that the Bible contains not only God's word, but also human words. Consequently, the Bible is not read literally in all cases.

Kimberly, a first-year mathematics major, had a hard time understanding how one could be Christian, yet not fundamentalist. She had been raised in a Bible-believing family. As she saw it, the Bible either was God's word or it wasn't. If it was, then people were obliged to regard the whole book as true and to apply it to their lives. These were the true Christians. If the Bible wasn't God's direct word, then there was no basis on which one could be a believer in God, let alone be a Christian. As Kimberly explained to a classmate, "I know what I believe is true because the Bible tells me so, and that's good enough for me." People who didn't adopt this position seemed to Kimberly to be people who either did not have faith in God or were trying to water down God's message to humanity.

Debbie, a sophomore English major, didn't agree with Kimberly's understanding of the Bible. Furthermore, she did not appreciate the fact that Kimberly equated her rejection of fundamentalism with a lack of true faith. Debbie explained her approach to the Bible this way: Sure, the Bible is inspired. That means, Debbie said, that the insights and values contained in the Bible are not simply the creation of human beings, but are the expression of human beings under the influence of God's spirit. Debbie believed that God really was revealed in the communal and individual experiences of the religious communities that produced the biblical texts. She believed that the Hebrews really experienced God's mighty hand in their remarkable liberation from slavery in Egypt, just as followers of Jesus experienced the powerful presence of God in Jesus' ministry and resurrection. For Debbie, the Bible records in human stories the experiences of God that ancient Jews and Christians had. Insofar as those stories reflect the limited or culture-bound perspective of their human authors, they were not necessarily literally true. Debbie believed that she could say that the Bible is true, without meaning that it is literally true in all its parts. And she thought it was possible to hold her view without being a bad Christian or a person of weak faith.

Kimberly's and Debbie's readings of the Bible reflect their different presuppositions about what the Bible is. And basic presuppositions are such that they cannot be strictly proven. One simply assumes the presupposition to be true and then uses it as the starting point from which to draw "logical" conclusions. This is what happens, for example, in geometry. We start with certain basic definitions or axioms (which are assumed, not proven), upon which basis we can then draw (and prove) certain conclusions. The issue of a fundamentalist versus a non-fundamentalist reading of the Bible is similar. Unless each side is compelled to recognize the weakness of its presuppositions about the Bible, each side assumes that its position is absolutely correct. Each side remains completely convinced that the other position is either overly skeptical or overly credulous. Insofar as it is not possible to prove in the strict sense that the Bible either is or is not the inerrant, direct word of God, debates that attempt such proof are futile. Reasons that seem to support one's presuppositions are the most one can offer in a discussion about the nature of the Bible. However that discussion might turn out, it cannot be denied that fundamentalism has spread in the past several years.

Fundamentalism

Fundamentalism is on the rise today because it has something attractive to offer. Many fundamentalist groups are permeated by a strong sense of caring for each other and by a religious fervor for "doing God's work." Being a part of such a group can give people a sense of belonging as well as a special sense of mission. Both elements are very attractive, especially to young people. In addition, fundamentalism generates a way of life that promises certainty about one's spiritual destiny and offers definite rules for living a Christian life. This, too, is something positive for many who are troubled by the direction of contemporary secular culture.

The world in which we live today is profoundly threatening. On the individual level, many people live in fear of contracting AIDS. Others are morally confused about the decisions they should make with regard to personal relationships, sexual intimacy, careers, etc. On the communal level, many people are keenly aware of the threat of total annihilation from the escalating nuclear arms race or the threat of slow death from ecological pollution. In so many ways, big and small, people are confronted with situations that produce anxiety. In a world of violence, greed, dishonesty, and personal and sexual irresponsibility, fundamentalism offers answers for which many people yearn. The answers are sure, simple, and definite. By professing Christ as their savior and by directly applying the literal meaning of the Bible's rules and exhortations to their lives, fundamentalists believe they are guaranteed protection from the destructive forces of the world. The certainty that fundamentalism offers can be very comforting.

Although many people find truth and comfort in the fundamentalist position, we wish to suggest that it is not the best approach for understanding the Bible or applying it to daily living. The fundamentalist option is, of course, an option. It is an approach that many Christians have taken, and one in which people have found direction and peace. Still, we think it is based upon some assumptions about the nature of the Bible that are unfounded. An inappropriate use of Scripture can cause people to become excessively rigid in their own lives as well as intolerant of others. Consequently, we will begin to make our case for a more critical, historical approach to the Bible by critically examining some of the fundamentalist assumptions about the nature of the Bible and the fundamentalist use of Scripture.

A Critique of Fundamentalism

Fundamentalism justifies its specific use of Scripture by claiming that the Bible itself supports the fundamentalist interpretation of Scripture. One biblical text (2 Tim 3:16-17) commonly believed to support the fundamentalist perspective reads: "All Scripture is inspired by God and profitable for teaching, for reproof, for correction, and for training in righteousness...." The conclusion that is usually drawn in fundamentalist circles is that the entire Bible is inspired by God and is therefore without error. As the distinguished professor of Hebrew James Barr has argued, such an interpretation goes far beyond the probable intent of the text's author. Moreover, it ignores the context of the passage.

Barr makes three important points that challenge the fundamentalist approach: 1) This passage does not say anything about the inerrancy of Scripture. An interest in the question whether all historical statements in the Bible are accurate did not surface until long after the biblical age. 2) The passage does not say that since Scripture is inspired, it ought to be the controlling criterion for defining Christian faith. Again, the text betrays little interest in this question. What it does assert is that Scripture is "profitable," that is, it is capable of instructing a person how to live properly. This is a far cry from the idea that Scripture is the absolute touchstone of everything that is to be said or done in Christianity. 3) When the author of the text refers to "all Scripture," he did not have in mind the same collection of Hebrew and Christian books that make up the modern Christian Bible. In fact, for the first generation of Christians, "Scripture" usually meant only the sacred Hebrew writings.

Barr draws two conclusions about the fundamentalist case. On the one hand, the notion that 2 Timothy 3:16 or similar texts such as 2 Peter 1:20-21 lay the foundation for a Christianity of evangelical fundamentalism arises from a simple cause, namely, the practice of reading single passages in isolation from their context. On the other hand, the biblical evidence itself makes it clear that the inspiration of Scripture was not a central concept for the writers of the major works of the Bible. The inspiration of Scripture receives explicit mention only in the text from Timothy; it is not mentioned in any of Jesus' statements recorded in the gospels; it is not found in the major epistles (Romans, Corinthians, Galatians, Ephesians).

When people make critical comments such as Barr's about biblical inspiration and the probable intent of biblical authors, many fundamentalists conclude that these people have been duped into believing that the historical-critical interpretation of the Bible is the only correct one. Some fundamentalists may even believe that these critics are somehow motivated by an anti-Christian spirit. It is important to remember, however, that the historical-critical interpretation of the Bible was developed for the most part by confirmed Christians, most of whom were Christian ministers. This type of interpretation applies to the biblical books the same kind of critical tools used in history for determining whether a historical document really was written by the alleged author, for exploring the historical context in which the document was written, and for assessing the historical reliability of what is reported therein. And even if no such thing as the historical-critical method existed, the fundamentalist position would be nothing more than one possible interpretation of Scripture. The scriptural materials themselves, however, suggest that the fundamentalist interpretation of Scripture is not the best. A few examples may clarify this point.

If we look closely at the four canonical gospels, we notice that there are differences in the events reported and in the way they are reported between the synoptic gospels (the first three gospels) and the gospel of John. Whereas the gospels of Matthew, Mark, and Luke describe Jesus' one-year ministry in Galilee, the gospel of John presents Jesus' activity as spanning three years and as located primarily in Jerusalem. Whereas the synoptic gospels record Jesus' teaching in the form of short sayings and parables, John's gospel has Jesus delivering long speeches. Moreover, a number of significant events reported in the first three gospels, such as Jesus' baptism in the Jordan, his temptation, and his transfiguration, do not appear at all in the fourth. And when we examine some of the *same* events recorded by all the evangelists, we notice differences in their respective versions of those events. These facts offer us some important information about the nature of the gospels.

The "cleansing of the temple" by Jesus is a well-known episode from the gospels. It relates how Jesus drove out of the temple area those people who were engaged in commercial activity. In the gospels of Matthew, Mark, and Luke (Mt 21:12-13; Mk 11:15-17; Lk 19:45-46), the incident occurs at the beginning of the final week of Jesus' life; it comes immediately after Jesus' triumphant entry into Jerusalem. In John's gospel, however, the event is located at the very beginning of Jesus' ministry (2:13-17). John says nothing about a cleansing of the temple at the time of Jesus' entry into Jerusalem a few days before his crucifixion. If it is unlikely that Jesus performed the expulsion twice, once at the beginning and once at the end of his ministry, what does this difference in the gospels tell us about their nature? Let us look at another example.

The gospels of Matthew and Luke are the only two that say something about the circumstances of Jesus' birth, yet each offers a different genealogy or list of Jesus' ancestors, and each describes the situation differently. In Matthew's gospel (1:1-17), Jesus' family line begins with Abraham and ends with Joseph, Jesus' legal father. In Luke's gospel (3:23-38), Jesus' family line begins with Adam and ends with Joseph. The two lists, from David down to Joseph, have only two names in common. Why are there so many differences between the two genealogies? Why does it seem that Jesus' Israelite roots are emphasized in Matthew's list, whereas his universal connection to all humanity (through Adam) is emphasized in Luke's? Are the authors trying to make a theological point?

There are other differences as well. In Matthew's version of the story, there is no advance notice to Mary concerning the miraculous birth that is about to occur (Mt 1:18-25; cf. Lk 1:26-38). Unlike Luke, Matthew gives no indication that Jesus' family was merely making a temporary visit to Bethlehem when Jesus was born; rather, Matthew implies that Bethlehem was their home. The family changes its residence to Nazareth, according to Matthew (2:19-23), only to escape the possible vengeance of Herod's son, Archelaus. Luke, on the other hand, reports that Jesus' family lived in Nazareth and made the trip to Bethlehem to abide by an imperial decree concerning a census (2:1-6). What can the differences in these texts tell us about the nature of the gospels?

The conclusion to which these and other examples lead us is that the gospels, and, by extension, the other books of the Bible, do not report merely what is historically true. It seems that at least some writers of the biblical books felt they could be free with the "history" of actual events in order to make a point. Does that mean that the incidents they relate have no truth value? Or that the events they relate have no historical basis? Not necessarily. Some events they report do have a *historical* core, which the gospel authors have embellished to fit their own aims or the needs of their community. Other events, which may have little or no historical basis, are presented in the gospels to make a *theological* point, that is, to say something about the significance of the Jesus story for our relationship to God and to each other. Is it possible to communicate an important, real truth by means of fiction? Of course it is. Good literature—the so-called classics—does that all the time. Truth need not be expressed solely in scientific terms or in historical terms; truth can also be expressed poetically. Consequently, before we can decide whether a statement or a text is true, we must first determine what the statement or passage is trying to communicate.

The Uses of Language

Language, whether spoken or written, has different functions and uses. To understand what a speaker or writer intends to communicate to us, we need to know what kind of language or speech is being used. There are four principal elements involved in written communication: a writer, a reader, a text, and a referent (what the writer is writing about). Depending upon which of the four elements is emphasized, we can distinguish four basic types of speech.

1. When the writer is emphasized, we are dealing with "emotive" speech. "Emotive" does not mean "emotional"; it is much broader than that. "Emotive" speech intends to communicate to us the state of mind, perceptions, and feelings of the writer. When an author writes, "I was disgusted by their behavior," he or she is describing what he or she thinks of the observed action and how it makes him or her feel. Emotive language, however, is not always signaled by the use of the first person. It can be mixed in with apparently referential language. For example, the statement, "The weather is beautiful," also says something about the writer's perception of the state of affairs.

2. When the reader or audience is the primary focus, we are dealing with persuasive speech. This use of language, common in advertisements and political campaign speeches, attempts to influence or affect the reader. "If you want to experience the thrill of driving, this is the car for you," and "For effective leadership and fiscal responsibility, vote Smith" are examples.

3. When the referent is emphasized, we are dealing with referential speech, that is, talk about objects and things. The intent is no longer to tell us about the author's state of mind or to persuade us to adopt a particular course of action. Rather, the intent is to inform us about things, topics, and states of affair. A manual describing the operation of a computer is filled with referential language.

4. The fourth basic use of speech is poetic. Here the focus is upon the words themselves, their shapes and sounds, as the very means of communication. For example, the words in Gerard Manley Hopkins's poem "Pied Beauty" have been carefully selected to create in the reader a strong sense of the beauty of creation and a feeling of worshipful gratitude toward its maker.

Glory be to God for dappled things—
For skies of couple-colour as a brinded cow;
For rose-moles all in stipple upon trout that swim;
Fresh-firecoal chestnut-falls; finches' wings;

Landscape plotted and pieced—fold, fallow, and plough;
And all trades, their gear and tackle trim.

All things counter, original, spare, strange;
Whatever is fickle, freckled (who knows how?)
With swift, slow; sweet, sour; adazzle, dim;
He fathers-forth whose beauty is past change:
Praise him.

What does all this have to do with the Bible? In his *Introduction to the Hebrew Bible* (1988), Michael Dick makes the connection eloquently. First, we need to identify what kind of language is being used in a biblical book or passage in order to understand what the author is trying to communicate. Once we know what kind of speech is being used, we should expect only what is appropriate for that type of communication. For example, if we assume that a biblical story is using referential language (attempting to inform us about an objective state of affairs) when it is not, then we will come to conclusions not intended by the author. In short, we will misunderstand what is being communicated. Dick offers an example from literature that clarifies this point. If we interpret the function of Jonathan Swift's *Gulliver's Travels* (1726) to be referential (that is, Swift thinks that there really are such places as Lilliput), we will conclude that it is a false story. We will miss the point that the novel is a satire that tries to convince the reader that many contemporary social customs are absurd. Similarly, if we read George Orwell's *Animal Farm* (1945) at face value, we will find in it nothing more than a fable about animals who take over a farm from their oppressive owner, Farmer Jones. We won't perceive the story as an allegory about the Bolshevik Revolution and its aftermath. Correlatively, it makes a big difference whether we understand the primary literary function of the creation story in Genesis to be referential (telling us about the factual origin of the universe) or persuasive (trying to convince us that everything comes from God and everything is good).

Second, we need to identify the kind of truth that is being

communicated through the use of a particular kind of language or speech. Not every truth communicated may be referential, that is, descriptive of a state of affairs that could be objectively confirmed by anyone through empirical observation or scientific testing. For example, when someone yells at you, "You're a jerk!" what is being communicated is not necessarily accurate information about you, but rather the anger of the speaker. The point is that sometimes the structure of a statement (as in this example) is referential, while the actual function of the statement is emotive (expressive of the speaker's mind and feelings). Similarly, the biblical authors may sometimes be communicating their own perceptions and feelings even though the structure of their statements is referential. Fundamentalism does not always distinguish carefully between the various uses of language in the Bible. It tends to collapse most uses into the referential use. The Bible, however, is filled with emotive and poetic language, as well as referential language. The historical-critical and the literary-critical approaches to the Bible, unlike the fundamentalist approach, recognize this fact. These modern forms of biblical interpretation make use of a variety of critical tools developed in the past few centuries in order better to understand what is being communicated in the Bible. Let us turn now to consider some of these critical, helpful tools.

Tools for a Critical Study of the Bible

In Chapter Nine we spoke of historical theology as one of the four major types of Christian theology. One very special branch of historical theology is biblical studies. This branch of historical theology attempts to explain how the Bible came to have its present form. It also seeks to understand the significance of specific biblical books and passages for the people for whom they were originally written. The following section will sketch some of the basic forms of criticism that have enabled Jews and Christians to better understand the Bible.

The principal critical tools currently used to interpret the Bible can be divided into two categories. The first category, in which source criticism, redaction criticism, and tradition criticism belong, is particularly appropriate to the study of the Bible. The second category, in which historical criticism, form criticism, and literary criticism belong, is useful in the study of any piece of literature. Let's begin with the first category.

Source, redaction, and tradition criticism are particularly well suited to the study of the Bible since they attempt to identify the successive stages through which a biblical book has passed. From the perspective of biblical criticism, nearly all the books of the Hebrew Scriptures are the product of centuries of anonymous composition and editing, just as the gospels of the New Testament are the product of decades of oral and written composition. Each of these three forms of criticism makes a distinctive contribution to understanding the development of the biblical books into their final form.

1. *Source* criticism divides a finished text or passage into its component written sources. By focusing upon the different terminology found in the same biblical book and by paying attention to apparent contradictions or twin passages in the book, this form of criticism theorizes about the different sources used in the production of the book in its final form. Source criticism has been developed particularly with regard to the first five books of the Hebrew Scriptures (Pentateuch) and the first three books of the New Testament (synoptic gospels). A source-critical analysis of the story of creation in the book of Genesis yields interesting results. Such an analysis reveals that there are two accounts of creation, not one. Source criticism has determined that the first account (1:1–2:3), attributed to what is called the P (or priestly) writer, is not as old as the second account (2:4-23), attributed to what critics term the J (or Yahwist) writer. The differences in the two accounts inform us about the different religious and social perspectives of the authors. For example, P stresses the fact that God is transcendent and unapproachable, while J describes God in anthropomorphic (human-like) terms and writes of God's relationship with human beings as concrete and intimate. And whereas P's style tends to be monotonous, dry, and repetitive, J's style tends to be simple, vivid, and colorful (as, for example, in the stories of the Fall and Sodom and

Gomorrah). P holds a God-centered point of view and tends to refer to God by use of the term *Elohim* (the generic Hebrew term for divine being). J, on the other hand, adopts a people-centered point of view and uses the personal name Yahweh (or "Jehovah") to refer to God. Correspondingly, the focus of the first account of creation is God's creation of the universe from nothing in the course of six days, whereas the making of Adam and Eve from the dust of the earth is the primary subject of the second account of creation.

2. *Redaction* criticism builds upon the work of source criticism. This critical tool is used to investigate why the pre-existing written sources were put together in this *particular* final form. Redaction refers to editing, and redaction criticism attempts to discover what the final editor of the text wanted to communicate by putting together his or her sources the way he or she did. The following analysis of two accounts of Jesus' baptism can serve as an example of redaction criticism:

> Mark 1:9-11
> In those days Jesus came from Nazareth of Galilee and was baptized by John in the Jordan. And when he came up out of the water, immediately he saw the heavens opened and the Spirit descending upon him like a dove; and a voice came from heaven, "Thou art my beloved Son; with thee I am well pleased."

> Luke 3:21-22
> Now when all the people were baptized and when Jesus also had been baptized and was praying, the heaven was opened, and the Holy Spirit descended upon him in bodily form, as a dove, and a voice came from heaven, "Thou art my beloved Son; with thee I am well pleased."

Careful comparison of the two accounts indicates that Luke has changed his source, Mark, by emphasing the role of the Holy Spirit. Whereas all the emphasis in Luke's version is on the descent of the Spirit upon Jesus, in Mark's version Jesus' actual baptism and the descent of the Spirit receive equal weight. The author of Luke's gospel apparently believes that Jesus' ministry began not with his baptism, but with the descent of the Spirit. By relating this conclusion to other observations about the way Luke has used his source(s), redaction criticism can formulate a theory about the particular theological perspective that has guided the writing of Luke's gospel.

Norman Perrin, a twentieth-century New Testament scholar, has observed that the ministry of the church begins in exactly the same way as Jesus' ministry did. In Acts of the Apostles 2, the ministry of the church begins with the descent of the Spirit at Pentecost, which in Acts 1:5 is interpreted in advance as a baptism. Perrin, using redaction criticism, has concluded that the author of Luke's gospel clearly intends to set the ministry of Jesus and the ministry of the church in close and formal parallelism with one another. This is an important clue to understanding Luke's theology.

3. *Tradition* criticism is the most comprehensive of the critical tools in the first category of criticism (the category that is particularly well suited to the study of the Bible). Utilizing the results of source and redaction criticism, tradition criticism attempts to draw a picture of the entire process of a biblical book's development from the oral stage to the stage of written sources to the final stage of redaction or editing of the sources.

The critical tools in the second category (those that can be used in the study of any piece of literature, including the Bible) include historical criticism, form criticism, and literary criticism.

1. *Historical* criticism, as the name suggests, investigates the historical context in which a work was written. It seeks to determine as much as possible about the background and social situation of the author. Historical criticism uses knowledge of other ancient texts (Near Eastern and Roman) and archaeology to shed light upon the possible influences working upon the author of the biblical texts.

2. *Form* criticism examines how the actual form of a biblical passage or story has been shaped by the content of what is being expressed and by the social context. The first concern of form

criticism is to identify distinctive literary forms within a biblical book. Form critics who have studied the gospels have identified the miracle story, for example, as a popular literary form. They have discovered that this type of story was used in ancient Greek, Jewish, and Egyptian culture to proclaim the importance of some local hero. The second concern of form criticism is to speculate upon the social or cultural context in which the form has a definite function. Michael Dick underscores the importance of social context with an example from everyday life. He notes that language (vocabulary, grammar, etc.) that is appropriate with friends over a beer might well be inappropriate in a university seminar, even if the topic of conversation is the same in both instances (an upcoming presidential election, for example). Conversely, the power of the Davidic king in Jerusalem (content) might well be described differently (form) when expressed in a hymn to be recited in the royal temple (context) or in a hostile diatribe of a prophet (context).

3. *Literary* criticism is the final critical tool in this category. Rather than dissecting a biblical book into its component parts or theorizing about the social context of a particular literary form within the book, literary criticism looks at the biblical book as a whole. It wants to understand how the parts have been assembled to convey meaning. Literary criticism and redaction criticism are closely related. Once biblical scholars realized that the final author of a biblical book was a real author, and not just a transmitter of tradition, it became inevitable that they would inquire into what the author's overall purpose and theological perspective was. Thus, redaction criticism tends to shade over into literary criticism.

The literary-critical approach to the Bible is the one we are most likely to find in courses taught at state universities. There the concern is not so much to present the biblical books as a depository of divine revelation as it is to appreciate them as pieces of literature. Anyone, whether a religious person or not, can approach the Bible in a literary-critical way and profit from considering what the biblical books have to say about life. In the past twenty years, literary criticism has become one of the most popular tools for understanding the Bible. One recent development in this field is the recognition that "the meaning" of a biblical text is not necessarily limited to what the author intended or what the original audience understood the meaning to be. The meaning of the text can also be found in what the text says today to you and me. In a sense, the meaning is not buried in or behind the text; rather, it lies in front of the text and happens in the reader.

What kind of light do these various critical tools shed upon the nature of the Bible? How do they inform this branch of historical theology known as biblical studies? It is impossible to describe here the entire course of biblical criticism as it has developed in the past two centuries. But we can summarize some of its general conclusions by focusing upon the critical insights that have been gained into one specific part of the Christian Bible, the gospels.

Critical Approach to the Bible: Some Conclusions

Scholarly study of the Bible has led to the insight that the books of the Bible, including the gospels, were formed gradually. The Bible is not the product of a few inspired individuals who wrote down their texts in one sitting. Rather, it is the product of a religious community (either Jewish or Christian), that passed on stories about their experiences of God in their lives and stories about their history, first by word of mouth (from generation to generation) and then in the form of writings that could be adjusted for new circumstances or supplemented with new insights. In the case of the gospels, most scholars have come to the conclusion that the gospel of Mark is the earliest gospel (probably written between 60 and 75 C.E., or approximately forty years after Jesus's death). Careful analysis of the plot line and language of the first three gospels led to the further conclusion that the gospel of Matthew is based upon Mark's, a source of sayings from Jesus called Q (for example, the Beatitudes: Mt 5:3-12), and certain materials peculiar to Matthew. The gospel of Luke is believed to be a rewriting of Mark, together with elements from Q and certain materials peculiar to Luke.

This means that the authors of the gospels selected and assembled material that had been passed on to them by earlier members of the Christian community. Although each has inherited stories and sayings about Jesus, each author presents them from his own particular theological perspective.

Scholarly analysis of the biblical texts has further suggested that, at least in some cases, books may not be written at all by the person whose name they bear. It was apparently an accepted practice among the ancient Jews and Christians to ascribe works to a revered figure of antiquity, whose own style, interest, or concerns were similar to those reflected in the works. Moses, for example, was long held to be the author of the first five books of the Bible, the Pentateuch; his name was usually associated with the various legal prescriptions cherished in Hebrew society. Just as scholars no longer believe that today, so, too, they doubt that Matthew's gospel and John's gospel were written by the original apostles Matthew and John. Moreover, they have determined that the connection, if any, between Mark's gospel and the John Mark mentioned in the Acts of the Apostles (12:12) is uncertain. In short, critical study of the New Testament suggests that we should not think of the authors of the gospels as people who saw the same event or heard the same teaching of Jesus and then wrote it down in their own words. The authors of the gospel did not have this kind of direct access to the events. They were reinterpreting traditions about Jesus that had been passed down to them by the early Christian community.

If the Bible did not fall from the sky complete, and if the Bible contains elements that are not historically true, then why should Christians believe it? Why turn to it as a source of knowledge about God and a source of spiritual and moral enrichment? To address these questions, we need to examine more carefully the nature of truth and the power of story.

Truth, Myth, and Story

When I suggested to my class that there are myths in the Bible, some reacted in horror. Kimberly, the first-year college student I mentioned earlier, gave an immediate response: "But myths are lies, and God doesn't tell lies." Kimberly's reaction is quite natural when one thinks of the usual understanding of myth. For most people, myth means one of two things, both of which are seen to be negative. On the one hand, myth can mean a (modern or ancient) fictitious story or erroneous belief. This is the connotation that most often comes to mind when we hear, for example, that young people hold many myths about how pregnancy occurs. On the other hand, myth can refer to a story filled with gods and fabulous creatures, used by primitive people to explain their world. This is the meaning that comes to mind when we think of Greek mythology, that ancient collection of stories that attempted to explain how the world came into being, how it operates, and how history develops as the result of the actions of the gods and other beings. In both cases, "myth" appears to be something that ought to be rejected today. Either it is a false story or it is a primitive view of the world that is no longer tenable in a scientific age.

A Christian's reaction to the claim that there are myths in the Bible will usually be negative if myth is understood in one of the two senses just defined. But "myth" can have a very different meaning. In what follows, I would like to propose a positive understanding of myth, one that recognizes that myths still exist today and that that is a good thing. This positive understanding is based upon the analysis and insights of many different scholars, anthropologists, historians of religion, and sociologists. It may be helpful to sample some of their insights.

Although the phenomenon of myth has been intensely studied in the past two centuries, there is no one commonly accepted definition of myth. Ian Barbour, a contemporary physicist and professor of religion, defines myth as a way of ordering our experiences; more specifically, he says it is a vision of reality that interprets the present in the light of certain formative events. The distinguished historian of religions Mircea Eliade adds that myths do not only explain or structure our understanding of life, they also provide us with models of behavior. According to Eliade, the characters in a mythic story behave in an exemplary manner; they become a model of behavior for all who share the story. Rudolf Bultmann, a twentieth-century Lutheran theologian and biblical scholar, defines myth as a story or imagery that expresses the other-worldly in terms of this world and the divine in terms of human life.

All of these different perspectives provide us with pieces for constructing a more positive definition of myth. Kevin J. Sharpe, a chaplain and professor of mathematics, has pulled these pieces together to create a list of some of the general properties of myth. The most important properties include the following: A myth is usually a story that proposes an understanding of the *origin* and *operation* of our world. A myth is shared by an entire *community* of people (a society or a religious group) and it provides them with *models for behavior* today. In addition, a myth usually involves the *whole person* by appealing to the emotions as well as the mind; it is experienced as authoritative and true. That is, people who share the myth do not necessarily reflect upon it in a detached, critical way, for it is part and parcel of the way they look at the world and the way they live.

Sometimes the supernatural content of myths makes them appear to be nothing more than fables, but such an appearance is deceptive. Myths are not the creation of a single individual. Rather, they arise from the consciousness of a group. Moreover, myths have a more serious content than fables. Instead of trying to convey a piece of folk wisdom or to teach a lesson, myths usually describe as well as proscribe a community's general orientation to life. Some myths, such as the creation myths of ancient Israel and ancient Mesopotamia, tell how the world came to be. Thus, they not only explain human origins, but also identify the powers (the gods) with whom humans have to deal if they are to survive and prosper. Other myths, such as national myths, instill a sense of identity and purpose into a social group by situating them as a special people among other nations and by defending their particular "mission" in human history. Myths, then, deal with very important issues: the origin of the world or of particular social groups; the purpose and role of entire communities in human history; the kinds of attitudes, patterns of behavior, or values a group should adopt.

At the beginning of this chapter, we pointed to some of the lingering effects of the Genesis story of creation upon Western society. That story of creation, special to Jews and Christians, is a myth in the positive sense proposed here. It is a story about the origin of the world, a myth that identifies God as the source of life and describes the attitude and behavior people must adopt if they are to have fellowship with God. The myth gives to the people who share it a sense of belonging to a world in which there is purpose, not just chaos. It also establishes a powerful code of behavior for the proper relationship between human beings and for the proper relationship between humankind and the rest of the animal world.

Myths, however, are not confined to the ancient world, nor are they to be found only in religious literature. People today continue to live by myths, even if they do not realize it. An example from our national history may clarify this point. "Manifest destiny" was a powerful idea used by American expansionists in the nineteenth century to justify continued territorial expansion westward to the Pacific Ocean. The idea could be and was expressed in the form of a myth, a story about the purpose former European settlers, now Americans, were believed to have in human history. The story expressed and promoted expansionist sentiments. John L. O'Sullivan, who coined the term in 1845, claimed that Providence (that is, God) had given the new nation the purpose of "overspreading the continent." How could nineteenth-century Americans have believed that God wanted that? It must be, came the answer from the new nation, that their form of government, their manner of religion, their form of life were the best. This sense of superiority and mission was so strong that it could justify the risk of war with Mexico over land annexation as well as justify taking land away from the native peoples (the so-called Indians). Although the expansionist rhetoric is not strong today, something of the mythic force of manifest destiny remains. It lives on in the myth of the American Dream, the story that, since this is a land that offers everyone an equal opportunity to prosper, people can materially succeed and be happy in this country as in no other. Such a belief leads many Americans to conclude that it is the destiny and purpose of the United States to spread its economy and form of government throughout the world.

As these examples make clear, myths are interpretations of reality in the form of stories that explain our experience of the world, shape our attitudes, and mold our behavior. The question, however, naturally arises: Are these interpretations true? This is a complex question to which there is no simple answer. Our example of manifest destiny can underscore the complexity. Was the myth of manifest destiny experienced as true by native peoples (Indians) and Mexicans? Hardly. Yet the majority of United States citizens at the time believed it to be true. Is America the greatest nation in the world? Perhaps. Does America offer equal opportunity to everyone, as the American Dream suggests? In theory, but not always in fact, for there is racism and sexism in this land of opportunity.

What are we to conclude about the truth of our myths? It seems that whether or not we accept a myth as true depends on the success of the myth in accounting for our *own* experience. Manifest destiny did not make sense of native Americans' own experience of themselves and their traditions; it did, however, make sense of the experience of the frontier people and their sense of mission. For some, the myth was true; for others, it was not. Does this mean that truth is relative? In a sense. Let me outline two ways we can approach the question of a myth's truth.

First, we can follow the suggestion of Norman Perrin, the twentieth-century Scripture scholar mentioned earlier. He suggests that we not think of a myth as true or false, but rather as effective or ineffective. According to Perrin, a myth has to arise out of the consciousness of the people; it has to correspond to reality as they experience it or make sense of a significant part of reality. If a myth does these things, then it is "true," or "effective."

Second, we can attempt to establish criteria for determining which myths are *worthy* of acceptance as true. Some possible criteria are: that the myth in question can make a reasonable claim to have some basis in reality, as confirmed by the experiences of others than ourselves; that the attitudes, feelings, and patterns of behavior evoked by the myth are capable of transforming ourselves *and* our world for the better. The more successful a myth is in meeting these or related criteria, the more likely it is that the myth is "true." These judgments about truth are not scientific. They are not capable of strict proof by means of logic or empirical observation accessible to everyone of sound mind. Nor are these judgments of truth confined to what is literally and entirely true. There can be degrees or levels of truth. Truth is not necessarily black or white. Truth, just like life, is more complicated than that.

These insights into the complex nature of truth are helpful when we examine both types of myth, that is, those that don't involve an element of history (myths of creation, which by definition occur before the beginning of history) and those that do (the foundational myths of the Jewish people and of the early Christian church). They remind us, for example, that the question, whether God really created the world in six days, is not necessarily the most important question. Creation may not have occurred literally in six days and Eve may not have been made from Adam's rib, but it can nonetheless be true that God is the source of everything that is and everything God created is good. The importance of myth in the life of a religion can be disclosed by examining the foundational myth of Christianity.

The Foundational Myth of Christianity

The foundational myth of Christianity is the story that God was uniquely active in the ministry of Jesus of Nazareth and that, by his death, Jesus reconciled all of humankind to God and to one another. This story, like the foundational myth of Judaism, is a mix of history and mythic interpretation. History is to be found in the fact that Jesus of Nazareth was a real person, that he spoke of God's reign, and that he was put to death. Myth is to be found in the interpretation by Jesus' followers that Jesus' death was redemptive for humankind and that Jesus' resurrection confirmed the fact that he came from God, that he was, in fact, the Son of God. Let us take a closer look at this interweaving of history and myth.

Like the exodus story, the narrative of Jesus' passion, death, and resurrection has the appearance of an historical account. The gospel authors seem to be using referential language. And, as we have seen, a fundamentalist approach would accept this appearance as accurate. A critical approach, however, would regard the narrative as a mixture of historical fact, religious conviction, and mythic interpretation. The way in which the two key events in the narrative (Jesus' death and resurrection) are presented underlines the complex and intricate interweaving of history and interpretation.

On the one hand, the crucifixion is probably the most fully attested historical fact in Jesus' life. Virtually no one, including non-Christians, doubts that Jesus was a real human being who was put to death. Although the details of the story differ, all four canonical gospels agree that Jesus was put to death and was buried. It is not surprising, moreover, that tradition and source criticism indicate that a passion narrative was probably the most extensive unit of traditional material inherited by the synoptic evangelists. In fact, the first gospel (Mark's) is often referred to as a passion narrative with an extended introduction.

On the other hand, historical and literary criticism suggest that not all the details of even Mark's passion narrative are historically true. For example, Mark takes details from Psalms 22 and 69 to portray Jesus as a righteous sufferer whom God will vindicate. Let us compare the texts.

Mark 15:23-30

They offered him wine mixed with myrrh, but he refused it. Then they crucified him, and shared out his clothing, casting lots to decide what each should get. It was the third hour when they crucified him. The inscription giving the charge against him read: "The King of the Jews." And they crucified two robbers with him, one on his right and one on his left. The passers-by jeered at him; they shook their heads and said, "Aha! So you would destroy the Temple and rebuild it in three days! Then save yourself: come down from the cross!"

Psalm 69:21
They gave me [God's servant] poison for food, and for my thirst they gave me vinegar to drink.

Psalm 22:18
...they divide my garments among them and cast lots for my clothes.

Psalm 22:7-8
...all who see me jeer at me, they toss their heads and sneer, "He relied on Yahweh, let Yahweh save him! If Yahweh is his friend, let Him rescue him!"

Perrin has observed that these narrative details (offering wine mixed with myrrh, the dividing of the clothes, and the mocking) are not true at the level of factual history. They are included because Jesus' crucifixion is being interpreted as the death of a righteous sufferer whom God vindicated—hence, as the fulfillment of Psalms 22 and 69. The point is that early followers of Jesus experienced him as someone who was righteous and who had suffered unjustly, and they attempted to express this experience by telling Jesus' story with these details included.

Since their experience of Jesus as messiah was contrary to popular conceptions of the messiah, early Christians were compelled to scour Hebrew Scripture for support of their interpretation of Jesus. The idea of a crucified messiah was scandalous at best, inconceivable at worst. Despite the fact that there was no trace of a suffering "Son of Man" in Hebrew Scriptures or tradition, Jesus' followers proclaimed, in the classic words of Mk 10:45, that "the Son of Man did not come to be served but to serve, and to give up his life as a ransom for many." Christians did eventually find resources in the Jewish tradition to express what they felt was the significance of Jesus. The suffering servant songs in Isaiah (especially Ch. 53), the traditional sprinkling of blood as the means of ratifying the covenant with God (Ex 24:4-8), and the Passover celebration all provided resources for making intelligible to their contemporaries what early Christians thought and believed about Jesus' death. Later generations of Christians found other ways besides this sacrificial model for expressing their conviction that Jesus' death was redemptive. (Recall the discussion of Augustine's devil-ransom theory and Anselm's satisfaction theory in Chapter Nine.)

Aside from the saving character of Jesus' death, his resurrection is also an element in the Christian narrative that defies scientific verification. Unlike his crucifixion, his resurrection was not a publicly observable event that anyone could verify if he or she were alive then and present at the right place. In fact, none of the canonical gospels describes the actual resurrection. Rather, they report stories of the reappearance of Jesus after his death and burial. Jesus, moreover, appears only to his followers, not to unbelievers. Nonetheless, Jesus' resurrection has been, since the time of St. Paul (see 1 Cor 15:14-19), the cornerstone of Christian apologetics.

A historical and literary critique of the gospels' post-resurrection stories reveals differences in the details of the stories, as well as different theological perspectives. The original version of Mark's gospel (ending at 16:8), for example, has no description of post-resurrection appearances. Both Matthew's and Luke's gospels, on the other hand, record two appearances. But even in these two gospels, differences exist. Whereas Luke is more concerned with what the risen Jesus looked like (24:36-43) and with emphasizing that Jesus' resurrection was in "fulfillment of the Scriptures" (24:13-35), Matthew stresses the fact that Jesus appears after death in order to commission his followers (28:16-20).

What do these differences mean? What kind of speech are the evangelists using? The structure of the narratives seems referential and objective, but is that the real function of the language used? Is it possible that the language is emotive, describing not so much the change in Jesus, but rather the change in the disciples' understanding of who Jesus is? Christian Scripture scholar

Raymond Brown points out, for example, that the post-resurrection confession is not simply "We have seen Jesus," but "We have seen the *Lord*" (Lk 24:34; Jn 20:18; 21:7). Brown's point is that, insofar as "Lord" is a christological term of interpretation, the evangelists are telling us that they came to enjoy not only sight of Jesus, but also and primarily *insight* into Jesus' signficance. Do not the apologetic elements (that is, the appeal to Hebrew Scripture to justify the notion of a suffering messiah, the attempt to deflect objections to the resurrection story) suggest that the passion-death-resurrection narrative employs persuasive language, at least in part? That is, the narrative is attempting to convince the reader to adopt the same understanding of Jesus that the authors hold. Is not the Christian foundational story a myth in the positive sense proposed in this chapter?

As you will recall, myths propose an understanding of the way the world operates, they speak to the human heart as well as to the mind, they offer models of behavior, and they bind a community of people together by shaping as well as expressing their attitudes and values. The story of Jesus' passion, death, and resurrection expresses the conviction that selfless love for the sake of others is redemptive. It proclaims that a person who spoke and lived as Jesus did must be divine. It affirms that the spirit of Jesus lives on after his death and burial. It challenges people to adopt Jesus' way of dealing with others so that they too can "be perfect just as" their "heavenly Father is perfect" (Mt 5:48). In short, the Jesus narrative is a myth—a very powerful myth indeed.

In our modern, skeptical, scientific age, people clamor for certainty and for proof. Contemporary Christians, however, cannot verify the truth of the Christian myth in a scientific way. They were not present to witness Jesus' life or his resurrection. The truth of the myth of Jesus' redemptive death and resurrection can be proven today only to the extent to which his spirit is still experienced and expressed in the life of the Christian community. That is, the myth is true to the extent that the Christ's presence is experienced in community and in the celebration of the eucharist; it is true to the extent that people experience the fact that self-sacrificing love in service of God and neighbor is capable of healing divisions and reconciling people with one another and with the God who is love. As Anglican theologian John Macquarrie argues, acts of God are not publicly observable events open to perception by the senses, though they manifest themselves in and through such occasions. Even if we could prove the story of the empty tomb to be historically true, that would still not establish the fact that God had acted in the resurrection of Jesus. The Christian story that proclaims it to be true is a myth, in the positive sense we have argued for throughout this chapter.

How then are we to approach Scripture and tradition? How are they to be used in theology? To the first question, our answer is that we should approach these sources of Christian life neither credulously nor skeptically. To approach them credulously means that we accept Scripture and tradition at face value, that we take the language in which they express themselves to be literally true, referential language. To approach them skeptically means that we refuse to accept Scripture and tradition as bearers of Christian revelation, that we understand the language in which they express themselves to be false referential or emotive language. The approach we have advocated in this chapter is one of critical openness: critical, because this approach does not take Scripture and tradition blindly at face value; open, because this approach is open to believing that Scripture and tradition convey special insights into the nature of reality, God, life, and human purpose. This approach, though not fundamentalist, still affirms that the insights, values, and stories contained in the Bible and reaffirmed in the Christian tradition are indeed inspired by God—in the sense that they express something of the truth about *ultimate* reality.

More specifically, this critically open approach maintains that before Scripture and tradition can be used appropriately today as resources in theological reflection, we need to examine them and their contexts very carefully. We need to learn as much as possible about the historical, social, and cultural situations in which they were formed and about the communities that formulated them. We need to approach Scripture and tradition with attention to the types of speech they use and their intended functions, the literary forms or genres employed, the sources (written and oral) that lay behind them. In short, to arrive at the most relatively adequate understanding of the Bible and Christian tradition, we must make use of the various critical tools described earlier in this chapter.

To the second question, how Scripture and tradition are to be used in theological reflection, our answer is: with fidelity and intelligence. Fidelity means that Christians today continue to shape their attitudes, basic beliefs, and moral practices in conformity with the essential thrust and fundamental themes of Scripture and tradition. Insofar as Christians want their statements and practices to be an expression of *Christian* theology, they must see that they are appropriate to the Christian tradition affirmed by the Christian community. Intelligent use of Scripture and tradition means that Christians today are not to take the statements and practices expressed in these two sources out of context. They may not take the statements and practices uncritically at face value; they must not be allowed to twist the sources to say what they want them to say; and they must never forget that Scripture and tradition, insofar as they have been formulated by human beings and therefore reflect those limitations, can of necessity only express *part* of the truth about God.

Questions for Reflection and Discussion

1. How did different perspectives on the place of Scripture and tradition in Christian life develop within the three major Christian groups (Catholic, Orthodox, Protestant)? If Protestants agree on "Scripture alone," why did so many Protestant denominations develop?

2. Do you think Kimberly is right to say that if a Christian is

not a fundamentalist, he or she does not have *true* faith in God? Describe how your own approach to Scripture compares with the approaches of Kimberly and Debbie.

3. To what extent do the fundamentalist and the critical approaches to Scripture find different kinds of truth in the stories of the Bible? Can you identify a story or poem that you believe says something true about reality, even though it is not dealing with historical facts?

4. What does it mean to say that the foundational story of Christianity is a myth in the positive sense? A myth in the negative sense? How would you decide whether the Christian myth is true or not?

SUGGESTED READINGS

Barr, James. *Beyond Fundamentalism: Biblical Foundations for Evangelical Christianity*. Philadelphia: Westminster, 1984.

Barbour, Ian G. *Myths, Models and Paradigms: A Comparative Study in Science and Religion*. New York: Harper & Row, 1974.

Brown, Raymond E. *The Virginal Conception and Bodily Resurrection of Jesus*. Mahwah, N.J.: Paulist Press, 1973.

Dick, Michael Brennan. *Introduction to the Hebrew Bible: An Inductive Reading of the Old Testament*. Englewood Cliffs, N.J.: Prentice Hall, 1988.

Eliade, Mircea. *Myths, Dreams and Mysteries: The Encounter Between Contemporary Faiths and Archaic Realities*. New York: Harper & Row, 1960.

Perrin, Norman. *The New Testament: An Introduction*. New York: Harcourt Brace Jovanovich, 1974.

____. *The Resurrection According to Matthew, Mark, and Luke*. Philadelphia: Fortress Press, 1977.

Sharpe, Kevin J. *From Science to an Adequate Mythology*. Auckland, New Zealand: Interface, 1984.

Williams, R. Rhys. *Let Each Gospel Speak for Itself*. Mystic, Conn. : Twenty-Third Publications, 1987.

CHAPTER ELEVEN

Human Experience and Its Role in Theology

When many people, especially young people, hear the words "religious experience," they think of the dramatic events reported about a Moses or a St. Paul. Since most people, however, have not heard God speaking from a burning bush and have not been knocked to the ground by invisible forces, they might conclude that they have never had an experience of a truly religious nature. Or, they might conclude that religious experiences, when they do occur, have little to do with their everyday lives. In this chapter, we will investigate these conclusions by exploring the nature of "religious experience" from a Christian perspective. In particular, we will examine the current role our experiences play or ought to play in doing theology as well as consider the role of past experience in the formation of Christian doctrines.

We will begin by investigating the interaction between experience, Scripture, and tradition in the formation of traditional

Christian doctrines. We will then turn to consider the question, whether people today continue to experience God as did their forebears, and how people's experiences today can be interpreted as pointing toward God. After this inquiry into the religious dimension of our common experiences, we will examine the ways in which some contemporary experiences have called traditional Christian doctrines and practices into question. Specifically, we will look at the ways in which our experience of suffering and radical evil, on the one hand, and the experience of contemporary women, on the other, have challenged the traditional conceptions of God and the traditional structure of the Christian churches.

Experience, Scripture, and Tradition

In a very real sense, human experience has always been the fundamental resource in Christian theology. At first glance, this statement seems to contradict the impression Chapter Ten may have made about the importance of the Bible in Christian churches. But, you may recall, we made the point that the Bible itself is a collection of the experiences that the Israelites and early Christians had of God. The description of those experiences was so profound and insightful that Scripture came to possess a special aura of holiness. Nonetheless, the words in the Bible are human words, reflecting human ideas about and human experiences of God and reality. In a similar fashion, the tradition of Christianity is also an embodiment of the religious experiences of those who preceded the present generation in Christian faith. The tradition we receive is comprised of beliefs, practices, and rules that express the meaning of Christian faith and its implications for living as perceived by Christians of past ages.

Viewed from this perspective, the triple division of Scripture, tradition, and experience is both artificial and deceptive. Scripture and tradition can be subsumed under the category of experience in the sense that both are witnesses to experiences of God's saving power. To claim that experience is the *primary* category is not, however, to assert that it is the *only* criterion for contemporary Christian theology. As contemporary theologians George Lindbeck and Sallie McFague point out, we don't experience reality apart from the context of the community that has formed us. Most Christians, as well as most members of other religions, are born into their particular religious community. And that community, by giving people the basic concepts, images, and language with which to interpret and express their experiences, forms people at the most basic levels of their existence. It leads people to interpret their experiences of reality in ways they cannot fully control and often in ways that they do not recognize. Consequently, just as it is "natural" for a person living in a Buddhist culture to think of ultimate reality in terms devoid of God, so it is "natural" for a person growing up in a Western culture to think of ultimate reality in terms of God.

If both the Bible and the rest of Christian tradition are expressions of past religious experiences, how is it that they have come to possess greater practical authority than our own experiences today? Why are they regarded as normative in a way that contemporary experience is not? Sallie McFague and Gordon Kaufman suggest that neither Scripture nor tradition *should* be regarded as absolutely normative. They propose to think of theology not as the process of interpreting these past records of religious experience, but as the creative construction of God images and metaphors appropriate to contemporary experience. Most Christian theologians, however, continue to regard Scripture and tradition as normative in some sense for their theological reflections. That means that they use Scripture and tradition as reference points. Either as the starting-point or finishing-point for their reflections, Scripture and tradition are held to be indispensable resources for answering our ultimate questions about God and life's meaning.

Why is that? Of the numerous reasons that might be given, let me highlight two. First, the Christian tradition, but most especially the Bible, has been acknowledged by millions of people throughout time to have expressed insights into the nature of God and the meaning of life with such depth and power that it demands to be regarded as "inspired" and authoritative. The Bible is a classic that we can ignore only to our own impoverishment. Second, since the early days of the Christian church, Christians have appreciated the need for some foundational expression of the basics of Christian faith. The demands from outside the church for an explanation of the Christian faith, as well as the necessity to distinguish appropriate manifestations of the faith (orthodoxy) from inappropriate manifestations (heresy) within the church, led to the formulation of canonical or approved Scriptures, creeds (the Apostles Creed and the Nicene Creed), and basic doctrines (the trinity). Accepting the meaning of these earlier expressions of the faith as true has been the central means by which later generations of Christians have been able to define themselves as "Christians," people who could be distinguished both from non-believers and other believers in God. Like all people, Christians have had the sense that preserving their past was central to maintaining their identity.

Scripture and tradition, then, do have an authority that demands to be recognized. To the extent that we wish to be known as Christians, we must relate our contemporary reflections to these past classic expressions of Christian faith. We must be able to demonstrate some basic continuity between our attempts today at witnessing and expressing Christian faith and those earlier expressions of Christian witness. Scripture, tradition, and contemporary experience, then, are related to each other dialectically. That is, they interact critically and creatively. Scripture and tradition raise questions about the validity of our interpretations of contemporary experience just as contemporary experience raises questions about the continuing validity of Scripture's and tradition's past expressions of the faith. Scripture, tradition, and contemporary experience take one another seriously.

In the next section, we will examine how earlier Christians made use of their experience in formulating their basic beliefs about God and Jesus.

Experience and the Making of Christian Doctrine

Contrary to what some people might believe, Christian doctrines such as the trinity did not descend fully formed from heaven. Christian doctrines are the result of years, sometimes centuries, of reflection upon the Christian community's experience of God in the light of the preceding tradition. A brief look at the formation of the distinctive Christian doctrine of the trinity can illuminate the interaction of experience, Scripture, and tradition in the life of the Christian churches.

Since the first century, Christians had affirmed that Jesus was different from other human beings. In fact, he was declared to be different even from other prophets who claimed to speak God's word to humanity. Early Christians attributed such high stature to Jesus, expressed in the titles Christ ("the anointed one" of God), the Son of Man, and the Son of God, because in him they had encountered the power and reality of God. But just as they were convinced of Jesus' special character among other human beings, the early Christians were equally sure that the God of the universe was one. Both of these convictions were rooted in their "experience."

It is important to remember that "experience" is a very broad concept. It can refer to the personal thoughts, emotions, and perceptions that result from living through an event right now. But "experience" can also refer to the totality of events in the past of an individual or group and the knowledge gained from them. I am using the word "experience" in both senses: personal, lived experience, and inherited knowledge from the past that now shapes the way we perceive reality. These two senses of the word, however, are related, for there is no such thing as "raw experience." Every experience is an interpreted experience. And the tools we have for interpreting our experiences are largely, if not entirely, inherited tools (that is, the past experiences of others). This kind of interplay between present, personal experience and past, inherited experience was involved in the development of early Christian ideas about the nature of Jesus the Christ.

On the one hand, monotheism was part of the legacy bequeathed to Christians by their Jewish ancestors. Monotheism was part of Christian experience, in the second sense of the word. That is, monotheism had become the accepted lens through which Christians interpreted all of their present experiences. Consequently, Christians, like the Hebrews before them, believed the world and its history to be in the hands of one mighty, yet loving God. And they interpreted their present experiences to be confirmations of the activity and providence of the one God.

On the other hand, the earliest followers of Jesus had a personal experience of the redemptive effect of Jesus' ministry. Although later generations of Christians could not have that kind of direct experience of Jesus, they could still experience something of his spirit when they gathered together as a community of love and service. The fact that Christians did feel Christ's spirit, especially when they gathered for the celebration of the eucharist, seemed to confirm the claim of his earliest followers, namely, that he was from God. As 1 Corinthians 16:22 and Philippians 2:5-11 attest, Jesus was clearly invoked in worship as "Lord" from the very start of the church's life. The title "lord" (*kurios* in Greek) was the usual translation of the divine name in the Hebrew Scriptures. To call Jesus "Lord," therefore, was to give him a divine name whose glory was not to be shared with any creature. In other words, Christians experienced the Christ as divine, yet they believed that God was one, not two.

A number of attempts were made in the second, third, and fourth centuries to reconcile belief in the oneness of God with belief in the divinity of the Christ. Some Christians, in an attempt to defend themselves against the charge of being believers in two gods, denied that Christ was truly divine. Theodotus of Byzantium, a second-century Christian, proclaimed that Jesus was a man who received a share of God's power at his baptism. Arius, a fourth-century priest in Alexandria, Egypt, explained that Christ was given the dignity of Son of God by the Father, but that he was not God by nature. This seemed to preserve the oneness of God. But what about Jesus' divine character? To maintain the Christ's elevated status among God's creatures, Arius claimed that the Christ, although created and not eternal, was different from all other creatures in that he was the instrument used by God the Father in creating the rest of the universe. Although their views could find some support in Scripture, both Arius's and Theodotus's explanations failed to account adequately for the liturgical experience of most Christians. As Oxford professor Maurice Wiles has pointed out, the continuing practice of invoking the name of Jesus in worship, both in informal prayer and in hymns, argued against Arius's explanation of who the Christ was. The practice of Christian worship demanded that every doctrinal definition of Christ be consonant with the fact that he was being directly addressed in prayer. The point was that Christians prayed only to God, not to creatures. And if Christians felt natural in praying to Jesus, then he must somehow be God.

Arius's teaching caused such agitation among the masses of Christians in the Roman Empire that the Emperor Constantine felt compelled to convene a general council of church leaders to resolve the controversy. This Council of Nicea, which met in 325, rejected Arius's teaching by proclaiming that the Christ was the Son of God, begotten of the Father from eternity and "of the same substance" as the Father. In short, the council members proclaimed Christ to be truly divine. But the way this was expressed in Nicea's Creed seemed to obliterate distinctions between Father and Son. If both Father and Son were divine, did this mean that Christians believed in two Gods? To many Christians, the formulation of Nicea did not answer this question sufficiently. Furthermore, it did not adequately express the conviction (tradition) they had inherited from their predecessors, namely, that Jesus and the Father were distinct.

Previous attempts to defend the divinity of Christ by eliminating real distinctions between him and God (the Father) had already faltered. Sabellius, a third-century Roman theologian, had suggested that the Son was simply an alternative mode of the Father's being. Such explanations, while justifying the church's practice of praying directly to Jesus, failed to do justice to much scriptural evidence that made it clear that Jesus and God the Father were not the same. And Scripture had already become a lens through which Christians saw and interpreted their experience of God, the world, and themselves.

As a result, the so-called trinitarian controversy raged in the Roman Empire for half a century after Nicea. Some defenders of Arius won the support of Constantine's successor. Others proposed a position between Arius's and that of Nicea (saying that the Son was of a *similar* but not of the same substance as the Father). By the time of the Council of Constantinople in 381, Christians finally found a way to express their faith that did justice to their experience of the divinity of the Christ and to their monotheistic tradition. They proclaimed that the Father and the Son, as well as the Spirit, were one in substance or being. That is, they all shared the same *divine* essence. They were, however, distinct persons. The Father was not the Son, and the Son was not the Spirit. In this way, the orthodox doctrine of the trinity came to be formulated.

It would be simplistic to suggest that the formation of the doctrine of the trinity (or of any other Christian doctrine) was simply the result of Christians' reflecting upon their experience, personal or inherited. Already at Nicea and Constantinople, politics, personal rivalry, and ideology were involved. The emperor supported a particular doctrinal position, at least in part, because it was politically expedient. Bishops accused brother bishops of heresy sometimes out of jealousy, at other times out of ignorance. Factors such as these would continue to influence the shape of Christian doctrines and practices in succeeding centuries. Nonetheless, what was initially at the root of the development of most doctrines was an experience, an experience whose expression in words, of course, was always shaped by a particular cultural and religious context.

As Christianity aged and grew in size and influence, the doctrines of the past, especially those formulated in the first five centuries, came to have a life of their own. No longer was their acceptance dependent upon their ability to correspond well to the Christian community's present experience. Instead, ancient doctrines and practices came to be the touchstone by which contemporary ideas, beliefs, and experiences were judged. And the church, which had become a powerful institution by the Middle Ages, could compel assent to these orthodox doctrines and rules (threat of excommunication, the inquisition). The inherited doctrines of the past were to be accepted without question. Moreover, their meaning was to be expressed only in the very same hallowed words of the first few centuries.

As a result, contemporary experience seemed to have less and less of a part to play in expressing what it meant to be a Christian. One knew that a person was a "Christian" if he or she confessed the beliefs, doctrines, and norms that were first formulated in earlier centuries and were now a part of the church's tradition. But even in the Middle Ages, people's experience continued to have some effect upon the way past doctrines were understood. As we saw in Chapter Nine, Anselm of Canterbury's experience of a feudal society influenced the way he understood Christian redemption.

This influence of human experience upon the teachings of the church, however, remained hidden or continued to be ignored for many centuries. In more recent times, Christians have appealed to their experiences more explicitly and self-consciously as a source of insight into the meaning of life and the meaning of Christian faith. But do our experiences put us in touch with *God*? Or is belief in God something we have to accept on the word of others, for example, parents, religious leaders, teachers, the Bible? In the next section, we will explore answers to these questions.

Religious Experience: What Is It?

The impression that an experience must be dramatic or extraordinary in order to be termed "religious" has been around for a long time. The notion was reinforced in the West by the American philosopher William James (1842-1910). In his book, *The Varieties of Religious Experience* (1902), James attempted to demonstrate that personal experience rather than general "philosophical" views about human destiny was the backbone of the world's religions. In the process, James made frequent appeal to reports of the very intense religious experiences of individuals. The following report of the experience of a nineteenth-century man is typical:

> I know not how I got back into the encampment, but found myself staggering up to Rev. ______'s Holiness tent—and

> as it was full of seekers and a terrible noise inside, some groaning, some laughing, and some shouting, by a large oak, ten feet from the tent, I fell on my face by a bench, and tried to pray, and every time I would call on God, something like a man's hand would strangle me by choking. I don't know whether there was any one around or near me or not. I thought I should surely die if I did not get help, but just as often as I would pray, that unseen hand was felt on my throat and my breath squeezed off. Finally something said: "Venture on the atonement, for you will die anyway if you don't." So I made one final struggle to call on God for mercy, with the same choking and strangling, determined to finish the sentence of prayer for Mercy, if I did strangle and die. The last I remember was falling back on the ground with the same unseen hand on my throat. I don't know how long I lay there or what was going on. None of my folks were present. When I came to myself, there was a crowd around me praising God. The very heavens seemed to open and pour down rays of light and glory. Not for a moment only, but all day and night, floods of light and glory seemed to pour through my soul, and oh, how I was changed, and everything became new. My horses and hogs and even everybody seemed changed.

James justified his belief that the more extraordinary experiences, such as this one, held the best clues for discovering the nature of religious experience by claiming that their intensity displayed more clearly the psychological processes involved in all religious experiences. Just as we go to scientists, and not average citizens, in order to learn the secrets of nuclear physics, so too we must go to those who have had the more extreme religious experiences, not to the ordinary members of an organized religion, in order to learn what "religious experience" really is. This was James's argument.

If we accept only dramatic experiences as examples of religious experience, however, we are led to the conclusion that only a small portion of the human race has had a religious experience.

Recent polls in the United States support such a conclusion. A 1986 Gallup Poll reveals that only 32 percent of the adult population claim to have had the dramatic experience of being "born again," the experience of a powerful turning point in one's life as one makes a personal commitment to Christ. A Gallup poll conducted a decade earlier shows that an even smaller number of people, less than 5 percent, reported seeing visions of God or hearing God's voice, as Moses did. Does this mean that God is experienced by only a very small number of people? If so, why is that? Or is it possible that many people have experiences that can disclose something about God or an ultimate reality?

In order to answer these questions, we must decide what makes an experience "religious." James said that religious experiences are those in which we are aware that there is something wrong with us as we naturally are, yet feel that we are saved from this wrongness by making the proper connection with "higher powers." Such a description surely fits the profound "conversion" experiences of such Christians as St. Paul, St. Augustine, and Martin Luther. Perhaps it even fits Bill Russell's experience described in Chapter Five. But as that same chapter made clear, religious experiences need not be abrupt or overwhelming. A broader conception of religious experience comes into focus when we look at what the world's religions have in common.

It seems that all the world's great religions share a belief that our visible world is part of a more spiritual world from which it draws its primary significance. The religions also believe that a harmonious relation with that spiritual world is the end of human existence. If that is the case, then "religious experience" might generally be described as any experience, intense or mundane, that supports or enhances this belief. Such a broad definition of religious experience clearly includes experiences that can be encountered everyday by anyone. The experience of the beauty of nature, the sense of wonder at the complex process of human embryonic development, the experience of life as a great gift when we feel the genuine love of a friend, all of these experiences can reinforce our belief that there is something more to reality than the visible world of matter. These experiences can point in the direction of a deeper or a transcendent dimension to life.

Of course, an objection can be immediately raised to such a broad concept of religious experience. Why should these everyday experiences be interpreted as religious, a critic might ask? A sense that life is a gift or a sense of awe at the beauty and complexity of life seems to be quite natural. Why bring God or a transcendent reality into it? And that is a very good question. From the outset, we must confess that there is no way to prove definitively that these experiences are evidence of the reality of God or a higher, spiritual realm. Fundamental theologians, however, have the task of attempting to demonstrate that it is at least possible, if not plausible, to interpret these experiences in that way. As you might recall from our discussion of the four types of theology in Chapter Nine, fundamental theology has been constrained ever since the Enlightenment to find ways to assert the reality of God other than through the use of "logical proofs." In the next few sections, we will explore some of the ways in which contemporary fundamental theology seeks to affirm the reality of God. We will notice in the process how each of these attempts makes prominent use of our own experiences of ourselves and of our world.

Experiences of Limits and of Transcendence

Karl Rahner, one of the most influential Catholic theologians of the twentieth century, insisted throughout his life that we cannot speak about human beings without speaking about God, just as we cannot speak about God without speaking about human beings. His point was that human persons are built in such a way that they are, knowingly or unknowingly, in relation to God. From Rahner's perspective, human nature has an inherent openness to God. The more we learn of the human, the more we learn of God. Although this bold claim is not self-evident, Rahner argued to this conclusion on the basis of his analysis of human beings as questioners and knowers. You might recall that we introduced some of these ideas in Chapter One, where we referred to Rahner's reflections upon the horizon of our experiences and our experience of limits.

Rahner's point may be made by examining the dynamic quality of our knowing. If we examine our own intellectual activity, must we not admit that, no matter what we already know or have learned, we always seem to want to know more? Even if we understand the basics of physics, the fundamentals of accounting, or the operation of motor engines, do we not naturally seek to know more? Rahner explained this natural desire in us as a drive to know God. His reasoning is that our insatiable desire to know is fueled by the awareness, often not conscious, that no finite object we have ever known has satisfied our inquisitive minds. Only an infinite reality, with infinite depth and richness, could finally and fully satisfy such an intellectual thirst. Like Thomas Aquinas many centuries before him, Rahner believed that this orientation of the human mind to the infinite would be in vain unless there really existed an infinite object we could know. Refusing to accept this natural drive as futile or absurd, Rahner claimed that it did point in the direction of something very real, namely, the Infinite or God.

The question immediately arises that if Rahner is right, if in every act of explicit knowledge we implicitly know God, how could atheism be possible? And why has atheism spread in the modern age?

The first part of a response to these questions would be to clarify in what sense Rahner means that *everyone* knows God. Rahner held that the knowledge of God to which he referred was very different from the usual way in which we know things. Usually we claim to have knowledge of something based on sense experience. We see this desk, we can touch it and feel its hardness. Bumping into the desk forces us to take notice of it. That is, our knowledge of the desk is explicit, conscious, and sensible. The knowledge of God that Rahner ascribes to every human being is not of this sort. It is not based on sense experience; it is not a knowledge we are *forced* to notice, like being forced to know that a desk is in our way by bumping into it.

Rather, we become consciously aware of our natural knowledge of God only when we freely choose to attend critically and reflectively to the basic structure of our intellectual and moral activity. If we refuse to reflect at all or if we suppress this kind of reflection, then we won't be explicitly conscious of the implicit intellectual movement of our nature toward God. Since this natural knowledge of God is one that we can ignore or suppress and since it is different from the way we know other realities, Rahner termed this kind of knowledge "transcendental." It transcends or goes beyond our usual way of knowing. It makes us transcend or go beyond the mere appearances presented to our senses. It points in the direction of a reality that is beyond the sensible world.

Atheism (denial of the reality of God) and agnosticism (denial of the possibility of knowing whether God exists) are possible, then, to the extent that people ignore the experience of transcendence. Rahner held that this experience could be evaded in a number ways. For example, people might get so caught up in their daily routine that they don't bother to reflect on anything that is not part of the daily ritual of sleeping, eating, and working. Or, some people might be aware of the infinite horizon built into the human person, but postpone thinking about what it means until they get enough leisure time or develop enough intellectual maturity to appreciate it. Still others may acknowledge the drive for more, but refuse to name the drive as movement toward God because they find that the concepts of God presented to them by parents or teachers are unbelievable, childish, or alien. If such people live morally good lives, they are Christians of a sort. Rahner called these "atheists" anonymous theists (believers in God) because their actions showed, even though their words did not, that they had responded unconsciously to God's call to transcend their own narrow concerns in order to meet the needs of others.

Fundamental theologians reflect upon other human experiences that might intimate the reality of God. Another such experience is our basic sense of the worthwhileness of life. Let us now consider this theological argument.

Worthwhileness of Life and Reality of God

If we examine the events in our own lives or in the life of the world community, we must admit that there is much suffering and tragedy. Loved ones die, innocent people suffer, nations engage in war, a few countries thrive while many more languish or decline. Yet, if confronted with the question whether life is worthwhile, do not most of us believe that it is? How is that possible? If we look only to the major events of the twentieth century, it would seem that we could reasonably argue, as some people have, that life is meaningless and absurd. Life appears to be a struggle to survive, in which might makes right and good guys suffer. Think of the two world wars, the dropping of atomic bombs on Hiroshima and Nagasaki, the Holocaust in which six million Jews and others were murdered, the drought and famine that has killed hundreds of thousands of people in Ethiopia and elsewhere, the young people killed on our highways in accidents or incidents of drunk driving. It all seems so senseless. So why do we believe that life has worth, dignity, and purpose? Theologians such as Protestant Schubert Ogden and Catholics Hans Küng and David Tracy have sought to explain this basic trust in the worthwhileness of existence in terms of our awareness of a transcendent ground of meaning and purpose. In short, they argue that this experience of basic trust points in the direction of God.

Seen from their perspective, religion is the response to our need to make sense somehow of our basic faith in the ultimate worth of life. In Chapters One, Five and Nine, we claimed that it is a natural human need to trust that there is an enduring meaning for our individual lives and for the life of all as a whole. As you will recall from Chapter Five, the psychologist Jung and others consequently assert that without some form of religious faith psychological health is not possible. Along similar lines, fundamental theologians point out that religious language (talk about God, human destiny, etc.) functions to reassure us that the world *is* a meaningful home and that the future *is* trustworthy. The experiences of suffering, hatred, and death threaten our basic faith in life's worth; they create a profound need for reassurance that our basic faith is not wrong. In a Christian context, the symbols of resurrection and immortality provide the needed reassurance as to the ultimate value of life. Retelling the Christian story of God's love for us as it is manifested in the life of Jesus reminds us that our life has meaning and value.

One does not have to be an expert in religion or psychology, however, to observe how pervasive our basic trust is. Recall the example of the mother and child mentioned in Chapter Nine. The mother hopes to reassure her upset child by telling her of her own trust in the goodness of reality. The mother's response to her child's distraught condition is spontaneous and natural. Critical reflection upon what makes her response possible and natural leads many fundamental theologians to a double conclusion: 1) The mother is speaking honestly to her daughter, when she says "Don't be afraid, everything is all right," only if life and its intrinsic worth *can* somehow be trusted, and 2) Life can be trusted or held to have worth only if there is a basis for such confidence. Fundamental theologians propose God as that basis.

After I had made a presentation like this in class, Rich, a bright first-year student, asked whether basic trust was valid. How do we know that we are not engaged in wishful thinking? Some students, I am afraid, did not find my answer very comforting. We don't know for sure, I said. That's the difference between faith and absolute certitude. As you may recall from Chapters One and Five, faith or trust involves more than the rational element. It is also a matter of feeling. But to say that something is a matter of feeling does not mean that it is make-believe. A colleague expressed this point well. He explained that religious experience means finding oneself trusting that there is something that makes life worthwhile. One feels it. But then by living one's life on the basis of such trust, the person finds, gradually and never definitively, that the trust is indeed worthwhile.

Let us examine one final area of experience that offers hints of transcendence: the area of morality.

Moral Living and the Question of God

Every normal human being has some sense of right and wrong.

We get our ideas of moral action from our parents, from school, and from society. We are taught to keep our promises, to be honest and fair, and to do what is just. Initially, as small children, our motivation to do what is "right" is based on a desire for pleasure and avoidance of pain. As we grow up, we find other motives for being good. If we have matured morally, we do what is right because we think it is right, not simply because we fear the consequences if we don't. Hence, the question arises: Why ought we be moral? We are once again face to face with a limit or ultimate question, that is, a question of primary importance that defies being answered by using our usual, limited methods, such as empirical observation. As philosopher Stephen Toulmin has argued, we cannot really produce a *moral* argument for being moral. The limit character of such a question, its inability to be answered by a direct appeal to sense experience or common sense, suggests that it be described as a religious question.

The traditional Christian response to the question has been to appeal to the reality of God. We ought to be moral because God has created us with a moral structure and nature. God is the basis and ground of what is right and wrong; and, as the book of Genesis proclaims, people are created in God's image. For Christians, this means that religion and morality are closely connected. Since the Enlightenment, however, there has existed the tendency simply to collapse the one into the other. Immanuel Kant (1724-1804), in his epoch-making critiques of pure and practical reason, maintained that we cannot know whether God exists or whether there is an afterlife. But, Kant went on to say, we must act *as if* both are real. This was the only sure and rational way to insure moral living and prevent chaos in society. For Kant, the only real service religion provided to society was the justification for leading a moral life. Friedrich Nietzsche (1844-1900), writing at the end of the nineteenth century, claimed that if there is no God, everything is permitted.

Many contemporary thinkers would reject Nietzsche's stark assertion. Even if there is not a God, they contend, there are good reasons for being moral: a personal sense of satisfaction from doing what one thinks right, preservation of order in society, etc. Some theologians, however, respond that none of these reasons can make sense of moral obligations that we experience to be absolute.

To experience an obligation as absolute or unconditional means that the particular action we feel called to do admits of no evasion. We feel compelled to do it not because the state is watching and we want its approval, or because we have been told to do it by parents or teachers and we don't want to disappoint them. Whenever we experience an obligation as absolute, we feel constrained to act in a certain way without regard for whether it serves our own selfish interests.

A number of fundamental theologians argue that this experience of unconditional obligation points to the reality of God. Their point is that only the existence of an absolute reality (God), capable of giving meaning to our obedient response to an unconditional obligation, could justify our feeling that this particular ethical claim is absolute and unconditional. Swiss theologian Hans Küng states this point most emphatically. He contends that although an atheist can lead a morally good life, the one thing that the atheist cannot do is to justify the absoluteness of his or her sense of obligation. The atheist, according to Küng, can give only a relative or conditional response to the question: Why should I observe any norm unconditionally, especially if it is completely at variance with my interests? The atheist might reply: because it is good for humanity as a whole or because the action promotes peace and justice. Those are good reasons. But they are reasons proposed by human beings, and they compel obedience only to the extent that other human beings choose to go along with them. An example might clarify Küng's point. Let us consider the issue of "inalienable human rights" or human dignity.

Christians generally feel a sense of absolute obligation to respect the dignity of other human beings. Christians believe that they ought to respect others' rights not only when it is convenient or when it serves their own interests. Rather, they feel that the dignity of all human beings ought to be respected and protected because people have been created in God's image. If there is no God, why should we respect others unconditionally? Why should we regard their lives and their rights as precious, something not to be violated or tampered with? Even critics of this moral argument for God, such as contemporary philosopher Anthony O'Hear, concede that in the absence of any transcendent perspective on human life (in which each person is seen as a child of God), it is difficult to see why people are to be regarded as worthy of the individual respect moral theorists generally insist on. As O'Hear notes, a purely biological perspective gives no grounding for individual rights. Rather, it tends to a sort of social Darwinism, in which the value of individuals (and therefore the respect due them) depends upon their contribution to the survival and improvement of the species or society. Similarly, the tactic of appealing to the fact that human beings are centers of consciousness, pleasure, and pain will not serve as a basis for any rights we are not equally prepared to accord animals. In a scientific, purely biological perspective, severely disabled people, people with genetic defects, and others are expendable. But that is not the case when people are viewed as created in God's image and when God is believed to be the ground of what ultimately is right and wrong.

What, then, are we to conclude? Does our experience of ourselves as insatiable knowers and moral agents or our experience of life as worthwhile prove the reality of God? Clearly, these experiences raise questions that can rightly be called religious. And the Christian answer to these questions can be defended as a possible and reasonable reply. In the final analysis, however, the Christian interpretation of these experiences, although good and reasonable, is still an interpretation. And interpretations are always open to question and revision, as well as to affirmation and agreement.

Against Rahner's interpretation of our desire to know, it can be argued that his analysis only demonstrates that we have a natural curiosity. Against Ogden's argument for the reality of God (upon the basis of our basic trust in the worthwhileness of life), one could reply that this is simply a human projection. The psychologist Sigmund Freud (1856-1939) made this point in his work, *The Future of an Illusion* (1927). Freud believed that people invent a father god in order to feel more secure in an alien and hostile world, but that this invention was an act of repression, a failing to come to grips with reality. Since repression, from Freud's perspective, can lead to psychological sickness (neurosis and even psychosis), the religious answer had to be abolished as an illusion. And to the argument from moral experience, one could reply that without God, there is no absolute foundation for being moral, but that is simply the way life is.

The point we want to make is that the interpretation of these experiences as pointers to God, as well as the denial of this interpretation by religion's critics, are just that: interpretations. Each one of us is forced to decide which interpretation makes more sense of our experience, which rings truer to life as we know it, which enables us to make this world a better place in which to live. There is no absolute guarantee that our interpretation will be the best, just as there is no final proof that any particular interpretation is *the* correct one. But each one of us must risk making some interpretation our own. In the words of Hans Küng, statements about the reality of God have to be tested against the background of *our* own experience of life. Affirmation of the reality of God will probably not be done as a logical deduction from a supposedly obvious experience, but rather as a *decision* we feel called to make because it illuminates our experience. Chapter One, you may recall, spoke of faith as a gift and as a holistic response. In making our own decision, we may be encouraged by the thought that the Christian interpretation of human experience is one that has resonated with people throughout the centuries. It is one that has provided meaning and purpose to the lives of millions of people.

In the next section, we will examine how contemporary experience has challenged some of the traditional images and doctrines of God and church.

Suffering and the Image of God

Perhaps more than any other experience, the experience of

unjust suffering and radical evil has challenged traditional Christian claims about God's goodness and omnipotence. The experience of suffering is certainly not new. What is new in this century, however, is the fact that increasing numbers of Christians find the past explanations for reconciling God's goodness with the reality of evil no longer credible. In the past, the suffering of good people was explained as a test by God of one's faith, as a way of causing people to appreciate through contrast the good things in their lives, or as a hidden part in God's overall plan for the welfare of the world. Today, many Christians feel that those explanations clash with their experiences of personal tragedy and global disasters.

Of course, the suffering caused by moral evil (murder, robbery, etc.) can still be plausibly explained in traditional terms. Moral evil is the evil and suffering caused by the actions of other rational beings. The traditional explanation for why God does not stop such bad actions is that God created us free. Without free choice, human beings would be little more than living robots; humans would not exist with the dignity God intended. God therefore refuses to take away our freedom, even when we misuse it.

But there is another kind of evil that Christians have had a harder time reconciling with their belief in an all-powerful, all-good God. That is natural or physical evil. This is the type of evil that is not intentionally caused by people. Hurricanes, earthquakes, and genetic defects are examples. Over the centuries, Christians have pondered questions such as: If God is all-good and all-powerful, why doesn't God intervene to stop the floods, hurricanes, and earthquakes that kill people? Why does God allow innocent children to be afflicted with serious genetic defects?

One Christian answer in the past was that events of physical evil were God's way of reminding us that life and health are gifts, and that we need to learn to appreciate who we are and what we have. Another answer was that God wanted to admonish us for self-centeredness. Another traditional solution was to admit that the purpose of this kind of suffering is hidden from us, but that God certainly does have a good purpose. We may not understand that purpose now because we, unlike God, don't see the whole picture.

In the twentieth century, especially in the past few decades, these traditional explanations have lost much of their persuasiveness for many Christians. The explanations of physical or natural evil, in particular, have been re-examined in light of the contemporary experience of relativity. Just as the science of physics in this century has come to recognize that there is relativity and randomness in the universe as well as order and pattern, philosophers and theologians have also come to acknowledge relativity and change in the life of human individuals and societies. Perhaps not everything in our world happens according to some fixed, absolute plan. Why did the bolt on this plane's wing come loose? Why should a drought occur here, but not there? Perhaps there is no reason intended by God; maybe it just happened.

When this kind of thinking is used to reconcile belief in God and the existence of physical evil, some new theological perspectives emerge. Harold Kushner, a rabbi, describes one such new perspective in his very popular book, *When Bad Things Happen to Good People*. The idea for the book began with an experience very close to home, namely, the suffering and early death of Kushner's young son from progeria (a rapid-aging disease). This experience of unjust suffering made Kushner reevaluate the traditional explanations of evil he had learned in the seminary, explanations very similar to the traditional Christian ones. In the course of his reflections, Kushner felt forced to choose between retaining his belief in God's total goodness or in God's absolute control of the world. If God were in total control, then God must have wanted his son to suffer the ridicule of other children, to endure much pain, and to die an early death. But such a God was not the God in whom Kushner believed. He concluded, therefore, that although God was good, God was not all-powerful.

Such a perspective might make it seem that God sits aloof from the world and, as a helpless bystander, merely watches physical evil kill people and shatter families. Kushner, however, rejects this understanding of God. In light of his own experience of getting through the loss of his son, Kushner believes that God *does* "intervene" in the world not by suspending the laws of nature, but by coming to us in the form of other people in times of trouble. Kushner also believes that it is God who fills up our reserves of strength when they are sapped by suffering. God does not make all our problems or all life's tragedies disappear, but God gives people the strength and courage to survive them.

Kushner's proposal for a new way of thinking about God finds a close parallel in the thought of "process theologians." These Christian thinkers are so named because they have been strongly influenced by the philosophies of Alfred North Whitehead and Charles Hartshorne, who asserted that everything that is actual is a process. The parallel is that both process theologians and Kushner understand God to be dynamic, not static. And both hold that God's involvement in the world never takes the form of coercion or absolute control.

Process theology, however, adds another aspect to this new way of conceiving God. It emphasizes the social and relational character of God. Traditionally, God has been thought of as a changeless being who, although unaffected by the events of our world, affects or causes everything that happens. In a process perspective, God is a reality who both affects as well as is affected by everything that is. But if God can be affected by us, does that not mean that we can manipulate God in some sense? And if God can be manipulated, is God really God, that is, an utterly supreme being worthy of worship?

Charles Hartshorne replied to these objections in his book, *The Divine Relativity* (1948). First, he argued that the process conception of God did a better job making sense of the biblical picture of God than did the traditional ones. The Bible depicts God as active in history and as love itself. Hartshorne's point was that to be in love is to be in relation. And to be in relation means being capable of being affected by the experiences of the beloved. Whereas traditional conceptions of God describe the divine-human relationship as a one-way affair (God knows, loves, and affects us), the process understanding of God declares that the relationship goes both ways. God enjoys our happiness and suffers with us when we suffer.

Second, Hartshorne replied that although God is affected by us, our thoughts and actions will never cause God to divert from God's holy purpose. God will always seek to promote what Hartshorne called "the highest cosmic good." To do that is God's nature. Our successive actions will influence God to adapt the divine purpose to changing circumstances in the world, but they can never cause God to abandon the divine will to do what is good for the world.

Third, Hartshorne pointed out that his process conception of God still preserved God's absoluteness in certain respects. Hartshorne's God is still a perfect and supreme being. God's perfection consists in the fact that God, unlike every other being, knows perfectly and is related to *every* being at one and the same time. Human beings, by contrast, can be in relationship with only a limited number of beings at any given time. Insofar as relationships are enriching, all beings will grow as a result of them. Since God, however, is related to all, no being can ever surpass the enrichment or perfection in God. And there is more. God is not only perfect; God is also absolutely reliable. That makes God worthy of our trust and reverence. God's absolute reliability does not mean in Hartshorne's view, as it does in the traditional Christian perspective, that God arranges all events according to a completely detailed plan. Rather, it means that God can be relied on to do for the world all that *ought* to be done for it, leaving for the members of the world community all that *they* ought to be left to do.

At this point, the similarities of Kushner's and Hartshorne's reflections about God are obvious. Just as Kushner denies that God is all-powerful (in the sense of controlling every event in the world), so does Hartshorne. Both of them suggest that we should not assume that what ought to be done in and for the world *by God* is everything that ought to be done *at all*. We humans have a very important part to play. Kushner and Hartshorne believe that when what God intends "ought to be done" does not get done, it is because of the lack of human response. God's power, however, is still maintained in both of their perspectives. God is powerful in the sense of *persuasive* power (that is, the power that encourages, persuades, and nudges other beings to do what they ought), not in the sense of *coercive* power (the power that controls by force), as the traditional images suggest.

The point of this exploration of process thought is to underline the ways in which contemporary experience can function as a fruitful resource in thinking theologically. Process reflection upon our experiences of the social, relational, and dynamic character of the world leads to new ways of visioning God, and it underlines the way in which we all are responsible for the course of history. Kushner's reflections upon the experience of unjust suffering led him, in a similar way, to a new conception of who God is. God does not cause all the tragedies and suffering that people experience; rather, God gives people the strength and courage to survive them. Process reflection adds that God does more than that: God gives us not only the strength to survive, but also the ingenuity and hope to draw good from evil and to change the world's suffering.

In the next two sections, we will explore how the experience of feminist women has also brought about a rethinking of the traditional Christian ideas about God, self, and world. We begin by studying the problems that have precipitated feminism and the women's movement.

Women's Experience, Religion, and Theology

Although feminism and feminist theology are highly controversial, the fact that gives rise to them is undisputed: the actual subordination of women to men. In recent years, women around the world have come to see that they have been denied equal access to positions of power in society and church on the basis not of competence and ability, but on the basis of their sex. They feel that their experiences, their thoughts, and their work have been trivialized or not valued at all by men. Feminism refers to that movement which demands for women the same rights granted men politically, socially, economically, and religiously. Although there are wide differences among feminists concerning what women's liberation means and how it is to be achieved, all feminists acknowledge that the problems with which they have to deal are sexism, androcentrism, and patriarchy.

Sexism refers generally to discrimination against women. It is often fueled by attitudes that promote the stereotyping of social roles based on gender. Statements such as "Washing clothes and cooking, that's women's work" or "Women are so emotional; they are not equipped to rule a country" are examples of sexism. Androcentrism is a related problem. It literally means "man-centered"; and it connotes a situation in which men are used as the norm for what it means to be human. Androcentrism ranks men higher than women. Patriarchy is what results from sexism and androcentrism in society. In the narrow sense, patriarchy means "father rule." In the broader sense, it means male domination. In other words, it insists that men ought to be dominant in society and that women ought to be submissive and subordinate to them.

When I addressed the problems of sexism and androcentrism in one of my theology classes, I ran into an immediate objection. Mike, an intelligent junior majoring in economics, asked me what these problems had to do with theology. The status of women in society, the merits or demerits of the Equal Rights Amendment, are political issues, Mike said, not religious ones. Many students agreed. In my response, I attempted to show how religious traditions had been used throughout history, either explicitly or implicitly, to support the social inferiority of women. The Christian tradition was no exception. In the Christian Scriptures, for example, one finds passages in Ephesians, Colossians, 1 Peter, and 1 Corinthians that suggest the subordination of women to men. And the subsequent tradition is replete with statements from influential theologians which denigrate or malign women. Speaking of all women as Eve, Tertullian (160-225) charged that they were "the gate of the devil, the traitor of the tree, the first deserter of divine Law," whose sin required that the Son of God die. Two centuries later, St. Augustine (354-430) affirmed that in women the good Christian "likes what is human, loathes what is feminine." And he asserted that woman's only purpose was to help in the work of procreation; in all other aspects of life, a male friend was better. Similar statements can be found in other centuries. As Scripture scholar Elisabeth Schüssler Fiorenza has demonstrated, the Bible and the Christian tradition have played key roles in the argument against women's emancipation.

Sexism and the subordination of women, then, is not simply a social or political issue, although it is that as well. The Christian tradition has been used to support androcentrism and patriarchy. Even though it has not always been explicitly admitted, countless Christians throughout the centuries have concluded that society should be male-dominated since God, who rules the world, is (conceived of as) a male, God our Father. If God's qualities are the stereotypical masculine ones (power, strength, reason, etc.) then those who possess these qualities are most like God and, therefore, the ones most entitled to rule on this earth. So the thinking goes.

It must be admitted, however, that this way of thinking and its practical results in society are not simply the doing of ambitious, power-hungry men. As many feminist women point out, the exploitation of women could not be perpetuated without the consent of the victims. And women give their consent when they refuse to see the problem or when they acquiesce in sex-role socialization. This socialization is a conditioning process that begins to operate from the moment we are born; it defines, often in subtle or unconscious ways, what it means to be a boy or a girl, a man or a woman. To be a man means to exhibit "masculine" qualities; to be a woman, "feminine" qualities. But sex-role socialization operates on the basis of stereotypes. According to these stereotypes, the masculine implies cool rationality, objectivity, competition, and aggressiveness; the feminine, emotionalism, subjectivity, and passivity. According to Mary Daly and others, sex-role socialization is generally supported by the institutions of family, school, mass media, and toy and clothes manufacturers. Sex-role socialization works to reinforce the assumptions, attitudes, and stereotypes of a sexually hierarchical society (with men on top).

The pervasiveness of these assumptions and stereotypes quickly became apparent one day in my class. We were discussing whether women ought to be priests or ordained ministers. Kathy, a second-year pre-med student, said that if women wanted to be priests, they ought to be allowed. But when I asked her how she would feel if the priest in her church were a woman, she replied, "I'd feel kind of funny. I don't know why, but I don't think I would like that." Another student, Lois, immediately challenged Kathy. Lois accused her of secretly thinking that a woman couldn't do the job as well, that a woman would not have the same authority as a man. And that was a notion that Lois would not accept: "I'm sick and tired of people assuming that women can't be just as rational and objective as guys. I am a lot better at academics and public speaking than most guys I know. But look who's on student government. Mostly guys." Ann, a sophomore psychology major, added another twist to the discussion. She expressed anger at being treated as stupid simply because she was very pretty. "Why do guys assume that if you're ugly, you're probably smart? But if you're pretty, you've got to be an airhead? Why can't a woman be 'feminine' and good-looking, and also intellectual and competitive?"

Sex-role conditioning and sexism, however, are not just women's issues. Sex-role stereotypes hurt men as well as women, even though many refuse to admit it. Think of the way most people react when they see a man express his emotions. What do people think when they see a man cry? What if a man is interested in pursuits (nursing, cooking, crafts, sewing, etc.) that stereotypically have been relegated to the domain of women? Does society generally allow a paternity leave, to give fathers time to spend with their newborn children? As some feminists point out, the women's movement seeks not only the liberation of women, but also the liberation of men from repressive stereotypes.

In the words of Mary Daly, women's liberation implies universal human becoming; it seeks to promote the becoming of androgynous (having both masculine and feminine characteristics) human persons. It does not seek to diminish male humanity by elevating female humanity as the norm. Rather, feminism, or at least some forms of it, is reaching for an expanded definition of inclusive humanity, one that is inclusive of both genders. Rosemary Radford Ruether indicates the universal scope and relevance of her understanding of feminism when she argues that it rejects any principle of religion or society that marginalizes one group of persons as less than fully human. In rejecting androcentrism, she says, women must also criticize all other forms of chauvinism: making white Westerners the norm of humanity, making privileged classes the norm of humanity, even making Christianity the norm for all religions.

One way to contribute to the overcoming of androcentrism and sexism is to challenge its past Christian underpinnings. And that means, first of all, to re-examine the dominant images of God in the Christian tradition.

Feminism and Alternative Images of God

How we imagine and speak about God has a tremendous influence not only on what we think about God, but also on the way we conceive of our relationship to God and to one another. For this reason, many feminists have advocated finding other images for God besides the traditional images of God as father, king, and lord. The images of God as king and lord suggest that our relationship to God is one of servant to master. Insofar as God is also spoken of as male, the inference has been drawn, often unconsciously, that males are the masters in this world and females their servants. The human social-political situation then mirrors the so-called divine ideal. And the master-servant model is not necessarily restricted to male-female relationships. It can and has been extended to all relationships. Thus, some people think that all human interaction can be defined in terms of dominance-subjection, command-obedience, aggressive power-meek compliance.

Aware of the power of images and of language, increasing numbers of Christian men and women in recent years have sought to avoid exclusive, sexist language when referring to human beings (rejecting, for example, "mankind" in favor of "humankind"). In addition, they have attempted to formulate more inclusive images of God. One image or metaphor that has been proposed is to imagine God as Mother. When I made such a suggestion in one of my introductory theology courses, the immediate response of a number of students was "That's ridiculous!" They were apparently reacting to the novelty of the image. Clearly, the image is unconventional and unfamiliar. When I asked my students what was wrong with imagining God as Mother, one replied, "That's not what we believe. God is our Father, not our Mother." Is God literally our Father, I wanted to know in return. Greg, a pleasant, thoughtful freshman, replied "No." But he went on: "We all know that God is not male. That's just an image. So, what's the point in making God female? Why get hung up on images?" Greg was right, at least about one thing. Sophisticated thinkers throughout the history of the Christian church have never identified God with a "super father" in heaven. They have recognized that "father" is an image, a cherished image, for God in our tradition. It is a way of speaking about God that highlights some of the qualities people experience or conceive God to have.

So why should we tamper with such a special image? Well, it's not really a matter of tampering with the father image. Rather, it is a question of creating other images of God in addition to that of father. It is a question of forming other images that might reflect more fully or in a better way the relationship Christians feel that they have with God. Not all feminists are demanding that male images for God be replaced by female images. And, in my opinion, we need both. Why?

There are at least three important reasons for using female images for God in addition to male images. The first reason might be called a negative one. Simply stated, if exclusively male images for God continue to be used in the Christian church, many women will continue to feel their humanity diminished and their female identity oppressed. For if we are all made in God's image, but God is conceived solely in male terms, what does that say about the full humanity and worth of women? The other two reasons are positive ones. First, creating more images for God, far from reducing God to our human conceptions, actually emphasizes by their very multiplicity that God is always more than what we can express in any *single* image. God is ultimately a mystery transcending any and all language we might use to express it. Second, since we are made in God's image, and since we are male and female, both male and female images for God should be used.

If these reasons are plausible, then why is there such resistance to female images for God? One explanation is the sheer "novelty" of the image. Although feminine qualities are occasionally ascribed to God in the Bible, God is never addressed as Mother. This way of talking about God is new to most Christians. Contemporary theologian Sallie McFague offers another explanation. She suggests that many people are uneasy with female metaphors for God since they seem blatantly sexual, whereas the sexual character of male metaphors is usually cloaked. But the ways in which our understanding of God can be enriched through the use of female images argues for overcoming this uneasiness.

It must first be noted that God should be imagined in female, not feminine terms. "Female" refers to gender, whereas "feminine" refers to qualities conventionally associated with women. The difference is important, as McFague points out in *Models of God* (p. 99):

> The problem with introducing a feminine dimension of God is that it invariably ends with identifying as female those qualities that society has called feminine. Thus, the feminine side of God is taken to comprise the tender, nurturing, passive, healing aspects of divine activity, whereas those activities in which God creates, redeems, establishes peace, administers justice, and so on, are called masculine. Such a division, in extending to the godhead the stereotypes we create in human society, further crystallizes and sanctifies them.

Thinking of God as Mother can avoid falling into feminine stereotypes because "mothering" is a female—not feminine—activity. To give birth to children is something some females do. Some may do it in a so-called feminine way; others may not. Moreover, a maternal image of God does not imply stereotypes of maternal tenderness and "softness." As McFague rightly points out, the female experience of gestation and birth engenders in most animals, including human beings, not attributes of weakness and passivity, but qualities contributing to the active defense of their young. Mothers are tough. Whatever threatens the development of their children is fought, often fiercely, as mother tigers illustrate. That is why McFague says that mothers, and not just fathers or kings, can act as judges. A *maternal* image of God implies that God is a judge, not in the stereotypical masculine sense of passing judgment on our sins, but a judge who is angry when the fulfillment of a life she has given is thwarted. McFague writes that God as Mother becomes an angry judge of people and society when what comes from her being and belongs to her lacks the food and other necessities to grow and flourish.

The value of the mother image is that it balances the father image of God. Whereas the conventional father image has implied that God is primarily a God who requires our obedience, the mother image suggests that God is primarily the reality who gives life. Giving life and sustaining it is more fundamental than demanding that life be lived according to a certain set of rules. In that sense, God as Mother is a more fundamental image that gets to the very heart of who God is.

But the image of God as Mother has other benefits. To imagine God as Mother is, as in the case of the father image, to think of God in terms of a parental model. Such a model is appropriate to God, McFague claims, because parental love is the most powerful and intimate experience we have of giving love whose return is not calculated. Parental love wills life and when it comes, exclaims, "It is good that you exist!" In addition, parental love nurtures what it has brought into existence, wanting growth and fulfillment for its children.

McFague and others admit that the parental and maternal models are not perfect. For example, they have difficulty in expressing that God's love is impartial and inclusive; that is, that divine love is directed to the fulfillment of all, not just one's own children. Nonetheless, these models provide rich and powerful ways for imagining God's creative love. McFague makes this very clear by drawing out some implications for the doctrine of creation. When God is thought of as mother and creation is thought of as birth, then the close connection between God and the world is emphasized.

The traditional picture of creation, by contrast, stresses the distance between God and God's creation. That is, God is pictured as creating the world through an intellectual process, speaking the divine word and creating from nothing ("God said, 'Let there be light...' "), or through an artistic endeavor, molding human beings from the clay of earth, just as a potter molds earthenware vessels (Gen 2:7). Both of these traditional pictures highlight the difference between God and God's creation; they underscore the great distance between them. The model of creation from God as Mother, however, emphasizes God's closeness to God's creatures. There is a special affinity or kinship between God and the beings to whom God has given life. This way of imagining the God-world relationship does not make God and creation identical, but it does seem to reflect better the God whom Jesus proclaimed: the loving God who is very near to us.

There are still good reasons to search for other images of God besides the traditional male images, even for those Christians for whom the image of God as Mother is not fruitful and enriching. In the history of the Christian church, the image of God as king and lord has held a prominent place. But as was suggested earlier, thinking of God exclusively as king implies that our relationship to God is one simply of servile obedience and that our relationship to one another is based upon power. Jesus, however, turned these notions of kingship on their head. In his life he demonstrated that to be "lord" (*dominus* in Latin; "dominant" in English) really means to serve others (see Jn 13:12-16). Jesus' image of God as serving friend offers to transform all relationships, including relationships with God. In the words of Rosemary Radford Ruether, all power and domination relations in society are overcome by overcoming the root metaphor of relationship to God modeled on king-servant relations.

In this chapter we have examined the ways in which human experience has contributed to the shape of traditional Christian doctrines as well as to their reformulation today. We saw that, although it has not always been explicitly acknowledged, experience has been a very important source of theological reflection. Our study of fundamental theology in action led us to consider the possibility of discovering "pointers toward God" or "signals of transcendence" in our own everyday experiences. And we concluded our reflections by thinking about the ways in which the experiences of unjust suffering and androcentrism have caused some people to formulate new images of God.

In our final chapter, we will take a look at the ways in which contemporary theology has tried to deal creatively with three. crises that currently face our world. There we will continue our exploration of systematic theology as well as introduce practical theology.

QUESTIONS FOR REFLECTION AND DISCUSSION

1. What role did experience play in the formation of early Christian doctrines? Does experience continue to play a role today in theology? Explain.

2. Can you describe an experience you have had that fits our broad definition of "religious experience?"

3. Do you think that a sense of basic trust in the worthwhileness of life or a sense of absolute moral obligation is really a pointer to the reality of God? Or can these experiences be adequately explained without reference to God?

4. Do you find yourself in agreement or disagreement with Kushner and process theologians on the issue of suffering and evil? What points would you raise to criticize or to support their position?

5. Are androcentrism and sexism theological problems? Why do some feminists think it is important to supplement the king-servant model with other models for our relationship to God? In light of your own experience, do you find the image of God as Mother to be a helpful, fruitful image, or are you satisfied with the traditional image of God as Father and king?

Suggested Readings

Carr, Anne E. *Transforming Grace: Christian Tradition and Women's Experience*. San Francisco: Harper & Row, 1988.

Cobb, John B. and David Ray Griffin. *Process Theology: An Introductory Exposition*. Philadelphia: Westminster Press, 1976.

Daly, Mary. *Beyond God the Father: Toward a Philosophy of Women's Liberation*. Boston: Beacon, 1973.

Schüssler Fiorenza, Elisabeth. *In Memory of Her: A Feminist Theological Reconstruction of Christian Origins*. New York: Crossroad, 1984.

Hartshorne, Charles. *A Natural Theology for Our Time*. La Salle, Ill.: Open Court, 1967.

Kaufman, Gordon D. *Theology for a Nuclear Age*. Philadelphia: Westminster Press, 1985.

Küng, Hans. *Does God Exist? An Answer for Today*. Garden City, N.Y.: Doubleday, 1980.

Kushner, Harold S. *When Bad Things Happen to Good People*. New York: Shocken, 1981.

Lindbeck, George A. *The Nature of Doctrine: Religion and Theology in a Postliberal Age*. Philadelphia: Westminster, 1984.

McFague, Sallie. *Models of God: Theology for an Ecological, Nuclear Age*. Philadelphia: Fortress, 1987.

Ogden, Schubert M. *The Reality of God and Other Essays*. New York: Harper & Row, 1966.

O'Hear, Anthony. *Experience, Explanation and Faith: An Introduction to the Philosophy of Religion*. Boston: Routledge, Chapman & Hall, 1984.

Rahner, Karl. *Foundations of Christian Faith: An Introduction to the Idea of Christianity*. New York: Seabury Press, 1978.

Radford Ruether, Rosemary. *Sexism and God-Talk: Toward a Feminist Theology*. Boston: Beacon, 1983.

Trible, Phyllis. *God and the Rhetoric of Sexuality*. Philadelphia: Fortress, 1978.

Wiles, Maurice. *The Making of Christian Doctrine: A Study in the Principles of Early Doctrinal Development*. New York: Cambridge University Press, 1967.

CHAPTER TWELVE

Contemporary Theological Issues

In Chapter Five, we suggested that the basic trust in life's meaning that comes from belief in God can bring many benefits to humanity. Specifically, we claimed that religion could make a significant contribution to the resolution of serious social and political crises that currently confront us. Three crises in particular make our world today a "threatened village": the socioeconomic crisis, the nuclear crisis, and the ecological crisis.

In this chapter, we will explore contemporary Christian theological reflection upon these three issues, and we will identify the specific contribution theology can make to their resolution. In the process, we will be introduced to an example of the fourth type of theology described in Chapter Nine (i.e., practical theology) and investigate further the nature of systematic theology. We will begin with a sketch of "liberation theology," which will provide a basic introduction to practical theology. We will then examine theological responses to the nuclear and ecological crises; specifically, the ways in which these crises have moved some Christian theologians to re-conceive the traditional understanding of God and of responsible Christian behavior. In this way, our understanding of systematic theology will be expanded and deepened. In the case of all three issues, we will see that theology in all its forms involves critical and creative reflection upon the relationship between our human experiences and the Christian tradition.

Liberation Theology as Practical Theology

You may recall from Chapter Nine that practical theology underwent a significant transformation in the past century. It changed from being conceived primarily as reflection upon and instruction in the best techniques for *educating* others about Christian faith to being conceived as serious reflection upon how to *live* that faith in the current situation of global social injustice. Liberation theology is one current example of Christian practical theology.

Liberation theology can mean different things to different people. It can refer to any theology that pays primary attention to the experience of suffering and oppression, and is also committed to changing that oppression. The oppression can be racial, sexual, cultural, or economic. Consequently, the theological critiques of racism, sexism, ethnic discrimination, and economic injustice can all be forms of liberation theology. In the following sketch, however, I am referring to a specific form of liberation theology that focuses upon the situation of *economically* oppressed groups. In particular, the sketch will deal primarily with liberation theology as it has been developed in Latin America.

Why should the economically poor get such special attention? As liberation theologians Leonardo and Clodovis Boff point out, the socioeconomically poor do not simply exist alongside other oppressed groups (indigenous peoples, blacks, women), but actually make up the "infrastructural" expression of the process of oppression. By that they mean that the very survival of the economically poor is threatened in a more basic and fundamental way than the survival of other oppressed groups. Economical poverty makes up the heart of oppression. Non-economic types of oppression, however, aggravate already existing socioeconomic oppression. The poor are additionally oppressed when, besides being poor, they are also black, indigent, women, or old.

Liberation theology has arisen in the context of immense human suffering. It sprang up among Christians reflecting upon the staggering number of people who do not have the basic needs for survival. Currently, a half billion people are starving in our world. They have no access to the most basic medical care. They have no work or only occasional work. In Latin America, where the foundations of liberation theology (in the narrow sense) were laid more than twenty years ago, two-thirds of the population is severely undernourished. Children in cities scavenge through garbage on the streets; children in the country eat mud when the meager supplies of rice or beans cannot dull their pangs of hunger.

Suffering, of course, is not new in human history. Throughout the ages, many people have lacked the basics they needed to live a humane life. And Christian concern for the poor and suffering is not new. The church throughout the ages has attempted to supply some of the basic food and health needs of people in addition to their spiritual needs. What is new in our current situation, however, is the increased number of the suffering, the greater awareness of the problem by more and more people, and the recognition that this massive suffering need not be. Another significant new factor is the fact that the oppressed are rising up with the announcement that they are not going to put up with their degradation and oppression any longer. Liberation theology arose from this painful recognition not only of the misery of poor people, but also of the injustice of their misery.

Most of the poor people in Latin America are poor not because they choose to be poor (through an unwillingness to work or laziness), but because they live in social and political systems that deny them the chance to be anything else but poor. As Methodist minister and theologian Rebecca Chopp points out, five percent of the population in Latin America holds 80 percent of the wealth; two-thirds of the usable land is in the hands of a few Latin Americans and foreign multinational corporations.

Those people fortunate enough to work the land usually do so for almost nothing. Brazilian farmworkers make between 65 cents and two dollars a day for picking corn, cotton, or sugar cane. All too often, Latin Americans who call out for reform meet with arrest, imprisonment, even death. Some governments suspend basic human rights and torture their critics in order to maintain the unjust status quo.

The roots of liberation theology, however, are not simply awareness of massive suffering and outrage at social, economic, and political injustice; the roots are religious and theological as well. Vatican II introduced into the Roman Catholic church a new atmosphere of freedom and creativity that, among other things, gave Latin American theologians the courage to think for themselves about pastoral problems affecting their countries. More specifically, Vatican II's *Pastoral Constitution on the Church in the Modern World* (*Gaudium et Spes*) emphasized that the transformation of our world into something better was an important part of human salvation. This document stated that the Christian expectation of a new, eternal world at the end of history ought not weaken, but "rather stimulate our concern for cultivating this one [i.e., our earthly world]." It affirmed that earthly progress, insofar as it contributes to the better ordering of human society, is "of vital concern to the kingdom of God" (par. 39). This inspiration was taken up by the General Conference of Latin American Bishops. In their 1968 meeting at Medellin, Colombia, and their 1979 meeting at Puebla, Mexico, the bishops acknowledged the need for social change and agrarian form. These same conferences spoke out against the "institutionalized violence" of the rich against the poor, and they affirmed "liberation" as an important dimension of the church's mission.

The Protestant presence in Latin America is considerably smaller than the Catholic presence, but there, too, a similar theological movement has been taking place. In 1968, the Third Latin American Evangelical Conference focused attention upon the present problems in Latin America. In 1978, the Latin American Council of Evangelization examined the question of human rights and political structures of power. In short, liberation theology found support for its reflections and proposals in the concern of the institutional church, in both its Catholic and Protestant forms, for justice in the Third World.

Preferential Option for the Poor

Liberation theology represents something new in Christianity in terms of its aim, content, and method. Unlike the traditional theology of Europe and the United States, liberation theology is not concerned primarily with demonstrating the reasonableness and truth of Christian faith, but with changing the unjust structures of the world on the basis of Christian convictions. In this sense, liberation theology is concerned with what Jesuit priest and theologian Jon Sobrino calls the second phase of the eighteenth-century Enlightenment. In the first phase, Immanuel Kant argued for the liberation of the human intellect from blind obedience to any and all authorities. In response, theologians attempted to show that blind obedience to church authorities was not the only way to arrive at Christian faith, but that one could establish the truth of faith on the basis of an appeal to reason. In the second phase, Karl Marx argued for the liberation of people from the wretched conditions in which they lived and worked. He insisted that it is not enough to understand the world; the world must also be transformed into something better.

In response, liberation theology holds that the central crisis confronting Christian faith is not intellectual, but practical. The central question is not how is it still *possible* to be a Christian in a modern, scientific world, but what it *means* to be a Christian in a world of destitution. In other words, what are Christians to do in the face of the dehumanizing poverty that afflicts hundreds of millions of people? How are Christians to respond to the unjust disparity in living conditions between the First and Third Worlds? What does belief in God have to do with such widespread suffering?

The content of liberation theology is, therefore, formally similar to, yet substantively different from, other forms of modern Christian theology. Modern Christian theology generally has been characterized by a concern to formulate the Christian tradition in terms that are credible and relevant to modern people. It has generally rejected the presentation of Christian truths as supernatural propositions that simply needed to be stated in order to be accepted. Instead, modern theology has been concerned with presenting Christian faith in such a way that people can affirm it without having to renounce their intellects or reject science. Modern theology has displayed concern for the *subject* of Christian faith, who it understands to be the believer living in a modern, secular world.

Liberation theology continues modern theology's concern for the subject, but has radically redefined who that subject is. No longer is it the secular-minded, educated individual, but rather the economically poor as a social group. Those who have been marginalized in society, the starving and homeless poor whom society does not know by name, have become the subject of liberation theology.

Similarly, liberation theology continues the refrain of modern theology that Christian faith can set people free. But now that freedom means not only freedom from anxiety about the meaningfulness of existence, but also the freedom to eat, to have drinkable water, to have access to basic medical care, and to have political self-determination. The liberation Christianity offers is understood, from this new perspective, to be not only spiritual, but also social and political.

Since the poor are the principal subject and focus of liberation theology, it is not surprising that a "preferential option for the poor" is the most fundamental theme of Latin American liberation theology. A preferential option for the poor requires all Christians to see the situation of oppressive poverty not through the eyes of those who "make" history, but, in the words of Chopp, through the eyes of those who suffer history. To see oppressive poverty from the perspective of those who suffer from it means that Christians come to identify with the poor's own quest for liberation. A preferential option for the poor does not mean that the poor are the only subject of theology. The experience of others (for example, the middle class, the people of the First World, etc.) is also important. But, given the extent of their suffering, the magnitude of their numbers, and the ways in which they have been unjustly excluded from the basics of life, the experience of the poor must take first place in our current reflections on a Christian life.

It is crucial to recognize that this call to see the world's injustices from a new perspective is not a call for charity. The inadequacy of charity is that, no matter how well-intentioned, it treats the poor as collective *objects* of aid, but not as *subjects* who have rights and are the authors of their own liberation. In the words of the Boff brothers, the usual charitable approach fails to see that the poor are oppressed and made poor *by others*; and what they do possess—strength to resist and the capacity to understand their rights—tends to be left out of account. The preferential option for the poor requires solidarity with the poor in *their own struggle* for liberation. It is a call to go beyond charity.

The Method of Liberation Theology

Another distinctive characteristic of liberation theology is its method. According to the exposition we have offered in this book, all forms of Christian theology involve the critical correlation of our understanding of human experience with our understanding of the Christian tradition. Liberation theology also undertakes this correlation, but with a significant difference. Instead of placing the primary emphasis in this correlation upon *understanding*, liberation theology places it upon *action*. In addition, liberation theology offers a different understanding of the relationship between theory (understanding) and practice (action). In other forms of Christian theology, including traditional moral theology, theory comes first. One first determines what the Christian tradition means and what it has to say in this particular situation, then one applies that insight to the situation. Liberation theology, by contrast, holds that pertinent and fruitful theological reflection cannot happen unless one is already involved in liberating action on behalf of the oppressed. What we do (or don't do) affects what we think. Consequently, if we are not already involved in some way in the process of liberation, we cannot truly understand what theology is all about.

As the Boff brothers explain it, the first step in liberation theology is pre-theological (in the sense that it is prior to critical reflection upon Christian faith). This pre-theological step is a matter of trying to live the commitment of Christian faith. Thus, the movement in liberation theology is not from theory to practice, but from living practice to theory (reflection upon faith) and then back to a living practice that is nourished and deepened by this effective connection between practice and theory. Liberation theologians often signal this distinctive understanding of the relationship between theory and practice with the label "praxis." From a liberation perspective, theological interpretation is not something we do and then apply, but rather something that we are and by which we are continually transformed. This means that theology does not begin with academic theories, but with the real experience of those who suffer and those who listen to and work with the suffering. Liberation theology is a theology from below, a theology that arises out of the experience of suffering and oppressed people. And it is a theology that highlights action. As Sobrino expresses the point, to understand the truth is to do the truth; to understand Jesus is to follow Jesus; and to understand God is to journey to God along the paths of justice. Theology, in the liberation perspective, is a practical activity.

The tools that liberation theologians use to interpret the sources of theology (human experience and the Christian tradition) are also different from the traditional tools. Instead of relying primarily upon philosophy, liberation theology turns to the social sciences. The use of history, economics, and political science may at first seem strange in such a "spiritual" discipline as theology, but the point is this: If theology is going to be practical and pay attention to concrete situations of oppression, then it must use theories that can analyze the various factors involved in the situation of oppression. Specifically, liberation theology begins by informing itself about the actual conditions in which the oppressed live and by investigating the causes of socioeconomic poverty. This means that a historical, economic, and political analysis is necessary.

Liberation Theology's Analysis of Oppressive Poverty

In analyzing the causes of massive poverty, liberation theology rejects much of the so-called conventional wisdom. On the one hand, liberation theologians criticize the position that sees the causes of poverty as laziness or ignorance. Such a position tends to look at individual cases and fails to see the *structural* dimension of the problem. The fact that the poor make up whole masses of a people, and the fact that their numbers (at least in the Third World) are growing all the time, suggest that there is something in the socio-political system that helps to keep the poor poor. On the other hand, liberation theologians also criticize the view that poverty is simply the result of economic backwardness. This point of view believes that massive poverty will disappear as soon as more technology and foreign loans arrive on the scene in Latin America or other parts of the Third World. Although this approach sees poverty as a collective, not individual, phenomenon, it, too, fails to perceive the problems built into socioeconomic systems that allow the rich to get richer at the expense of the poor, who get poorer. Moreover, this perspective regards the poor as passive objects of charitable action taken by others.

The explanation of massive poverty that liberation theologians prefer is the *dialectical* explanation. According to Leonardo and Clodovis Boff, this point of view sees poverty as the product of the economic organization of society, which exploits some (the workers) and excludes others from the process of production (the unemployed). This explanation of the cause of massive poverty is called dialectical because it perceives the tension and conflict between the few who are rich, whom the economic and political structures of most countries favor, and the many who are poor, who are oppressed and exploited by these very same structures. In his encyclical *Laborem Exercens* (ch. 3), Pope John Paul II alluded to this explanation when he criticized the supremacy of capital over labor.

Since massive poverty in the Third World is propagated by the present social system, that system must be replaced with an alternative, more just system. According to liberation theologians, in the process of transforming the present socioeconomic order, the poor will not be passive recipients, but rather agents of the social and political transformation. This has caused confrontations between rich and poor, oppressive governments and the disenfranchised.

It is at this point, the talk of socio-political transformation and even revolution, that liberation theology has met criticism not only from politicians and economists, but also from other segments of the Christian church. Insofar as liberation theologians have used Marxist analysis to understand the roots of class struggle and the economic factors at work in political systems, they have become suspected of replacing the spiritual gospel with a secular, even atheistic, program for social revolution. Liberation theologians, such as Sobrino, the Boff brothers, and Gustavo Gutiérrez, have replied that they use Marxism solely as an instrument. They do not accept its atheism or its materialism. In fact, they criticize Marxism for ignoring the nature of sin, which is an abiding element in the human condition and is not removed even when class conflict diminishes. Marxism is, at the moment, a useful and perhaps necessary tool for social and economic analysis, but it is insufficient to explain the full meaning of our historical existence. In fact, liberation theologians accuse Marxism of making a false promise when it suggests that it can solve all the problems of history.

Many liberation theologians are aware that their emphasis on political action may lead people to disregard the mystical roots of Christian faith or to fail to recognize the continuity between liberation theology and the classic tradition of the church. But the actual lives of poor Christians in Latin America, who have joined together in base Christian communities (small groups dedicated to working, living, and praying together), make it quite clear that liberation theology is rooted in prayer, contemplation, and intimate contact with God as God is experienced in their life as a community. Liberation theology is a new kind of theology in many ways, but it is rooted in the tradition of Jesus and the church who have come to announce good news to the poor.

My Relationship to Liberation Theology

It might seem to some people that liberation theology is a type of theological reflection that is appropriate for Christians in the Third World. This is the way it seemed to a number of students in my class. Mike, an economics major, wanted to know what liberation theology had to do with Christians in the First World, such as Christians in the United States and Western Europe. To Tony, a sophomore English major, it seemed that liberation theology was nothing more than a program for political revolution. "Let's face it," he said, "the poor in these countries want a piece of the pie. We can't blame them for that. I guess I would do the same thing if I were in their shoes. But let's not call this religion. They are advocating political revolution. They're talking military action, not theology." Andrea, a usually quiet first-year student, chimed in: "Yeah, that's the way it seems to me, too. Liberation theology sounds a lot more like Marxism than it does Christianity." My students raised some important questions. And I suspect that their first impressions of liberation theology were not all that different from the first impressions of many other people. Although the introductory nature of our book prohibits the detailed discussion these questions deserve, let us explore at least some of the issues involved.

Liberation theology roots its conception of God as liberator and its insistence upon an option for the poor primarily in the Bible. In both the Hebrew Scriptures and New Testament, liberation theology finds affirmation of God's saving activity on behalf of the poor and oppressed. The most dramatic and influential illustration of this is the story of the exodus. In that narrative God hears the cries of suffering Hebrews and responds by liberating them from their state of slavery in Egypt. Exodus (3:7) describes God's concern this way:

> And Yahweh said, "I have seen the miserable state of my people in Egypt. I have heard their appeal to be free of their slave-drivers. Yes, I am well aware of their sufferings. I mean to deliver them out of the hands of the Egyptians and bring them up out of that land to a land rich and broad, a land where milk and honey flow...."

Although the exodus is the fundamental event of liberation in the Hebrew Scriptures, it is not an isolated example of God's concern for the oppressed. The Hebrew prophets often speak God's harsh word of judgment against those who believe that the performance of religious ritual, rather than acting justly towards others, is the principal demand God makes upon people. The prophet Isaiah (1:10-17), for example, proclaims that God is sick of the many animal sacrifices offered by people who continue to commit wrongs against others. Isaiah (1:16-17) describes what God wants this way: "Take your wrong-doing out of my sight. Cease to do evil. Learn to do good, search for justice, help the oppressed, be just to the orphan, plead for the widow."

This divine demand for justice and for the liberation of the oppressed is continued and intensified in the New Testament. According to Luke's gospel (4:18-19), Jesus begins his public ministry with the declaration that God has sent him "to bring the good news to the poor, to proclaim liberty to captives and to the blind new sight, to set the downtrodden free, to proclaim the Lord's year of favor." Throughout Luke's gospel, as well as in the other gospels, Jesus is portrayed as having a special compassion for the poor, the multitudes, and the marginalized. He welcomes society's outcasts into fellowship with him. And to those who treat others unfairly, he has sharp words of criticism. Jesus denounces those who "swallow the property of widows, while making a show of lengthy prayers" (Mk 12:40), and he rebukes children who deny support to their elderly parents (Mk 7:10-13). Jesus declares that those who fail to feed the hungry, clothe the naked, and welcome the stranger will be banished at the last judgment to "eternal fire" (Mt 25:31-46). Although this important theme in Jesus' life and preaching does not mean that Jesus' mission is completely reducible to the salvation and liberation of the poor, it does mean, as Sobrino suggests, that Jesus thought of justice as the only form of love.

Liberation theologians point out that this concern and option for the poor also appears in the life and teaching of the earliest Christian community. According to the Acts of the Apostles, the community in Jerusalem held all things in common (2:44-45) so that none of its members was ever in want (4:32-35). The early community believed that it would be unjust for some of their members to have more than what they needed for a decent life while others did not have enough. And, as you may recall from Chapter Four, James (2:14-17) reminded his fellow Christians that following Jesus meant more than simply having faith. Faith demands active love:

> Take the case, my brothers, of someone who has never done a single good act but claims that he has faith. Will that faith save him? If one of the brothers or one of the sisters is in need of clothes and has not enough food to live on, and one of you says to them, "I wish you well; keep yourself warm and eat plenty," without giving them these bare necessities of life, then what good is that? Faith is like that: if good works do not go with it, it is quite dead.

According to the witness of the Bible, faith must be active in deeds of justice and love. But, as my student Tony once asked, does that demand also require First-World and other Christians to support the kind of social and economic "revolution" that liberation theology seems to espouse? Or, as Meg, a business student, put it: "Let's first worry about the social problems in our own country. We have poor people here. We have homeless people and the unemployed. We've got enough to do to solve our own problems without meddling in the problems of people far away." A number of students felt the same way Meg did. "Charity begins at home," Sheila reminded the class.

My students were certainly right about one thing. There are serious social problems in the United States that require immediate attention. In Chapter Four, we examined some of the ways in which each of us can get immediately and concretely involved in working to rectify those problems. But the United States also has a responsibility to those beyond its borders. In our class discussion, I wanted to point out two things that I thought Meg and some others had overlooked. First, the issue both in the United States and in the Third World is not simply an issue of charity, but an issue of justice. Second, the United States has contributed to the socioeconomic problems in Latin America; therefore, it also has a responsibility to help rectify them. Some of the points I raised with Meg and Sheila are presented here. Although necessarily brief, they may be enough to provide an impetus to your further thought and discussion.

Since the nineteenth century, the United States has been involved in Latin America economically and militarily. In the 1890s it invoked the Monroe Doctrine (1823) against Great Britain's and Spain's involvement in South America and Cuba, respectively. Economically, the United States became involved in Latin America through investments in sugar plantations, the construction of railroads, and the importation of manufactured goods. Several times in the twentieth century, the United States intervened militarily in order to support or establish governments the United States favored: Nicaragua (1912-33), Haiti (1915-34), and the Dominican Republic (1916-24). More recently, multinational corporations have come to wield greater power over the economic state of Latin American countries. Despite international efforts, especially in the 1950s and 1960s, to help these countries to develop economically, the situation of the poor seemed to be worse by the 1970s. As Chopp reports, military dictatorships seized political control in a number of countries and suspended the basic rights of the masses. International investors, including many from the United States, took more profits out of Latin American countries than they put in, in aid. As the current U.S. policy in El Salvador and Nicaragua reveals, the United States continues to influence Latin America.

But it is not only in Latin America that the United States has had considerable influence. Throughout the world, the United States has made its economic and military presence felt. As you may recall from Chapter Four, the United States makes up approximately six percent of the world population, yet it uses more than 30 percent of the world's resources. By controlling and using a disproportionate amount of the world's resources, we can enjoy a comfortable life. On the other hand, this unjust distribution of resources means that thousands or millions of other people will lead lives of poverty and degradation. In addition, our affluent lifestyle contributes significantly to the ecological crisis. Whether we wish to acknowledge the fact or not, we are at least passively involved in maintaining the world status quo, which means suffering and death for many people.

Liberation theology provides a valuable service to Christians outside the Third World at this very point. It makes us aware of the ways in which our lifestyle is maintained by economic and political forces that cause others disadvantage or suffering. It reminds all Christians that their attitudes and behavior are shaped, at least in part, by the social class to which they belong and the privileges they enjoy. Thus, liberation theology calls the church and society to a critical examination of conscience. It points out that Christians everywhere can find many ways in their own neighborhood and country to make their faith active in love and justice. One does not have to go to the Third World to identify with the poor and the oppressed. The poor are among us in the First World. And many of them are poor because of the injustices of our social, economic, and political system.

Similarly, here in the United States, just as in Latin America, there are people who are fighting to overcome the injustices of the economic and political system. One can look to Cesar Chavez, for example, who has been fighting for several decades on behalf of the rights of migrant farm workers. Or one can look to the Community for Creative Non-Violence (CCNV), which not only runs the nation's largest shelter for the homeless (in Washington, D.C.), but also directs a campaign to get Congress to respond to the needs of the growing number of the homeless. At least five times in the past ten years, CCNV's most visible member, Mitch Snyder (d. 1990), fasted almost to the point of starvation in order to get his demands on behalf of the poor met. And in many urban areas, there are other groups of people dedicated to trying to meet the daily needs of the poor in their cities and committed to getting Congress to change our economic-political system to benefit the homeless and the poor. Thus, there is ample opportunity for us to pass over to the experience of the oppressed right here in our own country. And liberation theology reminds us that some such praxis is necessary if we want to be able to hear and to understand what the Christian tradition is saying to us in the present age.

Liberation theology, then, offers a serious challenge to the contemporary church. It calls on the church, institutionally and personally, to commit itself to undoing injustice, to joining in solidarity with the poor and the oppressed, and to integrating a "this-worldly" (social and economic) dimension into its understanding of salvation. It calls all Christians to become evangelically poor, that is, not to put themselves first, but to place themselves at the service of God and their sisters and brothers.

The Nuclear Crisis

For all of recorded history there have been wars, but the present threat of nuclear war is a new situation. The human race is now capable of committing what Chapter Five called "humanocide," the destruction of the entire human race. This new possibility of communal suicide has resulted from the invention of nuclear weapons and the continuation of the arms race by the world's superpowers.

Some Christian theologians suggest that the nuclear threat is the most important issue that our generation must face. They see it not only as the most pressing practical crisis, but also as the most urgent theological issue. Two principal ways of addressing the issue theologically are the doctrinal and the moral approaches. As you may recall from Chapter Nine, both of these approaches fall under the category of "systematic theology." Systematic theology attempts to relate the various Christian doctrines to one another in a coherent and systematic way. It also attempts to draw out the implications of these doctrines for the way Christians ought to live. In a nuclear age, some theologians perceive the principal *doctrinal* task of systematic theology to be the formulation of a new conception of God and of God's providential care for humanity. Theologians such as Gordon Kaufman propose that the new conception account for God's reality and power in such a way that *human* responsibility for our earthly future is not thereby diminished. The principal *moral* task, on the other hand, is perceived to be an exposition of the (individual and collective) behavior appropriate to saving the human race and the planet from annihilation.

Not just individual theologians, but entire church bodies have come clearly to recognize the threat of nuclear annihilation. The recent statements on nuclear weapons and peace by the Methodist Church, *In Defense of Creation: The Nuclear Crisis and a Just Peace* (1986), and the Roman Catholic hierarchy in the United States, *The Challenge of Peace: God's Promise and Our Response* (1983), are but two examples of this institutional recognition. These churches, as well as others, assert that Christian faith is active in love. In the current context, in which the present and all future generations are threatened with extinction, they acknowledge that Christian love must work for global peace. These churches also recognize that American Christians have a prominent role to play in the resolution of the nuclear threat because of the prominent role the United States plays as one of the nuclear superpowers. American Christians have not forgotten the fact that their country is the only one ever to have used a nuclear weapon against another country.

Many Christians believe that the church has an important and distinctive contribution to make to the resolution of the nuclear crisis. They hold that insofar as the church is called to be an instrument of the kingdom of God in history, the Christian church must make the peace of God's reign more visible in our time. Let us begin our study of the church's contribution by exploring its moral assessment of nuclear arms and war.

The Morality of Warfare

In the history of Christianity, two basic alternatives have been proposed as proper Christian perspectives on the use of lethal force. On the one hand, some Christians have insisted on strict obedience to Jesus' command to love everyone, including one's enemies. These Christians, usually called pacifists, conclude that the moral presumption against the use of force is an absolute duty admitting no exceptions. On the other hand, other Christians have held that the duty to love all admits exceptions. When oneself or one's country is unjustly attacked, or when an innocent victim is threatened by another, these Christians hold that they are no longer bound not to use force against the aggressor.

Christians representing both positions can be found in the various periods of the church's history. Christian pacifists, for example, existed in the early church. In fact, pacifists may have constituted the majority position in the first few centuries. These early pacifists included those who refused to join the Roman imperial army as well as those (martyrs, for instance) who refused to use physical violence to protect their own lives. Christian pacifism was also courageously championed by some members of the radical wing of the Protestant Reformation beginning in the sixteenth century (the Anabaptists and the Mennonites), by the Society of Friends (Quakers) beginning in the seventeenth century, and more recently by the Rev. Martin Luther King, Jr., and many of his followers in the 1960s civil rights movement in the United States.

The majority of Christians in every age, with the possible exception of the first three centuries, has thought, however, that deadly force may be used in some exceptional cases. These Christians include the medieval Crusaders, who sought to rout the "infidel" Muslims and to reclaim the Holy Land, as well as those people throughout the ages who have believed that a just cause does permit Christians to kill others.

Since a majority of Christians hold to some form of a "just war" theory, we will begin our survey with it.

The Idea of a Just War

Although the idea of a "just war" is rooted in ancient Stoic philosophy, St. Augustine (354-430) formed this idea into a Christian approach to the use of force. As the U.S. Catholic bishops point out in their 1983 pastoral statement *The Challenge of Peace,* Augustine was convinced that war was a consequence of sin in the world. As such, it was sinful as well as a tragic remedy for sin in some situations. Violence and war ought to be avoided as much as possible because they are sinful, that is, destructive of our relationships with God and with one another. But, faced with an attack on the innocent, the presumption that Christians do no harm, even to their enemy, yields to the command of love for an innocent neighbor. In such a case, the rights of an innocent victim take precedence over the rights of an unjust attacker. In dealing with the violence generated by the Donatist schism in the African church in the late fourth century, Augustine proposed three criteria for determining when it was permissible for Christians to use physical force. He suggested that the use of physical force had to be just (used for defense, not for aggression against another); it had to be waged by a properly instituted authority (the emperor, not vigilante groups); and the motive for the use of force or warfare had to be love. Augustine regarded this last condition as the most important. Love in this context meant that Christians, remembering the inalienable human dignity even of the enemy, had to avoid unnecessary violence and that they had to pursue reconciliation with the enemy as quickly as possible.

In the course of history, additions and refinements were made to Augustine's original theory. The medieval Dominican Thomas Aquinas (1225-1274) and the Dutch jurist and Protestant Hugo Grotius (1583-1645) made significant contributions to the development of the idea of a just war. Among the additional criteria, two of the most important and most controversial in our present nuclear context are the principles of proportionality and non-combatant immunity.

The first criterion, the principle of proportionality, means two things. First, it means that the good expected to result from taking up arms must be proportionate to the damage caused and the costs incurred by war. Second, it means that in fighting a just war the response to aggression must be proportionate to the kind of aggression. Referring to this principle, the U. S. Catholic bishops state that the destruction of civilization as we know it by waging a total nuclear war would be a monstrously disproportionate response to aggression on the part of any nation.

This statement is hard for many Americans to swallow, as the reaction of some of my students confirms. Jason, a first-year student, pointed out that the bishops' position "sounds nice," but is "totally unrealistic. Come on," he said, "do you mean to tell me that if the Russians launch their missiles first, we're not supposed to retaliate? Just sit there, and let them wipe us out?" The ensuing discussion considered whether the bishops' pastoral should be taken seriously as well as whether there was any point to nuclear retaliation. Mary, a sophomore education major, rightly pointed out that the bishops weren't saying that a nation should not defend itself against attack. The bishops' point was that legitimate defense ought not to escalate into the destruction of the entire planet. Rich, a first-year student, defended the bishops on this point: "If we respond to an attack with all our forces, and we obliterate the other side, what does that accomplish? If both sides are annihilated and the planet becomes uninhabitable, total war is stupid. Neither side wins, everybody loses." A few others supported Rich.

A second important, yet controversial criterion for fighting a just war in modern times is the principle of non-combatant immunity. This principle prohibits directly intended attacks on non-combatants and non-military targets. Concretely, this principle states that it would be immoral to respond to a missile attack, even against a major city of one's own country, by intentionally targeting an enemy population center for retaliation. This principle, like many of the others, is not easily applied. There can be serious debate about what constitutes a "military" target and who fits the description of a "non-combatant." We can ask, for example, whether the location of an aircraft engine factory in the heart of a city makes the entire city a proper military target. Despite the complexity and difficulty of determining the application of these terms, this principle of the just war theory requires Christians to use moral means in the pursuit of a just end.

Critique of the Just War

Christian pacifists in previous ages, but especially in the past twenty years, have voiced vocal criticism of the just war theory.

Many of them believe that the issue of war is the crucible within which a Christian's most fundamental religious convictions either emerge or collapse under the pressure of political expedience. As ethicist Richard Miller points out, the pacifist criticism has been of two sorts: theological and ethical.

Pacifists have generally levelled two theological criticisms against the just war theory. 1) They accuse just war theorists of using an inappropriate method in deriving their moral conclusions. Specifically, pacifists complain that the just war theory replaces Jesus' direct commands of love and nonviolence with arguments drawn from non-biblical sources, such as natural law. In the seventeenth century, for example, Grotius removed from theology the discussion of laws pertaining to warfare by locating the principle of justice in the unchanging law of nature. Pacifists, by contrast, claim to base their position on the clear, but hard sayings of Jesus, such as "Do not resist one who is evil" (Mt 5:39) and "Blessed are the peacemakers, for they shall see the kingdom of God" (Mt 5:9). Protestant theologian and pacifist John Howard Yoder insists that these sayings of Jesus do not refer simply to *interior* dispositions nor do they sketch an ideal above and beyond basic Christian duties. 2) Pacifists criticize the just war theory for implicitly denigrating trust in God's providential care of humanity and the world. Surely human beings have to bear responsibility for their own defense and for promoting peace in the world. But some just war theorists, by exclusively focusing on the role of people and governments, seem to leave God totally out of the picture. If that is the case, so argue many pacifists, the just war position makes the state, not God or Christ, the object of religious loyalty.

Two ethical charges have also been made against the just war theory. 1) Pacifists argue that the just war theory is obsolete in the era of total nuclear war. Catholic pacifist Gordon Zahn claims that we delude ourselves if we think that nuclear war can be fought on a limited scale. And, if nuclear war cannot be fought on a limited scale, then the principles of the just war theory (proportionality, non-combatant immunity, probability of success) are inapplicable and, therefore, irrelevant. 2) Many pacifists suggest that the just war tradition has legitimated war more effectively than it has restrained the use of lethal force. Zahn, for example, uses the case of the Catholic church in Germany during the period of Nazism to make his point. The church leadership was unwilling to use the moral principles of just war to condemn Nazism, although the injustices of Nazism seemed quite apparent. The hesitancy stemmed from the desire not to place German Catholics in a conflict of conscience as well as the desire to spare the church persecution by the state. Zahn concludes from this fact that Christian leaders have, and will continue to, set aside the principles of the just war for purposes of expedience.

These are serious criticisms, and defenders of the just war tradition have attempted to respond. Against the charge that they water down Jesus' hard sayings about loving one's enemy, just war supporters recall St. Augustine's point that war is a necessity that is sometimes required because of sinful human history. These Christians highlight the tension between the ideal goal (God's kingdom, in which there will be peace) and the reality of present history. They suggest that in the real world compromises are often necessary. Just war supporters have also replied to the other charges made against them. For our purposes, however, it is important to see what the pacifist alternative is and to identify the common ground between Christian pacifism and the just war theory.

Christian Pacifism

Christian pacifists generally identify Jesus' Sermon on the Mount (Mt 5-7) as the foundation upon which their position is built. In light of Jesus' words, the proper Christian response is to obey Jesus' command to put up our swords and to adopt a spirit of universal fellowship (that is, loving all people as our brothers and sisters). Christian pacifists have put these words into action throughout the ages. And, as a result, they have been harassed by the Christian majority and persecuted by governments, which perceive pacifists to be disloyal citizens or a threat to national security. From the pacifist perspective, the suffering they have endured because of their faithfulness to Jesus' commands reflects the suffering Jesus endured for preaching his message. True Christian discipleship entails suffering. Consequently, pacifists insist that God's presence is to be more readily found in the community that suffers for Christ's sake than among the powerful who rule the globe.

It is important to notice, however, that Christian pacifism is not the same thing as passivity. Christian pacifists are generally passionately committed to the defense of the rights of all human beings. The difference is that they choose to defend those rights and to resist injustice through nonviolent means. Civil disobedience, boycotts, and public demonstrations are all viable, yet nonviolent means for actively promoting peace and justice. Advocates of nonviolent action point out, moreover, that their techniques, unlike the use of violence, neither dehumanize nor alienate the adversary. The effectiveness of nonviolent resistance to injustice has been powerfully demonstrated in our own century by Nobel Prize recipient Martin Luther King, Jr. (1929-1968), who gave his life for the civil rights movement in the United States, and Mohandas ("Mahatma") Gandhi (1869-1948), who nonviolently worked for the independence of India.

Although it has been accused of being unrealistic or too optimistic about human perfectibility, pacifism has profoundly contributed to Christianity. It clearly gives powerful witness to Christ. In addition, it reminds the church that, in order for it to express prophetic criticism of society, it must make the interests of God's kingdom, not those of the earthly kingdom, its primary concern. Despite differences between Christian pacifism and the just war theory, both of these responses to violence share important common ground.

The ethicist Miller identifies three areas of common ground. First, Christian pacifists and just war supporters alike perceive war to be an exceptional affair. Both groups start from the moral presumption against the use of force. Second, both pacifists and just war defenders have critical reservations about the commonplace fascination with war. Both groups demand that instead of using our imaginations to dream up more ingenious weapons systems (both offensive and defensive), we ought to develop the positive requirements for peace in the world. And finally, the tenets of both Christian positions are structured to limit the kinds of total claims to obedience and loyalty that nations may make in the name of military or political necessity.

Rethinking God in a Nuclear Age

Some theologians today suggest that the radical nature of our situation (the possible annihilation of the entire human species) requires a radical theological response. Gordon Kaufman is such a theologian. He recommends that theology be judged not only by its reasonableness and coherence, but also by its pragmatic usefulness to human life. He alleges that the traditional conception of God and of God's providence is not useful, but is in fact dangerous in our current nuclear crisis. It is dangerous because it leads people to think that it is up to God to prevent a nuclear holocaust. We humans have nothing else to do but to trust that whatever happens is God's will. God's omnipotence and providence, traditionally understood, will see to it that a nuclear holocaust won't happen, unless, of course, it is God's will.

In his book, *Theology for a Nuclear Age,* Kaufman describes what he regards to be a more useful alternative. Instead of conceiving of God as external to the course of human history, yet determining it from the outside, Kaufman suggests that we think of God's own being and destiny as intimately linked with human history. Although God is active in human history, God does not irrevocably determine its course. Kaufman's point is that our fate is very much in our own hands. Kaufman seeks to justify this proposal by claiming that the doctrine of incarnation means that God's self is irrevocably bound to humanity, and that God is active in human history only through human agents. This does not mean that human beings are all alone in wrestling with the nuclear problem. Kaufman admits that, as Christians, we can and certainly should hope that the divine creativity working in history will bring forth possibilities for peace that we cannot now foresee or intend. Others, including myself, would add that God's power and presence can be found in us and that this divine presence not only strengthens but also enlightens us as we struggle for peace.

Kaufman's theological proposal entails not only a new way of imaging God; it also requires us to develop a new way of understanding ourselves and the meaning of salvation. As you may recall from Chapter Eleven, contemporary experience is one of the sources of theological reflection. And the most profound problem we experience today, according to Kaufman, is not individual estrangement from God, but the steady undermining of the conditions (social, political, and ecological) that make fruitful human life possible. Consequently, Kaufman recommends that we no longer conceive of salvation as a unilateral action from on high that works primarily through the church. Rather, salvation or saving work is to be found wherever a spirit of creativity and liberation and healing is at work in the world. To give ourselves over to such reconciling and healing work in human affairs is to participate in the salvific work of the divine spirit.

In a nuclear age, just as in previous ages, Christians therefore believe Jesus when he said that in losing ourselves we are saved. Insofar as we seek to help make human life more humane and fulfilling, we are continuing Christ's salvific mission. We may not be rewarded by others for our efforts, but we will know that we have been faithful to the Christ. Similarly, just as a radical *metanoia* (change of mind and heart) was required in order to hear and accept what Jesus had to say about God's reign, so too a radical *metanoia* is needed today. The change needed is the rejection of thinking simply in terms of my or our own objectives. Instead, we ought to think of life itself as interdependent. Consequently, we ought to set up as our goal not self-realization, but the fulfillment of all. Unless we learn to subordinate our particular interests as individuals, communities, or nations to a wider loyalty to ongoing life, we will surely perish. Such a vision, grounded in Jesus' own example of self-sacrifice, is needed in our perilous nuclear situation. Kaufman writes (p. 60):

> The Christian vision, with its understanding that ultimate-

> ly we are not our own—we come from and belong to God, that wider stream of self-giving creativity and life which has brought us into being and of which we are a part—and that we are called to live, therefore, in continuous self-giving to and for others, and in this alone will we find fulfillment, presents an orientation for human existence precisely appropriate to the most urgent demands of our time.

This kind of Christian vision is also an appropriate response to the ecological crisis that now faces us.

The Ecological Crisis

Although ecological problems have been around for some time, they demand attention today as never before. Beaches are closed because medical waste washes ashore; supplies of drinking water are threatened as more streams and rivers are polluted with industrial and toxic waste; acid rain destroys forests and harms crops; emissions from automobiles and factories pollute the air. In newspapers and popular magazines, we read of the depletion of the ozone layer, the "greenhouse effect," and the extinction of species. Bacteriological weapons are dumped into the ocean on the untested assumption that the water will sufficiently dilute their virulence; uranium-processing and arms plants, such as the ones in Fernald, Ohio and Hanford, Washington, routinely release vast amounts of radioactive particles into the air. In this century alone, one species of mammal becomes extinct every year. All these ecological problems are interconnected. Cumulatively, they threaten the survival of all living beings on the planet. For this reason, cultural historian Thomas Berry claims that the most immediate threat to survival on this planet is not *possible* nuclear war, but *actual* industrial plundering. The real threat is not from other nations, but from the retaliatory powers of the abused earth.

Many perhaps are convinced that if the problems are that serious and that obvious, their elected officials will take care of them. Some Americans might argue that we need not worry about pollution and these other problems because that is the job of the Environmental Protection Agency. Others may presume that no matter how bad the current situation is, science will find a way to clean up the environment and save the planet. Some people, however, are not willing to leave these important matters to others. They think that perhaps government is not vigilant or concerned enough to insure the safety of all. Consequently, movements such as Greenpeace work to mobilize governments to clean up our polluted water and to insure protection of the environment. Local citizens unite to protest against the waste disposal policies of nearby chemical companies and to protest against lax safety and security measures at nuclear power plants. Some have actually formed political parties dedicated to promoting ecological concerns. The Green Party, for example, has gained some power in the parliaments of Western Europe.

But what does the ecological crisis have to do with Christian theology? It is a fact that within the past twenty years Christian theologians have become aware of the gravity of the ecological crisis. A number have begun to write about it. Protestant theologians Jürgen Moltmann and John Cobb, Catholic theologian Thomas Berry, and others have become convinced that the ecological crisis is so comprehensive that it must be seen as a life-and-death struggle for creation on the earth. Official bodies of various Christian churches have also begun to attend to the problem. In 1987, the Pontifical Academy of Sciences issued the document, *A Modern Approach to the Protection of the Environment*. And the World Council of Churches is preparing a 1990 conference on "Peace, Justice, and the Integrity of Creation." But do these documents, conferences, and theologians believe that Christian theology has a particular responsibility and a special role to play in the resolution of this crisis?

Christianity and the Ecological Crisis

Some theologians are convinced that Christianity has a special role to fill in responding to the ecological crisis. They feel it has a responsibility to alleviate the crisis because Western Christianity contributed to the rise of science and technology, the careless use of which has been partly responsible for the current mess. As theologian Cobb points out, the Western Christian understanding of nature as the creation of an intelligent divine will provided the motivation for the sustained effort that carried Western European science from its infancy in the Middle Ages to the amazing achievements of the seventeenth century. One knew that creation embodied rational and intelligible order because nature was seen as God's creation. And the discovery of that order became supremely valuable since it led to knowledge of God. Moreover, the specific authorization (by the first Genesis account of creation) of human lordship over the rest of the world provided the justification for the technological manipulation of nature to serve human needs. Even after the authority of the Bible was thrown into question in the nineteenth century, few people doubted human dominance over the subhuman world.

Christian beliefs and Christian theology may have contributed to the ecological problem in other ways as well. Berry, for example, levels several indictments against the past Christian tradition. Thomas Berry accuses the Israelites and their spiritual descendants of making the natural world less sacred and, therefore, less valuable, by consistently emphasizing the transcendent nature of God. Other ancient Near Eastern peoples, by contrast, were attuned to the pervasive presence of the divine throughout nature. Christianity followed the Hebrew lead, and may actually have made the problem worse by making redemption and salvation its fundamental doctrine. This emphasis occurred, according to Berry, at the cost of the doctrine of creation. Insofar as one's *spiritual* salvation was paramount, the inherent goodness of the created, *material* world was thereby ignored or trivialized.

Christianity, of course, has not been the only, or even the most direct cause of the current situation. Modern industrial societies have generally shared the idea that every generation ought to live better, have a more luxurious lifestyle, and enjoy more technological conveniences than the previous generation.

Even though this "progress" is achieved by disturbing the atmospheric conditions; contaminating our air, soil, and water; depleting our limited quantity of fossil fuels; many people still clamor for it.

Many American families, for example, regard having two cars as quite natural. In 1986, there were 135,431,000 cars registered in the United States. That is more than ten times the number of cars in Brazil, 135 times the number in India, and more than a thousand times the number in Kenya. The impact of vehicles on the environment is, of course, considerable. The metals in the cars are non-renewable resources won from their ores with much use of energy. And the list of side effects from a vehicle's use is long. These effects, according to *National Geographic* (Dec. 1988), include pollution and ecosystem destruction from building roads, bridges, parking garages, etc.; and exhausts that contribute to eye irritation, emphysema, lung cancer, as well as to acid rain and the greenhouse effect. An average U.S. family affects the environment 40 times more than an average family in India or 100 times more than an average family in Kenya.

Corporations, moreover, are ready to respond to the demands of affluent consumers. Many businesses and corporations, however, are so driven by the desire to maximize their profits that they care little for how they might contribute to the contamination of the planet. If we are all dead in the long run anyway, why not maximize our profits and enjoy them now? Surely, there is enough blame to be shared by all—individuals, corporations, governments, society, and Christianity.

Although everyone can play a part in working to reverse the process of ecological doom, many believe that Christian theology can make a unique contribution. In the past, it supported that understanding of the relation between humanity and the rest of the natural world that justified the manipulation and exploitation of the natural and subhuman world. Now it can contribute to resolving the crisis by presenting a new conception of the relation between humanity and the rest of the natural world.

Theology's Ecological Contribution

Perhaps the most important contribution theology can make in response to our ecological crisis is the promotion of a new way of thinking about the humanity-natural world relationship. If, in addition to proposing a new way of thinking, theologians can find a grounding and justification for it in the Christian tradition, they can provide society with a powerfully influential vision of reality that simultaneously enhances reverence for the natural world and prohibits wanton contamination of the planet.

Thomas Berry presents three key elements for this new vision of the relation between humanity and nature. First, we need to recognize nature not as an object for our use and manipulation, but as a subject. Berry wishes to emphasize the fact that the natural world is the maternal source from which we emerge into being as earthlings. Our existence could not be sustained without the natural environment. Second, we need to adopt a biocentric, rather than a homocentric, perspective. This means that human beings should see themselves not as totally above nature and dominant over it, but as beings who are a part of nature. Our focus should be on the living planet as a whole, not simply upon humanity. This new perspective entails the third element, a new orientation in our behavior. When we work for "progress," that progress ought to include the entire earth community. Berry states that if there is to be real and sustainable progress, it must be a continuing enhancement of life for the entire planetary community. And that means that the purity and life-giving qualities of air, soil, and water must be preserved for the good of all, not just for human beings.

But, some may ask, does Christianity demand such a vision and orientation? Is this new vision even compatible with Christianity? Let us explore some of the resources in the Christian tradition for giving an affirmative answer to both questions. The Genesis story of creation, to which we have often returned, suggests that the goodness of other parts of nature is intrinsic; it is not dependent upon people. The other animals, the plants, the earth and water are good in themselves. This fact is signaled in the Genesis narrative by having God say at the end of each of the six days of creation that what had been created was very good. Taking this part of the creation narrative seriously can help to offset the usual literal reading of Genesis 1:28-29 (where God says to the first human beings: "Be fruitful, multiply, fill the earth and conquer it").

But Christian resources for a new biocentric vision are not confined to this and other parts of the book of Genesis. As biblical scholar Donald Senior comments, biblical traditions as varied as the Wisdom literature and the Pauline letters regard the earth as an effective revelation of God. Since nature reveals and bears the sacred, St. Paul, for example, believed that everyone could have some knowledge of God. In Romans 1:19, he writes that "ever since God created the world his everlasting power and deity—however invisible—have been there for the mind to see in the things he has made." Throughout the history of Christianity, the natural world has been regarded as a reflection and revelation of its creator.

What are some of the implications we might draw from this conviction? One implication might be that, insofar as nature reveals God, we ought to be careful not to mar or destroy that revelation through the contamination and destruction of our natural environment. Concretely, the extinction of species of animals can be regarded as a diminishment of God's presence in the world. Christian thinkers such as Thomas Aquinas have suggested that the existence of a multiplicity of life forms is necessary for us to appreciate the grandeur and infinite nature of God. In his *Summa Theologiae* (Part I, ques. 47, art. 1), Aquinas wrote that God brought things into being in order that the divine goodness might be communicated to creatures as well as be represented by them. He added that since God's goodness could not be adequately represented by one creature alone, God produced many diverse creatures so that what was lacking to one in the representation of God's goodness might be supplied by another. Thomas's conclusion was that the goodness of God is represented better in the universe as a whole than in any single creature. Ideas such as these could be drawn out to formulate a biocentric picture of our world.

Some, however, might fear that a biocentric conception of the world will mean that the value of human life will be set on a par with the value of plant life or the value of other animals. This is not a necessary consequence of a biocentric perspective. Paleontologist and Jesuit priest Pierre Teilhard de Chardin (1881-1955) proposed a theory of evolution in which all members of the cosmos are related, but in which the human person is both the axis of evolution and the key for understanding the universe. The human being can still be regarded as the apex of nature on account of its greater biological complexity and rational capabilities. The point, then, is that acknowledging the greater worth of a human being over other creatures does not reduce the value of other beings to nothing; it does not permit us to be ruthlessly indifferent to the consequences of our actions for the living environment. In Cobb's estimation, St. Francis of Assisi (1181-1226) and Dr. Albert Schweitzer (1875-1965) can provide us with models for a Christian, biocentric approach to life. Francis showed respect for his brother the wolf and his sisters the birds without abandoning Western rationality. As his "Canticle of Brother Sun" (1225) indicates, he saw all the creatures of the earth as expressions of God's mercy and greatness. Schweitzer, on the other hand, devoted much of his life to caring for the sick in what is now Gabon, Africa. He did this without repudiating society or the music, philosophy, and theology he loved. Schweitzer suggested that a person is ethical only when life *as such* is holy to him or her. Schweitzer devoted himself to the service of human need while living out a vision of *all* life as worthy of reverence.

As we saw in Chapter Eleven, how we image God affects not only our relationship to God, but also our relationship to others. That truth applies in the case of the God-world relationship as well. Theologian Sallie McFague proposes that one way to sustain an ecological approach to reality is to imagine the God-world relationship as similar to the relationship between our selves and our bodies. Just as our minds or spirits cannot think and will apart from its physical base (in the brain and in the neurological system of the body), so, too, suggests McFague, we ought not think of God apart from the world of nature. Her point is not to claim that the world is literally God's body, but to assert that it is metaphorically so. Such a radical conception overcomes the traditional dualism between spirit and flesh and between nature and humanity by insisting that God is expressed in the spiritual aspects of reality as well as embodied in the physical aspects of reality. Such a conception, moreover, implies that God's love extends not only to spiritual beings (humanity), but also to all other beings of the world.

The question, arises, however, whether such a vision is one that Christians may affirm. McFague clearly thinks that it is. She argues that her approach is not only more holistic and sound in evolutionary terms, but is also faithful to Christianity's Hebraic background (e.g., the idea that the created order is inherently good). And Cobb agrees with her that the extension of Christian love beyond human beings to other living creatures is a continuation and development of the Christian heritage, rather than its repudiation. Whether or not one agrees with them, it is clear that their proposals present a significantly new understanding of what it means to be a Christian today.

In this chapter, we have examined Christian theological responses to three major crises that confront us today: the socioeconomic, the nuclear, and the ecological. In each case, we have seen that Christian theology involves critical and creative thinking about our current situation, the Christian tradition, and the relation between the two. Some of the theological proposals we have explored are controversial since they challenge traditional ways of thinking about Christian faith. But all of the theological reflections we have considered are sustained by a very ancient and traditional Christian conviction, namely, that Christian faith must be active in deeds of love and justice.

As our examination of these three contemporary issues demonstrates, theology is not an activity removed from the concerns and the life of the world nor is it a pursuit necessarily confined to professionals. Rather, theology is a process of critical reflection and liberating action in which all Christians can engage, at least to a certain extent. And, by doing so, Christians can deepen their faith, help save our planet from destruction, and enrich life tremendously.

QUESTIONS FOR REFLECTION AND DISCUSSION

1. How is the content and method of liberation theology different from other forms of modern Christian theology? Do you think it is unfair to choose the poor for a "preferential option?" Explain.

2. How is liberation theology's explanation of the causes of poverty different from the usual explanations? Can you think of ways in which our own socioeconomic system is unfair to the poor?

3. In what way is the nuclear threat a theological issue as well as an important political issue? Which way of thinking about God's care for the world, the pacifist position or Kaufman's, is closer to your own understanding of what God will or will not do with regard to nuclear annihilation?

4. Is it possible for Christians to justify war morally on some occasions in spite of Jesus' command to love our enemies? Do you feel that Jesus' commands are unrealistic or that contemporary Christians don't deserve to be called his disciples?

5. Explain how the Christian tradition may have contributed to the ecological crisis and describe how you, too, may have contributed to it. What can Christian theology do to help resolve this crisis? What can you do?

SUGGESTED READINGS

Birch, Charles, and John B. Cobb. *The Liberation of Life: From the Cell to the Community*. Cambridge: Cambridge University Press, 1981.

Boff, Leonardo and Clodovis. *Introducing Liberation Theology*. Maryknoll, N.Y.: Orbis, 1987.

Chopp, Rebecca S. *The Praxis of Suffering: An Interpretation of Liberation and Political Theologies*. Maryknoll, N.Y.: Orbis Books, 1986.

Cobb, John B. *Is It Too Late? A Theology of Ecology*. Beverly Hills: Bruce, 1972.

Ferm, Deane William. *Profiles in Liberation*. Mystic, Conn.: Twenty-Third Publications, 1988.

Granberg–Michaelson, Wesley, ed. *Tending the Garden: Essays on the Gospel and the Earth*. Grand Rapids, Mich.: Eerdmans, 1987.

Gutiérrez, Gustavo. *A Theology of Liberation*. Maryknoll, N.Y.: Orbis, 1973.

________. *On Job: God-Talk and the Suffering of the Innocent*. Maryknoll, NY: Orbis, 1987.

Kaufman, Gordon G. *Theology for a Nuclear Age*. Philadelphia: Westminster Press, 1985.

Hall, Douglas John. *Imaging God: Dominion as Stewardship*. Grand Rapids, Mich.: Eerdmans, 1986.

Linzey, Andrew. *Christianity and the Rights of Animals*. New York: Crossroad, 1988.

Lonergan, Anne, and Caroline Richards, eds. *Thomas Berry and the New Cosmology*. Mystic, Conn.: Twenty-Third Publications, 1987.

McDaniel, Jay. *Earth, Sky, Gods, & Mortals: Developing an Ecological Spirituality*. Mystic, Conn.: Twenty-Third Publications, 1990.

McFague, Sallie. *Models of God: Theology for an Ecological, Nuclear Age*. Philadelphia: Fortress Press, 1987.

Miller, Richard B. "Christian Pacifism and Just-War Tenets: How Do They Diverge?" *Theological Studies* 47 (1986): 448-72.

National Conference of Catholic Bishops. *The Challenge of Peace: God's Promise and Our Response*. Washington: U. S. Catholic Conference, 1983.

Ramsey, Paul. *War and the Christian Conscience: How Shall Modern War Be Conducted Justly*? Durham, N.C.: Duke University Press, 1985.

Sobrino, Jon. *The True Church and the Poor.* Maryknoll, N.Y.: Orbis Books, 1984.

Teilhard de Chardin, Pierre. *The Phenomenon of Man.* New York: Harper & Row, 1959.

True, Michael. *Justice Seekers, Peace Makers: 32 Portraits in Courage.* Mystic, Conn.: Twenty-Third Publications, 1985.

Vanderhaar, Gerard A. *Enemies and How to Love Them.* Mystic, Conn.: Twenty-Third Publications, 1985.

Yoder, John Howard. *When War Is Unjust: Being Honest in Just-War Thinking.* Minneapolis: Augsburg, 1984.

Conclusion

In this book we have described the phenomena of faith, religion, and theology. We have attempted to understand these realities, to identify their relationship, and to appreciate their value.

Our starting point was experiential—the fact that all of us have faith in something or have some degree of trust. We have faith in ourselves, in others, in the future, in the worth of life. Such faith or trust is necessary to live life with a sense of meaning and purpose. Religious faith is integrally related to this basic trust, but it is also different. Religious faith is a trust in a reality beyond sensible observation and proof. Christian faith is a trusting response to the invitation of God to accept and follow Jesus. We saw that a positive response to God's invitation goes beyond mere belief in Jesus as savior; it involves a way of life and action, especially on behalf of the oppressed and marginalized.

We also explored the ways in which our development as human beings affects our faith. We saw that just as our personal identity goes through stages of conflict and growth, so too does religious identity. Although one's identity, personal and religious, is always an on-going process, we emphasized that the young adult period is a crucial transitional phase. In this stage, people confront and attempt to resolve a variety of important issues: self-image, independence, life options, and intimacy. We explored the ways in which faith relates to these different issues and challenges.

As we made the transition from our consideration of faith to our consideration of religion, we suggested that religious faith—although in many ways quite personal and private—needs to be lived out in a community and in engagement with social issues. We suggested that a completely private faith, a faith without works or community, was partial faith.

In our initial exploration of the nature of religion, we underlined again the importance of community and the experiential root of faith and religion. Religion is what comes about when people have some kind of experience of ultimate reality or "Something More," and then gather together to maintain and live that experience. Honesty, however, required us to recognize that there has also been a dark side to religion. In the course of history, religions have been used for ignoble purposes: to manipulate others, to maintain the social and political status quo, to prevent people from growing up. Even today, all too frequently, religion continues to be misused and abused. Consequently, many people find religion to be dangerous or irrelevant. Nonetheless, we argued that religion can and does have positive value. We suggested that religion has psychological value for the individual and ethical value for society. In particular, faith and religion can play a constructive role in confronting the socioeconomic, nuclear, and ecological crises that confront our contemporary world.

In our further reflections upon the nature of religion, we highlighted two important facts. First, there is a creative tension within all religions between the individual and the community. Insofar as religion is rooted in a personal experience of ultimate reality that calls people to transcend their egocentrism, individual faith cannot grow without community, and yet community cannot take the place of personal faith and responsibility. Second, there is a growing awareness today that there exists not only many religions, but that there is also great value in the plurality and diversity of religions. We suggested that this fact means that we ought to reflect upon our own faith and religion within a broader context of other religions. We think that it is possible to be fully committed to one's own religion, while being fully open to the possible truth and value in other religions. In fact, dialogue with and respect for other religions seems to us to be an essential part of living out Jesus' vision of love for others.

The imaginary conversation we heard between Jesus the Christ and Siddhartha the Buddha was intended to illustrate the possible fruitfulness of dialogue among religions. Our point was that the messages that these two religious figures brought into the world, although different, can make a difference. We examined how the experience of a God of love leads to work for greater love and justice among all peoples, just as the experience of the interrelatedness of Nirvana leads to lives of compassion for all beings.

In the final section of the book, we explored the phenomenon of theology as both a process of critical reflection upon and a product of religious tradition. Although our focus was Christian theology, we pointed out that theology occurs within all the major religions. Theology examines the faith content of religion and is, therefore, integrally related both to faith and to religion. But it is also different from belief. Theology asks tough questions of one's religious tradition and of one's contemporary experience of reality. We suggested that the many different categories of Christian theology could be distilled down to four major types: fundamental, historical, systematic, and practical.

As we studied one branch of historical theology, biblical studies, in more detail, we confronted the important issue of how Scripture and tradition should be understood. We saw that there is a significant difference between the fundamentalist and the critical approaches to Scripture and tradition. We suggested that the critical approach is a more appropriate way of reading the

Bible. Although it refuses to read the Bible in a consistently literal fashion, this approach nonetheless takes the Bible with utmost seriousness. A proper approach to Scripture and tradition, it seems to us, is neither credulous nor skeptical, since both Scripture and tradition express something of the truth about ultimate reality without ceasing to be limited, human expressions.

We pointed out, however, that Scripture and tradition are not the only sources of theological reflection. Human experience, both individual and social, is another important resource for theology. In the past, the role of human experience in theological formulations was not always recognized or explicitly acknowledged. But it influenced the language and even the perspective reflected in Christian doctrines and practices. Today we are much more aware of the pervasive influence of our experiences upon everything we think, feel, and believe. Fundamental theology examines these everyday experiences in search of an answer to the question about the reality of God. Besides investigating the nature of fundamental theology, we also turned our attention to two contemporary experiences that seriously challenge traditional understandings of God and reality: suffering and androcentrism.

We concluded our introduction to theology by returning to the three crises which confront our world and to the resolution of which we claimed that the religions could offer valuable assistance. First, we considered one form of a Christian theological response to the socioeconomic problem of systematic oppression of the poor. We reflected upon liberation theology as a form of practical theology, which is attempting to live out the truths of Jesus' mission and message in a new way. Second, we turned our attention to the threat of nuclear annihilation. We underlined the fact that we are living in a new situation: never before has humanity had the capacity completely to destroy itself and other forms of life on the planet. This new fact forces us to reconsider the adequacy of the traditional just-war theory and to assess again the value of Christian pacifism. Third, we turned our attention to the ecological crisis, a crisis that has been ignored for quite some time. After reviewing the role Christianity has played in the creation of this crisis, we explored the valuable contribution Christian theology could make to lessening it. In all three cases, we saw that the crisis had moved some Christian theologians to re-conceive the traditional understanding of God and of responsible Christian behavior.

Throughout this book, there has been a dialectic—a kind of creative tension—at work between opposite poles. One such dialectic is that between the individual and the community. One's decision to trust, to have faith, is personal; yet one does not come to such a decision by oneself. A community, whether it be our family, our peers, or a religious group, helps to bring us to such a decision. In a similar way, religious experience and religious commitment are both personal and social. As adults, we believe for personal reasons; yet our religious beliefs call us to move beyond ourselves in concern for other persons and other realities.

There is also a dialectic in our understanding of ultimate reality. On the one hand, it is something that transcends all our attempts to grasp it and describe it in our limited concepts and language. On the other hand, ultimate reality can be experienced here and now in our world. From a Christian perspective, we can say that God is both transcendent and immanent. God is always more than we can imagine, yet God is always present in us, in others, in all of created reality.

Another dialectic that underlies this book is the tension between tradition and freedom. We have seen how tradition is one of the sources of Christian theology. Fidelity to tradition is necessary for Christian theology to remain Christian. And yet we have also seen that the message and spirit of Jesus can be understood in ways that go beyond our past tradition. In fact, we have considered some of the ways in which our contemporary experiences and insights demand that we freely criticize our past heritage.

We are, then, both individual seekers and companions in community; we are both free in our creation of new visions for a better world and yet also constrained and enriched by structures of the past and earlier insights into the truth; we sometimes experience powerful manifestations of ultimate reality in our lives, while at other times we grope desperately for a God who seems to be hidden. In these various dialectics, we develop and grow. We are confronted with the question of faith; we are invited to be a part of a religious community; we are challenged to reflect critically upon our contemporary world and religious tradition. We hope that our book has been of some help as you begin or continue your journey.

Index